Enterprise-wide
Risk Management

FINANCIAL TIMES
Prentice Hall

In an increasingly competitive world, it is quality
of thinking that gives an edge – an idea that opens new
doors, a technique that solves a problem, or an insight
that simply helps make sense of it all.

We work with leading authors in the fields of
management and finance to bring cutting-edge thinking
and best learning practice to a global market.

Under a range of leading imprints, including
Financial Times Prentice Hall, we create world-class
print publications and electronic products giving readers
knowledge and understanding which can then be
applied, whether studying or at work.

To find out more about our business and professional
products, you can visit us at www.business-minds.com

For other Pearson Education publications, visit
www.pearsoned-ema.com

Pearson
Education

Enterprise-wide Risk Management

Strategies for linking risk and opportunity

JAMES W. DeLOACH

For Paul,
Best wishes for continued success.
Jim

ARTHURANDERSEN

FINANCIAL TIMES
Prentice Hall

An imprint of Pearson Education

London	New York	San Francisco	Toronto	Sydney
Tokyo	Singapore	Hong Kong	Cape Town	Madrid
Paris	Milan	Munich	Amsterdam	

PEARSON EDUCATION LIMITED

Head Office:
Edinburgh Gate
Harlow CM20 2JE
Tel: +44 (0)1279 623623
Fax: +44 (0)1279 431059

London Office:
128 Long Acre
London WC2E 9AN
Tel: +44 (0)20 7447 2000
Fax: +44 (0)20 7240 5771
Website: www.business-minds.com

_____

First published in Great Britain in 2000

© Arthur Andersen 2000

The right of James DeLoach to be identified as Author
of this Work has been asserted by him in accordance
with the Copyright, Designs and Patents Act 1988.

ISBN 0 273 64414 9

British Library Cataloguing in Publication Data
A CIP catalogue record for this book can be obtained from the British Library.

10 9 8 7 6 5 4 3 2 1

Typeset by Boyd Elliott Typesetting
Printed and bound in Great Britain

The Publishers' policy is to use paper manufactured from sustainable forests.

About the author

James W. DeLoach is a Partner of Arthur Andersen who has been with the firm for over 29 years. He has extensive risk consulting experience in a wide variety of industries and engagements. In his current capacity as the Global Leader of the firm's Business Risk Management Competency Development Center, he works closely with assurance, risk consulting and industry professionals to develop the firm's business risk management competencies. He is co-author of *Managing business risk: An integrated approach*, published by the Economist Intelligence Unit in 1995, and of several articles covering various aspects of business risk assessment and management. He has delivered numerous presentations on risk management to many companies and groups and has taught senior and graduate level courses at two major universities on a variety of topics over the years. Mr DeLoach is a sports enthusiast and an accomplished magical entertainer. He resides in Houston, Texas with his wife.

This book is dedicated to my parents,
James and Carolyn DeLoach, who
taught me that life is about magic.

Contents

Preface
A new and evolving approach to improving risk management capabilities

> *Nothing noble is done without risk.*
>
> André Gide, French novelist
>
> *The policy of being too cautious is the greatest risk of all.*
>
> Jawaharlal Nehru

CEOs are focused on investment and return, on opportunity and reward and on competitive advantage and growth. That's why business risk management is vital to their success:

- Investment and return? – No investment is without uncertainty. Embracing and mastering risk is one of the keys to managing investment and return.

- Opportunity and reward? – Risk is the partner of opportunity. Opportunity seeking behaviour is invigorated if managers have the confidence that they understand the risks and have the capabilities to manage them.

- Competitive advantage and growth? – Business risk management is much more than just avoiding and hedging bets. It is also a differentiating skill which is vital to selecting the most rational bets for a company to take in the face of powerful and dynamic forces in the new economy. These same forces present exciting opportunities for creating new sources of competitive advantage and growth.

> An enterprise-wide process will link risk and opportunity and position business risk management as a source of competitive advantage.

CEOs face many challenges. They must focus and motivate their organizations to capitalize on emerging opportunities. They must continually invest precious resources in the pursuit of promising – though uncertain – business activities. They must manage the business in the face of constantly changing circumstances. And, as they do all of these things, they must simultaneously be in a position to confidently assure investors, directors and other stakeholders that their organizations embrace and master risk while thriving in the new economy.

Our premise is this: An enterprise-wide business risk management process will help CEOs meet these challenges by improving the linkage of risk and opportunity and positioning business risk management as a source of competitive advantage.

Indeed, risk and opportunity are everywhere. An increasingly competitive global environment, emerging technologies and business models, changing customer values, mergers and acquisitions, new regulatory developments and ever-demanding shareholder expectations: these and other powerful forces are changing the global business landscape, transforming industries and creating incredible opportunities for growing a business, all at a breathtaking pace. Amid these shifting conditions, most firms – your competitors certainly – are and will continue adopting new and innovative business practices.

Every organization has a business model – and certainly your business model is critical to differentiating and positioning your company for success. But traditional business models often treat risk too much like an afterthought. Ultimately, it is your ability to manage the risks inherent in your business model that will determine whether or not you succeed. Risk is inherent in all opportunity, so risk management is the bridge between strategic concept and executional excellence. This book shows you how to bring risk into balance as a strategic imperative in a complex and fast-changing world. This book embraces and demystifies what we believe is a most compelling approach: Enterprise-wide Risk Management (EWRM).

THE FUTURE OF RISK

The current state of business risk management must evolve – dramatically.

As the rules of wealth creation and preservation evolve in the new economy, traditional risk management approaches will not get the job done unless they are robust enough – even holistic enough – to assure success. In fact, they may even contribute to failure.

Current risk management approaches are fragmented, treating risks as disparate and easily compartmentalized. While their tight focus on loss prevention is not necessarily a bad thing, neither is it a good enough thing because they are not adequately integrated with the evaluation and optimization of growth and capital. Moreover, current approaches are too firmly rooted in the command and control era – which means they have not yet found the means to balance management's desire for control with the need for agility and cross-functional co-operation. While they may create a somewhat comprehensive view of a company's risks of the recent past, they cannot adequately deal with the company's continually evolving risks and opportunities – its future. And they tend to focus on the risks to tangible, owned assets, ignoring the important exposures arising from the enterprise's intangible assets. Again, it is questionable whether they help managers harness a company's full potential.

Because risk is a reality of life and life is constantly changing in the new economy, the current state of business risk management must evolve – dramatically. A new strategic process is needed, one that identifies and addresses the full range of risks and opportunities.

The new model we propose is EWRM. It features shared organizational goals and broad co-ordination or 'strategic control' and yet provides freedom to act within well-defined boundaries. It facilitates the management of risk in a world of uncertainty, leading to broad optimization of opportunities, risk, growth and capital. It fosters continual feedback and re-evaluation, capitalizing on the enormous advances in technology and knowledge-sharing available today. The solution we envision lies in an evolution towards – a journey towards – EWRM.

EWRM is a structured and disciplined approach: it aligns strategy, processes, people, technology and knowledge with the purpose of evaluating and managing the uncertainties the enterprise faces as it creates value. 'Enterprise-wide' means an elimination of functional, departmental or cultural barriers. It means a truly holistic, integrated, forward-looking and process-oriented approach is taken to manage all key business risks and opportunities – not just financial ones – with the intent of maximizing shareholder value for the enterprise as a whole.

Our research has identified a significant and growing number of companies who are beginning the journey towards the risk-focused, EWRM-oriented organization. These companies believe – and we agree – that their transformation will result in superior risk-taking acumen and business results. Risk-conscious, fast-moving and entrepreneurial: these companies are positioning themselves to be among their industries' pacesetters for many years to come.

EWRM is not a 'one-size-fits-all' solution. Energy giant Enron's implementation differs from food and beverage giant Diageo's or from the British Post Office's in accordance with its business model and strategies, its organizational structure, its culture and its dedicated resources.

The ideal is an organization that understands and continually re-evaluates its opportunities and risks. Its leadership, processes and people are keenly focused on and motivated towards continually refining strategies and tactics to achieve superior results. It knows how to 'price' both its risks and its opportunities, and it allocates its capital – intellectual, financial and otherwise – accordingly. It is an organization with a shared, collectively developed vision, clear operating objectives and optimal communication both internally and externally. It is 'in control' and yet its emissaries are free to manoeuvre within the scope of their objectives and capabilities.

GETTING STARTED

The ideal is clear; the road ahead is becoming clearer. This book identifies the issues, details the evolving frameworks designed to address these issues and finally chronicles the trailblazers. Ultimately it is a trail guide for managers who are ready to recognize the role of risk in their organizations. These managers understand that some risks must be embraced as others are avoided. They grasp the need to begin the journey towards a holistic and dynamic enterprise-wide approach to managing business risks and opportunities.

Undoubtedly, improvement in many of the above areas is under way, but even so, advances are probably unco-ordinated. Treasury, Insurance, IS, Legal and Internal Audit: all are looking for ways to increase their relevance by broadening their focus to improving business performance. Topping the list, owners of the strategic management and business planning processes are seeking ways to make risk management more strategic by consolidating risk assessment and management into their activities. Somehow, the efforts of these seemingly disparate groups have to coalesce into integrated enterprise-wide capabilities. Our view is that your company can rely on chance and the gods, or it can lead the way from the top.

This book is a call for leadership. Companies should (a) adopt the view of optimizing risk, opportunity and capital to create value and (b) learn to focus the full spectrum of corporate resources co-operatively and effectively. Those that do so will most certainly enhance their prospects for future growth at superior returns. Our conclusion: if your business model does not address its risks on an enterprise-wide basis, it is probably suboptimal.

> **Your company can rely on chance and the gods, or it can lead the way from the top.**

WHO SHOULD READ THIS BOOK?

This book has valuable lessons for all companies. Business leaders and risk managers desiring to improve their organization's effectiveness will benefit from this book. As for companies just beginning their EWRM journey, they will find useful ideas to help navigate the way. Finally, for those companies which are well down the road on their journey to EWRM, this book is replete with valuable ideas that will aid, provide a 'reality check' and perhaps even accelerate their progress. Our ultimate aim is to help each organization either begin its journey toward assessing and improving its business risk management capabilities – enterprise-wide – or continue the journey it has already begun.

EWRM is a powerful management process. We believe the frameworks, tools and case examples in this book will prove compelling and inspiring to senior executives and practitioners everywhere – regardless of industry or industry position. We challenge you to evaluate what EWRM will mean to your business.

Acknowledgements

While fully responsible for any errors and omissions in this book, the author uses the pronoun 'we' instead of 'I' throughout because no book of this kind is possible without the help and support of many people. This book is no exception. First, I wish to thank Michael Bennett, Arthur Andersen's Managing Partner of Assurance and Business Advisory, for his help in getting this project started and encouragement and support through its completion.

Second, this book would not have been completed without the valuable input, editing, advice, counsel and case development of my good friend, Bill Millar. As evidenced by the reactions of executives who see his work, Bill has few peers when it comes to managing the process from arranging and conducting interviews to shaping and articulating ideas to completing the final written product. Bill, it was my good fortune you were available and willing to assist me and I will always be grateful for your unwavering commitment and tireless efforts during the eight months you have worked with me to complete this project.

Third, Bill Millar and I interviewed over 100 executives representing over 60 companies to gather material for this book. I am most appreciative to these executives for sharing their valuable time. I also wish to thank the companies consenting to the cases and vignettes included in this book.

Fourth, many of my colleagues at Arthur Andersen have provided valued advice to me during the past two years or during their reviews of the manuscript itself for which I am grateful and wish to acknowledge with my sincere thanks:

- Nick Temple of London for getting this project started in the first place and motivating me to take it on when I was reluctant to do so.

- Mike Onak, our North America Leader of Financial and Commodities Risk Consulting, for being a valued advisor and confidante over the last two years and during this project and for contributing significantly to several chapters in this book.

- Mike Dolan for his adaptation of the Carnegie Mellon Capability Maturity Model to risk management and integrating the components of risk management infrastructure into that adaptation.

- Greg Greiff for his meticulous and thorough review of the manuscript as well as his extensive contributions in several key areas that helped me shape this book.

- Paul Hoeve of Zurich for giving me opportunities to gain much insight into the EWRM journey and supporting me during this project.

- Elaine Miller for her input in the change enablement area and her capable management of the New Dimensions research in 1998 on which parts of this book are based.

- Bill Sacks for 'taking the calls' as I focused on completing this book, not to mention providing me valuable advice and input on the manuscript itself.

- Dan O'Keefe, Lou Grabowsky, Dave Tabolt, Bob Rinder, John Kuik, Peter Newman, Alberto Piedrafita and Steven Lim for their review of and comments on the manuscript.

- Everett Gibbs, Larry Rieger, Russ Gates, Bill Keevan, Greg Jonas, Mike Levin, Dick Gregoire, Gus Krause and Richard Ensbury for input and ideas that were of great value to me during the development of this book.

- Robert Hodgkinson for his advice and counsel 'from the shadows' on the approach to Chapter 3.

- Richard Boulton, Steve Samek, Barry Libert and Ed Giniat for including me as part of their working network as they wrote *Cracking the Value Code*, to be published in May 2000 by HarperCollins. My participation with their team helped me immensely in shaping my thoughts on linking risk and opportunity.

- Amanda Bailey for her invaluable assistance with managing this project from beginning to end, as well as Heather Hulsey and Vickie Mueller for their assistance in many ways throughout the project.

- Gina Baudat and her team in Arthur Andersen's Houston office for their assistance with the proofing process and Bob Kerfoot for his assistance with the index.

In addition, I also wish to thank my friends at Risk Management Solutions for their valuable input and insight on securitization. Thanks also to Martin Drewe, Kate Lodge, Boyd Elliott and the team at Financial Times Prentice Hall, for their support and commitment to a quality product.

Finally, this book would not be possible without the clients, partners and professionals of Arthur Andersen. It is their collective experiences and knowledge that provide the foundation for much of my learning.

Most importantly, my appreciation and thanks to my real partner, my wife Diane, whose patience with and support (and, yes, even tolerance) of my adventures during almost 30 years of professional life with Arthur Andersen has known no bounds. She has always encouraged me to pursue my dreams and, for that, I will always be eternally grateful.

James W. DeLoach, Jr

Mastering risk to create value: what is an enterprise-wide approach and why is it essential?

Without risk, there is no opportunity.

Ray Joy, Finance Director, Guinness

A rattlesnake may bite us every now and again, but we knew it was there and how much it might hurt.

Rick Buy, Executive Vice President and Chief Risk Officer, Enron

Imagine an organization where:

■ the board and senior managers are in a position to confidently make informed decisions regarding the trade-off between risk and reward, and daily business decisions at the operating level are made within the context of the company's strategies for bearing risk;

■ the risks relating to the firm's sources of value in the new economy such as its customer base, its distribution partners, its supply chain, its intellectual and knowledge capital, its processes and systems are acknowledged and optimized just as fully as its physical and financial assets;

■ the need for operational control is balanced with entrepreneurial empowerment;

■ risk management is actively integrated with strategic planning and risks are systematically identified and managed on an aggregated basis by executives who are accountable for their choices;

■ new – and existing – investments are evaluated on both a stand-alone and portfolio basis; and

■ the company understands its risk management capabilities so thoroughly and its processes are so well aligned, that it can move quickly on opportunities that would be cause for trepidation or failure in less sophisticated organizations.

This is no pipe-dream. These organizations either exist or are evolving rapidly today. The management process they are embracing is one we call Enterprise-wide Risk Management (EWRM).

EWRM redefines the value proposition of risk management. How? By providing firms with the processes and tools they need to become more anticipatory and effective at evaluating, embracing and managing exposures to uncertainty as they create sustainable value for shareholders and establish competitive advantage. Inasmuch as an EWRM environment provides better information for decision-making, performance variability and loss exposure are reduced as opportunities are optimized. These capabilities deliver at least two benefits.

■ First, they give management a more compelling, and potentially differentiating, story to communicate with investors, which in turn can lead to higher price/earnings multiples in share valuations.

Business risk management is integral to the achievement of your organization's value creation objectives and the successful execution of its strategies.

■ Second, they enable the firm to pursue strategic growth opportunities with greater speed, skill and confidence. Executives know that the risks inherent in existing operations are being managed effectively; they also bring skilled risk assessment and management to new risk-taking ventures.

All told, an EWRM approach differentiates the firm's business model and builds its image and reputation with customers, suppliers, employees and the capital markets, all of which are keys to sustaining a successful business.

If your approach to risk management is not enterprise-wide, your company is missing valuable opportunities or assuming undue risk. Why? Because business risk management is integral to the achievement of your organization's value creation objectives and the successful execution of its strategies. Those companies that emerge as 'first movers' toward EWRM are seizing the high ground of competitive advantage. They are better positioned to move rapidly to profitably exploit risks which intimidate their competitors, anticipate and manage critical risks better than their competitors and reduce the costs of managing risks below those of their competitors.

Redefining the value proposition of risk management is vital in this day and age. We are at the dawn of a new economy where successful companies use powerful technologies to create wealth from assets that currently aren't measured and reported on their balance sheets. For example, a firm's customer base, its distribution and outsourcing partners, its intellectual and knowledge capital, its supply chain, its processes and systems, its resiliency, its culture and values and its brand image and reputation, to name a few, are contributing in significant ways to its market value.[1]

These increasingly sophisticated ways of creating value mean one thing: risk profiles are changing – faster than ever. Risk is more significant and yet less understood than ever before. That is why managers need to be more systematic in their approach to risk management precisely because the dynamics of creating value are changing.

This chapter presents an introductory overview of what it means – in practical terms – to embark on a journey toward developing and improving EWRM capabilities. Dynamic, often volatile changes in the global economy are driving EWRM as a management strategy to link risk with opportunity and position business risk management as a differentiating skill.

This new management solution is emerging at a growing number of leading companies who are re-examining and revitalizing their approaches to identifying, sourcing, measuring and managing risk. This chapter highlights the specific shortcomings of traditional risk management programmes and presents EWRM as the solution of choice.

---

1. Richard E. S. Boulton, Barry D. Libert and Steve M. Samek (2000) *Cracking the Value Code: How Successful Businesses are Creating Wealth in the New Economy*. HarperCollins.

A NEW APPROACH: ENTERPRISE-WIDE

EWRM is a structured and disciplined approach: it aligns strategy, processes, people, technology and knowledge with the purpose of evaluating and managing the uncertainties the enterprise faces as it creates value. 'Enterprise-wide' means just that: an elimination of functional, departmental or cultural barriers. It is a truly holistic, integrated, forward-looking and process-oriented approach to managing all key business risks and opportunities – not just financial ones – with the intent of maximizing shareholder value for the enterprise as a whole.

EWRM is not a 'one-size-fits-all' solution. Enron's implementation differs from the Royal Mail's or from Diageo's in accordance with its business model and strategies, organizational structure, culture and dedicated resources. However, there are several essential elements of EWRM which are being implemented consistently by all companies undertaking this journey.

EWRM is not rocket science, but it is both comprehensive and powerful. It essentially enables the organization to capably integrate the need to preserve capital with the desire to generate return in a growing business. It also cannot be implemented overnight. But it can be observed that as firms develop their EWRM capabilities, they are focusing resources to address the following seven essential attributes.

> **EWRM is a truly holistic, integrated, forward-looking and process-oriented approach that aligns strategy, processes, people, technology and knowledge.**

Establish goals, objectives and oversight

EWRM is built on a well-defined organizational oversight structure and assignment of accountabilities to appropriate personnel. The purpose is to make risk an integral and proactive part of the culture of the business. Explains Nick Rose, Finance Director of Diageo, the UK's £12 billion food and beverage giant, 'anybody that doesn't understand the broader business risks around their business and isn't doing something to manage risk proactively, holistically – even opportunistically – frankly, they're not using good commercial judgment and practice.'

Risk management must be integrated with business planning and strategic management so that it becomes inextricably linked to those processes. Risk management goals, objectives and policies are clearly stated and communicated throughout the enterprise and aligned with overall business objectives, strategies and performance goals. A corporate level group supports the business risk management process.

Assess business risk

Under EWRM, risks are openly and freely acknowledged and discussed. It is clearly understood by all key managers that risks matter and that everyone is responsible for managing them or else a major business factor is being left to chance. Risk assessment entails three key elements – skilful risk owners, a common risk language and a forward-looking, continuous process for identifying, sourcing and measuring risks and opportunities. These elements are applied consistently across the enterprise to:

- understand the nature of the key risks impacting on business performance to avoid unacceptable surprises;

- determine the root causes or drivers of risks to provide a basis for measuring, controlling and monitoring them;

- price individual and aggregate risks taken in terms of capital, earnings and cash flow at risk;

- evaluate risk/reward trade-offs and the effectiveness of alternative strategies to bring risk into balance with established risk parameters and limits;

- better analyze operating performance across different types of risks, investments, products and business units; and

- separate 'emotion' from 'fact' during the inevitable internal competition for economic resources to fuel new opportunities for growth.

Once a consistent risk assessment framework is developed and implemented, comparison and risk aggregation become possible and capital allocation becomes more meaningful.

Develop risk management strategies

'Risk owners' are identified for each significant risk (or group of related risks). They are responsible for co-ordinating and continuously improving risk strategy, processes and measures enterprise-wide in accordance with established business objectives. They share knowledge and best practices, so the enterprise learns only once and captures intellectual capital.

Risk strategies are selected based upon a thorough understanding of business objectives and risk, rather than custom. All available options for managing risk are evaluated during rich, intensive dialogues to select the strategy that optimizes risk and reward with a view on the enterprise as a whole rather than a narrower divisional or functional perspective.

Decisions to transfer or accept risks are evaluated not only on a stand-alone but also on an aggregate basis. This practice leads to more (a) cost-effective hedging through a better understanding and exploitation of diversification opportunities, and (b) focused relationships with risk underwriters. For example, considering natural internal offsets and changes in operating and borrowing practices can reduce the need for hedging through financial derivatives.

Design and implement risk management capabilities

As the risk sensitivity of the firm's culture is increased, its best people are leveraged in building the most effective capabilities for managing risk. These people, the 'risk owners', implement the processes, reporting, methodologies and systems that execute the selected risk strategies and policies. Finite resources are efficiently allocated to the most significant risks, therefore redundant and unnecessary risk controls are eliminated. As MarineMax's CFO Mike McLamb explains, risk owners become invaluable in designing controls 'not in the negative sense', but rather in the sense that appropriate controls add value by 'helping managers run their businesses'.

Monitor performance

Performance measures are created to monitor the execution of risk management processes and risk controls. Relevant, actionable business unit information is gathered, evaluated and reported on a standardized basis for monitoring purposes, including formalized reporting to the board and appropriate levels of management. A continuous review process is in place to ensure achievement of objectives, successful execution of strategies, compliance with policies and identification of evolving 'best practices' for managing risk. As a CFO at a large US power generation company observed, 'strategies and policies without "monitoring teeth" may as well be called hopes'.

Continuously improve risk management capabilities

Plans for improving risk management are managed closely to final completion. Benchmarking, education and training are a priority. The flow of knowledge and information about risk up, down and cross-functionally across the enterprise is facilitated and supported by all levels of management and enabled by technology.

Common frameworks translate into numerous knowledge-sharing opportunities that can drive continuous improvement. Dow Chemical's Director of Risk Management Paul Brink points out that today's information technologies – the Internet, intranets and e-mail – create tremendous opportunities to share knowledge and experience. Finnish telecommunications firm Sonera uses cellular Internet communications technology to poll risk owners and their teams regarding the likelihood and severity of key risks. At Enron, EVP and Chief Accounting Officer Rick Causey says his group is looking at an intranet as the means of providing uniform business risk assessment tools for business managers.

Support the process with information for decision-making

Timely, relevant information, including measures of individual risks, are aggregated into an overall 'portfolio' framework for more informed decision-making and linked to enterprise performance. Data and information about the effectiveness of risk management capabilities and risk control processes are provided from risk owners all over the enterprise using web-enabled feeds to data warehousing facilities. The data and information is then extracted manually or electronically by a central group for analysis and reporting purposes.

These seven essential attributes of EWRM help firms increase their capabilities to master risk as they create value. The single most important benefit of EWRM is to provide greater confidence and relevant summary information to the board, CEO and management that risks and opportunities are being systematically identified, rigorously analyzed and effectively managed on an enterprise-wide basis – all fully aligned with the enterprise's business model for creating value.

IS YOUR RISK MANAGEMENT KEEPING PACE?

Seven essential attributes of EWRM help firms master risk as they create value.

The emergence of EWRM is being fuelled by a handful of *risk drivers*, as follows.

Business at warp-speed

Change is no longer linear, but exponential. Successful companies must innovate and produce total solutions that create new sources of value for their customers or they will lose ground to nimbler, more creative rivals. This cycle of innovation requires agility and an attitudinal shift, one from 'change is inevitable (but deferrable)' to 'change is a proactive way of life'. Never ending innovation also gives rise to new risks that should be evaluated virtually real-time.

Increasingly, companies are facing a 'strategic inflection point' which is defined as 'a time in the life of a business when its fundamentals are about to change. That change can mean an opportunity to rise to new heights. But it may just as likely signal the beginning of the end.'[2] The EWRM response is to make risk an active part of the business agenda with a balanced focus on the upside as well as the downside. Understanding the consequences of inaction versus action helps managers see the full picture. 'Protect the status quo' can be a dangerous mindset in the new economy.

---

2. Andrew S. Grove (1996) *Only the Paranoid Survive: How to Exploit the Crisis Points that Challenge Every Company and Career*. Doubleday, p. 3.

Do you know your greatest risks and opportunities, today, as they evolve? Is your organization and culture capable of adapting to change? Is it able to quickly adjust its strategies to capitalize on profitable growth opportunities and respond to competitive and other risks?

Obsolete business models

Business models are changing radically in the new economy. Risk is on the rise as the boundaries of traditional business expand to include intangible 'new economy assets' or sources of value that are neither owned nor ownable (customer and supplier relationships, for example). These intangible sources of value may very well present the greatest source of risk. As power shifts from suppliers to consumers, innovative companies are altering the competitive balance in their respective industries through revolutionary business models that are built on the Internet. 'Anything that can affect industries whose total revenue base is many hundreds of billions of dollars is a big deal.'[3]

What will become of video rental chains and similar businesses around the globe in the age of on-demand Internet or satellite-based digital movie downloads? Similarly, what will become of the music industry in an age where musicians can 'net release' their own recordings? Fredrick Matteson, Executive VP of Charles Schwab & Co., summarizes this point succinctly: 'The Internet business model offers a new level of speed and efficiency for those who get it – and huge problems for those who don't.' As another astute observer pointed out: 'Volatility isn't just a currency or stock market risk anymore. Labour markets, technologies, even business models oscillate at higher frequencies – their behaviour more and more resembling that of financial markets.'[4] Indeed, the life cycle of business models is compressing in the new economy.

Is your business model focused on the right strategies that emphasize your competitive strengths and core competencies? Are you managing the risks to your reputation, brands, channels, human capital and other 'new economy assets' just as you manage the risks to your tangible physical and financial assets? How do you know?

New business practices

Just-in-time inventories, sole-sourcing, outsourcing, Internet-based sales and procurement: these are just a few of the increasingly prevalent business practices which dramatically alter risk profiles. Steve Jobs, CEO of Apple Computer,

---

3. Ibid., p. 165.
4. Thomas A. Stewart (2000) 'Managing risk in the 21st century', *Fortune*, 7 February, pp. 202–6.

recently announced that his firm has reached a milestone objective: end-of-quarter inventory levels representing less than a day's supply. ('Under 15 hours, or 0.6 days,' says Jobs.) Dell Computer actually operates with negative inventories – taking orders for PCs without components in stock. Similar shifts are underway at many more companies. But as GM Director of Risk Analysis Tom Hunter observes, while these practices cut costs, they also create new risks, such as the 'increased likelihood of business interruption'.

While the Internet and related technologies are having a major impact on external relationships and commercial transactions, their impact on internal operations and communications is increasingly pervasive. It is inevitable that we will see a marriage of 'bricks and clicks': Internet retailing supported by the inventory and delivery capabilities of so-called 'old economy' companies. As your company increasingly sells, promotes, procures, designs, distributes, plans – in general, conducts all business virtually and electronically – risk controls and contingency plans become essential.

As you adopt new practices, have you also evaluated the new risk–return trade-offs of using them?

Converging financial services providers

Boundaries between traditional suppliers of capital and intermediaries are being eliminated. Capital market providers include insurers, commercial banks, mutual and pension funds, hedge funds and corporate treasuries. Intermediaries include brokers, agents and investment bankers. The convergence of these two groups is spawning new products (derivative-like insurance and insurance-like derivatives) for transferring risk. Major investment banks, for example, are developing securitized insurance products. Some insurers and banks are partnering to provide alternative risk transfer solutions. These developments create opportunities for non-financial companies to transfer risk at lower costs.

Are you confident that your organization is looking at its exposures from an enterprise-wide perspective and considering innovative ways of managing those exposures?

Increasingly demanding investors and regulators

The global economy is becoming truly market-oriented and increasingly efficient. The ability to define a company's future in terms of its opportunities – and its ability to anticipate and manage an uncertain future – is a powerful driver of share price. Furthermore, the push towards greater disclosure is snowballing. Policy-makers, standard setters, regulators, investors and advisors want more information relating to risk and internal control. For example, in the US, the SEC has been expanding reporting requirements for risk disclosures. Legislation in Germany now requires reporting on risk management for large companies. Firms listed on the London Stock Exchange and incorporated in the UK are now required to report to shareholders on a set of defined principles relating to corporate governance (known as the Combined Code, and recently supported with guidance provided by the 'Turnbull Report'). In the UK, a recently released report calls for more improved risk reporting.[5]

Are you prepared to communicate in a public forum what your firm's risks are and how effectively you are managing them? Will your revelations inspire confidence or raise more questions than they answer? Is your reporting keeping investors informed with no surprises?

Increasingly accountable – and demanding – directors

Finally, the boss wants to know – what are my risks? Boards, CEOs and other senior executives are increasingly being held accountable and are searching for more comprehensive, holistic techniques that give them greater confidence that their organizations are identifying, measuring, controlling and monitoring risk. Too often, the focus is on reacting to financial disasters: 'Can what happened to them happen to us?' But as investor and regulator 'curiosity' heightens, and as competitors develop and communicate increasingly value-added business models, it is imperative that boards begin demonstrating equal competence in managing the 'upside'.

Should you wait until the board starts asking these and other related questions before taking action or, conversely, should you take proactive steps to address them now?

As external environment and competitive forces drive the call for timely improvements in risk management, equally important is the emergence of *new risk management tools and processes*. These include the following.

Increasingly effective processes for risk identification

Companies from a broad range of industries are finding new ways to identify the risks associated with their business activities. One of the most pervasive is risk-mapping – the process of identifying and prioritizing risks so that improvement opportunities can be identified and appropriate risk management

---

5. Institute of Chartered Accountants in England and Wales (1999) *No Surprises: The Case for Better Risk Reporting.* ICAEW.

actions can be planned. The most effective use of risk-mapping occurs when it is integrated with business planning. At Guinness, for example, the risk-mapping process generates what the firm refers to as a 'risk footprint'. This, says Finance Director Ray Joy, 'provides a backdrop for our strategy and planning'.

Is your firm utilizing risk mapping effectively to ensure it is consistently and continually identifying the full range of risks? Is your organization making the achievement of its risk management objectives a key component of the business plan?

Increasingly effective measurement tools

Leading companies have realized the need to be more rigorous in their measurement – and 'pricing' – of risk in order to ensure that returns are adequate for the risk undertaken and capital is allocated optimally. A myriad of evolving tools, such as RAROC (Risk Adjusted Return on Capital), ECAR (Economic Capital at Risk) or VaR (Value at Risk) represent quantum improvements in the pricing of risk. Says Chris Wasden, Managing Director of Azurix, Enron's new water company, 'Our CEO will not even look at a project until it has survived the RAROC process.' At Microsoft, VaR analysis is not only evaluating existing pricing relationships but is now being introduced at the product development phase. Though such tools are not infallible and all the caveats relating to 'model myopia' apply, they are a vast improvement relative to 'tea leaves and best-guesses', says Microsoft Treasurer Jean-François Heitz.

Are you using the most effective measurement tools? Are you allocating capital to the best prospects for earning acceptable returns on a risk-adjusted basis? How do you know?

Increasingly effective information tools

One reason non-financial companies may not have pursued EWRM until now is that the informational tools were not available. With the advent of the Internet, that excuse no longer exists. Firms like Boeing and ABB have been using the Internet and intranets to form 'virtual' engineering working groups for many years. Given the complexity of engineering, by comparison, the sharing and dissemination of risk management information and expertise is easier to accomplish through these enabling technologies. Companies now, for example, have access to enterprise-wide resource planning (ERP) systems such as those available from SAP, Hyperion or PeopleSoft. While these are not yet configured to work seamlessly with the risk measurement systems mentioned above, they do consolidate a great deal more information.

Is your organization capturing and utilizing all data elements relevant to measuring and managing risk?

Increasingly effective scenario analysis and planning

Similarly, companies are recognizing the need to use 'probabilistic' as well as 'deterministic' views of the future. Financial institutions do not look at discrete forecasts. Instead, they view the future as a range of possibilities. Not only is this dynamic 'portfolio-based' view of the future vital to assessing business opportunities, it defines a value-added role for risk management – identifying, understanding and managing the uncertainties an organization faces as it seeks to achieve its value creation objectives.

Ron Dembo, President of risk management consultant Algorithmics, explains that the sophisticated tools utilized by financial institutions are now migrating to non-financial firms. According to Dembo, 'Instead of looking at things the way accountants do, instead of making "point" forecasts, you value the portfolio of the corporation based on the possible ranges for all of the variables.' The result is a view of the organization's full potential, both the upside and downside.

The key risk drivers and emerging risk management capabilities call for a new approach to assessing and managing risk.

CEOs and business planners should ask themselves:

- *Can we afford to bet our company on a single forecast or even on a few discrete scenarios?*

- *Is business planning focusing solely on the upside?*

- *Are business planning and risk management separate appendages?*

- *If an adverse scenario occurs, do we know in advance what actions we will take?*

The key risk drivers and emerging risk management capabilities call for a new approach to assessing and managing risk. EWRM is an effective response to that call.

Cadbury-Schweppes: risk and the three As

EWRM is not for the timid. Companies that are implementing these processes are making a conscious choice: they intend to improve their capabilities in risk assessment and management so that their organizations become enormously effective engines of wealth creation. An example of a company just beginning this journey is the $6.8 billion chocolate, sweet and soft-drink maker, Cadbury-Schweppes plc. Its strategies are typical of companies beginning the EWRM journey described in detail in this book.

Continued ...

The watchword: value creation

In September 1996, the firm's new CEO J. M. Sunderland launched an initiative the group calls 'Managing for Value'. One of the most critical planks of this programme is a call for behavioural changes among managers and processes. To this end, the group is implementing 'the three As', challenging its organization to become more Accountable, Aggressive and Adaptable. 'Our businesses are definitely being managed more aggressively, our managers are being held more accountable, and as for adaptable, yes, if they are aggressive and accountable, they also absolutely have to be able to move more quickly in the marketplace,' explains Director of Risk Strategy Peter Cartmell. Necessarily, this cultural change 'raises the profile of risk management and flags the need to improve capabilities.'

Like other companies heading down the EWRM path, Cadbury-Schweppes is moving to integrate 'the strands' of risk management capability. Achieving co-ordination and a degree of systematization for the various risk management groups – treasury, internal audit, health/safety/environmental, insurance, for example – is now a primary goal. At the same time, the company is reconfiguring its activities to satisfy the new risk reporting requirements in the UK. As Mr Cartmell explains, 'We are already doing 95 per cent of what has been directed by the Turnbull Report, but we are improving the co-ordination between the groups that manage risk.' Ultimately, says Mr Cartmell, 'We want to put our board in a position where they fully satisfy external reporting requirements. But even more importantly, we want to optimize our risk management and give our managers a framework – put them in the best possible position to identify and manage their risks.'

As for the common framework, the company is implementing an annual risk-mapping process utilizing a common risk language. 'Everything begins from business objectives,' says Mr Cartmell. But from there, 'We've created a prompt – an indication of the wider spectrum of risks and risk actions. It's a checklist where we document our risks and more importantly, reduce the chances that there is anything out there business managers have overlooked.'

The early results

Although a new exercise and just underway, the process is clearly focusing managers' attention on potential risks and opportunities. As risks are 'flagged'

Continued …

they are analyzed carefully. 'We're finding in most cases, the situation is already fine as is,' says Mr Cartmell. But also, in many cases, significant opportunities for improvements and refinements are being uncovered and resources are being allocated accordingly. 'Although there were those in the businesses who were initially sceptical, it has provoked a lot of critical thinking,' explains Mr Cartmell. 'We are getting real value from the process.'

As for the 'three As', EWRM dovetails perfectly with the newly evolving business culture. As Mr Cartmell explains, 'There's nothing wrong with being aggressive and taking on some risk. But you have to be able to measure it, you have to be able to justify your decision, you have to be able to adapt to changing conditions and – you have to take full accountability.'

Going forward, the company is investing in further training to gain broader acceptance and understanding of a common risk language and framework. Ultimately, the company will be able to pull together risk profiles for various processes, geographic units, business units or the group as a whole. In addition, the company is also looking forward for opportunities for cross-fertilization of knowledge and practices between business units, risk management groups and processes.

All of the above steps are typical of companies beginning the EWRM journey, and all of the above steps are described in detail in this book. 'We're just getting started,' says Mr Cartmell, 'but we're learning this is definitely the direction to go.'

THE EARLY LESSONS

Because risk and opportunity are inextricably linked, past conventions and attitudes about risk as a hazard or threat have resulted in too narrow a view of the role of risk management in business. Traditional approaches are fragmented, negative (risk is downside), reactive, *ad hoc*, transaction-oriented (or cost-based), narrowly-focused and functionally-driven – in effect, treating risk management as an afterthought and an appendage to the core business.

The new paradigm is an approach that is integrated, positive (risk is both upside and downside), proactive, continuous, value-based, broadly-focused and process-driven (see Figure 1.1), making risk management integral to creating value and managing a business. EWRM adopts this new paradigm in redefining the value proposition of risk management to a business, generating a broad spectrum of well-developed capabilities and equipping managers with needed tools and frameworks for evaluating the activities of the corporation.

Fig. 1.1 Enterprise-wide risk management – a new perspective

FROM	TO
• Fragmented	• Integrated
• Negative	• Positive
• Reactive	• Proactive
• *Ad hoc*	• Continuous
• Cost-based	• Value-based
• Narrowly-focused	• Broadly-focused
• Functionally-driven	• Process-driven

The current state of risk management at most corporations is suboptimal (for a more detailed assessment of current practice, see Appendix 1). But a handful of leading companies are blazing trails towards a more effective future state – they have begun the EWRM journey. Much is being learned, and we have attempted to capture these lessons in various cases and vignettes included in this book. Here are just a few examples of companies from the world's largest organizations that are featured in this book where a risk-focused, enterprise-wide approach is taking centre-stage:

■ *Diageo plc.* The vessel for the Grand Metropolitan/Guinness merger, Diageo presides over such household brands as Burger King, Guinness, Pillsbury, Johnnie Walker, Bailey's, Gordon's, Tanqueray, Smirnoff and Moet & Chandon. Each of its well-known divisions is intensively risk-focused and follows a defined set of uniform processes. For example, every business plan details specific objectives for risks highlighted in the business unit's 'risk footprint'. Says Guinness Finance Director Ray Joy, 'Risk is a focal point for our planning and evaluation.' The group adds 'teeth', says Diageo Group Director, Finance, Nick Rose, 'by integrating this risk-focused approach with our balanced scorecard.'

■ *Enron.* Among industrial companies, no one knows risk like the world's number one buyer/seller/producer of natural gas and wholesale power. With vast trading operations and merchant power plants throughout the US and the rest of the world – not to mention rapidly growing water and fibre-optics-based communications activities – the company focuses keenly on risk/return trade-offs. Its EWRM approach represents the state of the art for non-financial organizations, with features such as sophisticated controls for extensive trading operations, a capital allocation process driven by a rigorous and comprehensive risk evaluation, and a culture that fosters rich dialogues among managers about opportunities and risks. Says EVP and Chief Risk Officer Rick Buy:

> *Every company, I don't care if you're an oil company or a widget maker, you take on risk. You have to be thinking about how that risk can help you and how that risk can hurt you. What's interesting, people always say to me that because it looks like we spend a fortune understanding, monitoring and tracking risk, we must be risk averse. The truth is, we actually are one of the bigger risk takers in our industry, if not the world. But we do it with knowledge: knowledge of each business; knowledge of risk; knowledge of the enterprise.*

■ *Holderbank*. A leading maker of cement, concrete and related aggregates is yet another organization advancing towards EWRM. Like Hydro-Quebec, Diageo and others, the Swiss-based company has taken initial steps such as the development of a common language and the implementation of a uniform process. As implementation progresses, accoutrements such as technology-based knowledge-sharing and risk aggregation and optimization are being added. According to CEO Thomas Schmidheiny, 'We live with risk every day – everyone should be thinking about, understanding, defining, identifying, measuring and managing risk.'

■ *Hydro-Quebec*. Negotiating the path from a regulated state monopoly to a market-based international developer and power-provider, this organization recognizes that risk is the common denominator of all planning and activity. Accordingly, Hydro-Quebec has just received a mandate from the board of directors to pursue a multi-phased plan to implement enterprise-wide risk management (EWRM) and has begun increasing the risk sensitivity of its culture and defining its future state.

■ *The Royal Mail*. A £7 billion organization, the UK's postal service is undergoing a dramatic restructuring. Facing a fast-moving and increasingly competitive marketplace, the group is creating a larger number of business units enabling each to focus more clearly on its risks and opportunities. This reorganization, says Group Risk Manager Nick Chown, is also an opportunity for the Royal Mail to more fully refine and implement its already broadly embedded risk evaluation and management principles and processes. 'We're in business to take risks,' says Mr Chown. 'Enterprise-wide risk management is all about giving line managers the tools and techniques they need to make better decisions relating to both the group and their individual activities – and that's what we're doing.'

This case features a large organization that is integrating risk management and quality management.

In addition to the above comprehensive cases, highly-focused lessons come from mid-sized, entrepreneurial organizations where top management is still 'close to the risk'. Consider the following:

The art 'we strive for' is teaching the organization to 'turn competitive threat into business opportunity'.

- *Eidos*. Eager to followup on the success of icon Lara Croft, star of its top selling Tomb Raider interactive video game series, Eidos knows that exciting new 'titles' are its bread and butter. 'Game development cannot be a 9 to 5 job,' says Finance Director Jeremy M. J. Lewis, so his company's processes focus on its foremost risk and opportunity: getting the most from both internal and external creative resources. Similarly, the group realizes it must develop its brands. Says Mr Lewis, 'Mickey Mouse has been around for 75 years – we're here to see that Lara has comparable staying power.'

- *MarineMax*. A giant among recreational boating dealers (approaching $500 million in sales), this firm uses risk as one of its most fundamental organizing principles. Through uniform processes (e.g. risk mapping) and continual dialogue (utilizing a common business risk language), all of its affiliates understand the most critical risks in the industry and to MarineMax specifically. Incentives, via bonuses and business planning, drive executives to manage accordingly.

CEOs at these companies (and other companies that we will discuss in this book) recognize that their organizations face a difficult yet essential challenge – they must evolve risk management practices to master risk. The art 'we strive for', says Diageo's Nick Rose, is teaching the organization to 'turn competitive threat into business opportunity'.

All told, an effectively functioning EWRM environment stimulates the desired behaviours consistent with the firm's business and risk management objectives, strategies and performance goals. Once EWRM is fully implemented, the firm will have created a culture in which risk is viewed as an essential component of any major business decision.

CONCLUSION: A JOURNEY REQUIRING A CULTURAL CHANGE

A transition that cannot happen overnight, EWRM redefines the new value proposition for risk management. It is not a 'product' that will be available on a shelf after a number of visionary 'role model' firms achieve success. Why? Because its implementation requires an effective change process. 'It is a cultural change that must be driven from the top of the organization and be customized to each organization,' says Glen Labhart, Chief Risk Officer of Dynegy, a major US energy company.

We intend to help you take a fresh look at business risk management in your firm – the first step in a journey towards EWRM. In Chapter 2, we explore *how* EWRM is evolving and is implemented.

2

The evolution towards EWRM

> *You have to realize, managing risk is everyone's job. If the price of risk isn't understood, and if the fact that it's everyone's job to manage risk isn't understood, there is no way you can progress towards anything like EWRM.*
>
> Jean-François Heitz, Treasurer, Microsoft
>
> *This is not the elimination of risk, but rather, it is an unparalleled tool for strategic planning and control.*
>
> Thomas Schmidheiny, CEO, Holderbank

The waters ahead are largely uncharted, but through the efforts of companies seeking to master risk to create value, we have a clear path for increasing the value proposition of risk management. Indeed, the elements of and the conveyances towards a true EWRM state are becoming clearer. In this chapter, we will first describe the evolution of risk management beginning with a focus on the traditional risk management model (the early stages) to a true EWRM environment (the future state). From there, we will begin describing the stepping stones along the journey to EWRM.

> EWRM represents a shift to a new strategic perspective.

THE EVOLUTION OF RISK MANAGEMENT

There are no perfect prototypes, as a true EWRM environment represents a paradigm shift to a new strategic perspective. Paradigm shifts are important in that most significant advances begin with a break from traditional thinking. The shift towards EWRM is a natural evolution, responding to the environment risk drivers and emergence of new risk management tools and processes that we discussed in Chapter 1. The continuum illustrated in Figure 2.1 describes this evolutionary shift elevating the value proposition of risk management to a strategic level.

The three key stages of evolution are further described below.

Risk management

Most organizations view risk management primarily from the traditional model of managing selected financial and hazard exposures through products and transactions and appropriate internal controls. The risks being managed via products like insurance, derivatives and the like are largely financial in nature, but also in evidence are certain elements of operational risk management – health and safety, for example.

Often applied with a 'risk as downside' paradigm, the classic risk management model uses derivatives, embedded derivatives (derivative-like clauses in contracts, e.g. indexed price adjustments in a supply contract or currency risk-sharing agreements), insurance policies, contractual indemnities and the like to mitigate the potentially negative effects of discrete or closely related events. These tools transfer the financial exposures to an independent, financially capable counterparty. Internal controls, by contrast, are also applied to manage operating exposures that are typically kept in-house; they are primarily aimed at preventing risk incidents from occurring in the first place.

Fig. 2.1 The evolution of risk management to a strategic process

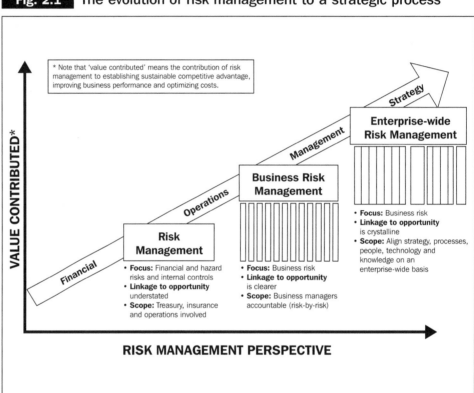

* Note that 'value contributed' means the contribution of risk management to establishing sustainable competitive advantage, improving business performance and optimizing costs.

Risk Management
• **Focus:** Financial and hazard risks and internal controls
• **Linkage to opportunity** understated
• **Scope:** Treasury, insurance and operations involved

Business Risk Management
• **Focus:** Business risk
• **Linkage to opportunity** is clearer
• **Scope:** Business managers accountable (risk-by-risk)

Enterprise-wide Risk Management
• **Focus:** Business risk
• **Linkage to opportunity** is crystalline
• **Scope:** Align strategy, processes, people, technology and knowledge on an enterprise-wide basis

VALUE CONTRIBUTED*

RISK MANAGEMENT PERSPECTIVE

Financial — Operations — Management — Strategy

Sophisticated examples of derivatives in use include hedging multiple risks with basket options, using cross-hedging instruments (that associate, for example, the level of interest rates with sales), trigger options and other structured products. In the insurance markets, products are used to manage the risks of natural disasters, environmental liability, health and safety, product reliability and other operations risks creating property, income loss, liability and human resources exposures. Under traditional risk management, 'lessons learned' are often applied to other areas. For example, techniques for managing foreign currency risk are applied with appropriate modifications to commodity price risk, e.g. energy risk management.

Many executives view the breadth and scope of traditional risk management as inadequate in the new economy. Three shortcomings stand out in particular, as follows.

Responsibility for risk management is often fragmented

A narrow focus on a few specific financial and hazard risks often leads to the view that risk management is a 'cost centre' managed by a small group of individuals rather than a broader enterprise-wide activity involving everyone. Managers are often taught 'don't worry about the foreign exchange risk – just manage your business in dollars and those guys in treasury will protect your budget rates,' explains John Fitzpatrick of Union Carbide. This feeds the view that risk management is 'someone else's job'.

While a fragmented approach of separate risk management units striving towards functional excellence may offer short-run contractual protection from discrete risks, a question arises. Are there more effective solutions or 'long-term' value-adding strategies that are more operationally focused? For example, some treasurers have hedged foreign exchange exposures associated with overseas sales, enabling operating personnel to focus on the core manufacturing business. But hedging may not always be the best answer. The risks arising from day-to-day operations can only be dealt with – over the long term – by solutions of an operational nature, such as changing R&D, inventory and labour sourcing to weak currency environments, establishing regional netting centres to 'net down' currency risk before hedging and addressing product pricing based upon elasticity studies.

The focus is on discrete risks, not the business portfolio

The application of the classic risk management model is sometimes based upon a view of risks in isolation, either by risk type or by the unit or activity potentially exposed to the risks. This approach ignores the benefits of netting exposures that offset on an enterprise-wide basis. As Thomas Hunter, Director of Risk Analysis at GM explains, 'In the past you would have various operating companies buying insurance with no one saying "hey, wait a minute, couldn't we do this better if we look at insurance needs from a company-wide perspective?"'

As Keith Johnson, Manager of Planning and Evaluation at Rio Tinto plc explains, 'the problem with a product or hedging focus is that you fail to see the effects on the company overall. You can hold back the river for a short while, but if it's a real flood, you're going to need something more substantial than derivative contracts.' At Rio Tinto, 'we have to think about *30 years* of iron ore or copper flowing from a mine. It is not practical to hedge 30 years of cashflow.' The company's response, therefore, begins by looking at its entire portfolio of metals exposure, leaving it only to deal with the residual risks from a more diversified portfolio. Companies need a strategy, not a finger in the dyke.

Risk management is not a product or a transaction

'Derivatives are useful, insurance is useful, but without putting in the time to really understand your risks these can do more harm than good,' says Ray Joy,

Finance Director of Guinness plc. 'You cannot "buy" risk management, you cannot delegate risk management to "a group over there", it has to become part and parcel of your overall culture.' We agree. Risk management is integral to, not independent of, broader corporate strategies.

Of course, a competent and well executed hedging programme can be very important. Even if the impact is merely the delay of adverse effects on the achievement of a business plan, the classic risk management focus on products and transactions has delivered significant value in many industries and companies. But following years of a narrow focus on a few financial and hazard risks, leading executives have begun to examine:

- the manner in which risk is viewed (differentiating operational versus contractual exposures, for instance);
- the process by which risk information is gathered and analyzed; and
- the means by which responsibility for managing risk is rewarded.

For example, says Paul Brink of Dow Chemical, 'Those closest to the risks have to be directly engaged in the management of the risks.' For this reason, cutting-edge treasury and insurance functions are taking a broader, more strategic view of the business, leading their organizations to a more formal and systematic approach to managing operational and other business risks.

Risk management is integral to, not independent of, broader corporate strategies.

Business risk management

The shortcomings of a narrow risk focus are leading many companies to a more comprehensive view on managing other risks in the business. This broader management approach effectively integrates the efforts of operating managers with the activities of risk managers. Business risk management doesn't view risk as an afterthought – or something to be delegated to separate functions such as insurance, treasury, finance or internal audit. Rather, as Microsoft's Jean-François Heitz asserts, understanding and managing risk becomes 'part of everyone's job'. 'Everyone accountable' becomes a fundamental operating philosophy.

Over the years, large highly publicized risk incidents in non-financial areas have caused firms to underperform. As these incidents occur, they increase awareness on the part of senior managers and their boards that many different types of risk, which are not addressed by traditional risk management, can impair business performance. These executives also realize that most, if not all, of these risks are manageable and that it is possible that many are not being managed effectively. Therefore firms evolve toward business risk management by implementing a more systematic risk evaluation process, assigning accountability for managing major risk areas to appropriate managers and applying proven risk management processes and techniques to all critical risks.

But the evolution to business risk management goes beyond the management of surprises. As they expand their own spheres of influence, there have been increases in the sophistication of both the treasury and insurance functions – the functions driving the classic risk management model described above. The most sophisticated companies increasingly apply risk modelling techniques such as Monte Carlo simulation and options theory not only to financial risks but also to broader strategic issues. Merck, for example, uses option-based measurement tools in managing the risks inherent in its lengthy research and development pipeline for new drugs, extending over many years. At Azurix, Managing Director Chris Wasden says his firm is adopting more sophisticated techniques. 'A lot of companies look at a project's NPV. But that's a discrete number based on a whole array of assumptions. We use assumptions too, but instead of generating a single NPV, we generate a probabilistic distribution. That is much more meaningful.' Insurance managers are increasingly using more rigorous tools while also improving their knowledge and use of multi-line, multi-year coverages.

At the same time, a business risk management focus means that risk and operating managers make their best efforts to get 'closer' to the source of risks. For example, Dow Chemical's Fernando Ruiz leads efforts to expand treasury's influence beyond currency and interest rates into commodity and perhaps other operating risks. He says, 'We are doing as much as we can to help line managers recognize their risks, and we, ourselves, are learning as much as we can about their businesses to help us with our decisions and strategies.' Companies like Dow, Intel, Merck, Motorola, MarineMax and Diageo are also facilitating knowledge sharing between their treasury and insurance functions and their line managers. As Chris Wasden explains, 'The risk managers need to understand the business; the business managers need to understand risk – so much so that risk and business management become indistinguishable.'

> 'The risk managers need to understand the business; the business managers need to understand risk – so much so that risk and business management become indistinguishable.'

Order versus chaos: the call for leadership

Myriad elements of every organization are evolving towards a more holistic approach. The choice for the CEO becomes: do we allow these 'pieces of the total puzzle' to transform themselves independently and chaotically, or do we provide leadership and co-ordination from the top? Examples of the functions that are expanding their circles of influence towards a more holistic enterprise-wide view include the following:

■ *Treasury and insurance functions* are proactively seeking to increase the value they contribute to the organization through their respective risk management roles.

Continued ...

- *Executive management* is seeking to consolidate risk assessment and management into strategic management and business planning processes. The desire is to move from an *ad hoc* approach (a strong treasury manager or internal audit function promoting comprehensive risk management and selling it up the organization), to a more broadly implemented approach in which risk identification, assessment and management is an integral part of everyone's job.

- *Operations personnel* are now recognizing that there are new processes, frameworks and tools available to help them identify, measure and manage risks. The challenge they face is that the forward-looking, anticipatory view of managing risk is a very different approach from the one they know best – the focus on managing cost, quality and time process performance.

- *Chief legal officers* are beginning to look at how they can add value beyond traditional compliance issues to address broader strategic issues.

- *Internal auditors* are emerging as key players in risk management. They are undergoing their own transition because the traditional compliance-driven approach of the past is not dynamic or forward-looking – which is inconsistent with the proactive mindset an organization needs to manage risk in turbulent times. For example, at GM, General Director of Audit Services Angie Chin insists 'internal audit is working very hard to become more value-added, more proactive, in the way it looks at the business'. At Marconi in the UK, internal audit is implementing a quarterly review process covering the full range of business risks and opportunities and making extensive use of risk mapping and related interactive processes. Internal audit is also supporting EWRM with technology tools at Charles Schwab and Pioneer International.

- *Chief risk officers* are emerging in non-financial firms with the responsibility of co-ordinating the integration of business risk management across the organization. Examples include Dynegy, Hydro-Quebec, Holderbank and Enron – to name only a few.

Overall, an integrated approach to business risk management is leading to the development of more sophisticated tools and processes to address individual risks. However, the above individuals and groups realize that the 'right answer' lies in a still more comprehensive approach – an enterprise-wide approach.

Enterprise-wide risk management

As risk management has broadened to business risk management, the focus has been limited primarily to managing individual risks and groups of related risks. Often, there is a lack of consistency across the enterprise in terms of the level of detail, reporting formats, management methods and guidelines; therefore, it is difficult for executives to evaluate risks in terms of their aggregate effects on the entire business. And while the linkage of risk to opportunity is not as understated as it was under the classic model, it must be clearer still.

Although the broader focus on business risk is a positive step forward, EWRM takes additional steps to raise the value proposition to the highest level. EWRM positions business risk management as a disciplined and rational process of pursuing opportunity which, depending on the nature of the firm's business model, may even increase the firm's exposure to performance variability. In addition, EWRM retains the traditional risk management focus on reducing loss exposure to an acceptable level.

An EWRM approach:

- implements a common language that facilitates internal and external communication;
- provides a consistent reporting framework for aggregating risk measures and information;
- fosters increased management confidence through a systematic approach that identifies all of the enterprise's risks;
- supports resource allocation through rigorous prioritization of risk;
- reduces transfer costs due to offsetting or pooling of risks; and
- creates a disciplined, structured process for making the vital decisions, e.g. accept/reject risk, pool risks for measurement purposes, select risk strategies and decide on risk management improvements.

EWRM also measures the portfolio effects of multiple risks that are beyond intuitive guesswork because of the complex interrelationships between risks and the factors affecting them, e.g. instrument terms, environment risk drivers and other variables.

As we have said, there are no complete EWRM prototypes to follow. But tools, techniques and processes are now available to companies that want to make a serious attempt at dramatically improving their risk management and, hence, their competitive capabilities. These include:

- *advances in information technology* allowing the collection and analysis of internally and externally available data, which can be efficiently converted into strategic, real-time intelligence and used to support measurement methodologies;
- *practical advances in the application of measurement and analytical methodologies* which, when combined with information technology, enable the use of a host of risk analytics and models;
- *cultural shifts* toward knowledge management and total quality which provide incentives – and capabilities – to continuously improve processes and strategies.

Once management teams understand the potential for increased effectiveness in their risk management, they will quickly recognize the advantages of combining these tools, interactive processes and techniques. Says consultant Ron Dembo, 'The day of industrial companies practising an enterprise-wide approach is dawning.'

An EWRM approach is anticipatory, proactive and supports the business model for creating value. While avoiding bad bets and hedging current bets is vitally important, business risk management is also about making the best bets possible in the new economy, consistent with the firm's stated business objectives, strategies and performance goals. Risk, therefore, is as much a 'friend' as it is an 'enemy'. Under EWRM, the opportunities targeted by the firm's business model give risk management a clear context – to assist the firm in managing its exposures to uncertainties that could impact on the successful execution of that model.

> **An EWRM approach is anticipatory, proactive and supports the business model for creating value.**

EWRM integrates business risk management activities with the strategic management and business planning processes so the organization:

- identifies the opportunities for creating value that present the most attractive risk/reward trade-offs based on a thorough understanding of the business realities in the external environment;

- designs a business model that is responsive to those opportunities;

- obtains a holistic, enterprise-wide understanding of the risks inherent in (a) the firm's assets and processes used to execute the chosen business model, and (b) the information used for decision-making;

- acquires the capabilities to effectively manage the risks inherent in the firm's business model, including knowledgeable people, effective processes and supporting technology;

- collects, analyzes and synthesizes relevant external and internal data to produce actionable, consistent and timely business risk management information;

- selects and implements the best strategy for exploiting desirable risks while concurrently mitigating or eliminating undesirable risks, all to enhance the prospects for successful implementation of the business model; and

- supports business units in achieving business performance goals in a proactive and empowered, yet well controlled, environment.

If organizations desire to create competitive advantage by taking risk management to a strategic level, they must raise the bar. The prescription is a comprehensive, transparent, consistent and continuously improved approach that aligns strategy, processes, people, technology and knowledge. The goal is to optimize risk, return, growth and capital for the enterprise as a whole.

Momentum for EWRM is already underway. Visionary leaders from treasury, internal audit and other functions – most often with support from top management – have helped their organizations to understand risk more clearly. Senior executives are supporting the implementation of integrated, cross-functional strategies, albeit focused on individual risks. But there is room for improvement. Although not every organization will adopt all elements of EWRM, it is the direction toward which many organizations will migrate over time. The question these organizations must ask is: when do we begin the journey?

TAKING AN ENTERPRISE-WIDE VIEW

So what does it really mean to take an enterprise-wide view? This question appears deceptively easy, but its implications are important. In a nutshell, taking an enterprise-wide view means that every decision made is meant to improve the organization as a whole, not any particular part. It will, at times, entail making significantly different decisions than one might make from within a specific function or department or even a single operating unit.

Managers might assume this is the normal course of affairs within their organization, but that is not likely. In many companies, information flows up and down the organization. Most managers are responsible for looking 'downward' over the people, resources and responsibilities for which they are accountable. They establish objectives and make the best choices they can over their span of control, as defined by the organization. On matters like corporate strategy, they look 'upward' to receive direction from more senior managers. However, rarely do they look 'horizontally' across different departments or operating units, or even at an 'angle' (to network and interact with more senior or junior managers of *other* operating units, for instance) unless there are processes that stimulate such behaviour.

In Chapter 7, we will stress the importance of four-way interactive information and knowledge sharing. Senior management typically must create the environment in which this kind of co-ordination occurs. The problem is, as information flows up the organization to more senior managers, it becomes more general; details are left behind, and hence, the opportunities for joint or co-ordinated action become blurred. The challenge of taking an enterprise-wide view is finding a way to understand the impact of every key decision at every level of the organization on every other decision. Hence, the choices managers make will always consider the interests of the organization as a whole.

This systematic approach can create dysfunctional behaviour if each manager's objectives and incentives and the firm's performance measurement systems do not also reflect an enterprise-wide perspective. The manager in charge of manufacturing, for instance, might have different incentives than the manager in charge of procurement. The manager in charge of procurement might be rewarded to find the best raw materials for the corporation at the lowest possible prices, even if that means being flexible with suppliers in terms of material specifications or timing of delivery. The manager in charge of manufacturing, by contrast, might

> Every decision made is meant to improve the organization as a whole.

be motivated to operate a consistent, reliable production schedule, and may not want to be constrained by the availability of input materials or the downtime resulting from retooling to accommodate variations in raw material quality.

If each of these, managers make the best choice for the organization relative to their own specific areas of responsibility, the result may not have the best consequences for the organization as a whole. Making the best choice for the organization as a whole, however, might make one – or both – manager(s) appear as if they were less effective at their respective roles. Hence, the ways in which their performance is assessed and rewarded significantly affect the implementation of an enterprise-wide view.

The firm's operating philosophy significantly influences the definition of an enterprise-wide view. For example, senior management may establish operating units to act as stand-alone profit centres or encourage competition among employees. In such firms, EWRM is applied at the operating unit level rather than to the organization as a whole. In order for EWRM to be appropriate, the objectives of all employees must be aligned, including the incentive to co-ordinate and integrate one another's activities, to generate and share information on their respective activities, and to take an active interest in the success and profitability of the larger organization.

Structuring such incentives is a change-enablement challenge requiring careful study of the needs of the larger organization. Before initiating the process of committing people to new behaviours outside their historical paradigm and modifying performance incentives accordingly, senior management should understand all the consequences of such actions and the economic justification. This issue should be addressed when defining the business case and shared vision for implementing EWRM, as discussed in Chapter 9.

There is another way to think about EWRM which may offer some insight into the nature of the firm itself. Senior management must find ways of turning many individuals with private self-interests into a unified force acting in the interests of the whole. As the organization gets larger or more complex, this becomes more difficult to accomplish. Therefore, one way in which we may rephrase the question as to the appropriate use of EWRM is to ask: how do the boundaries of the firm affect the ability of senior managers to implement an enterprise-wide approach?

This question of boundaries is a subtle one. Just what are the boundaries of 'the firm'? In recent years, some have argued that the firm is a group of stakeholders, i.e. people who have any interest or substantive involvement in the corporation. The new economy is certainly blurring traditional organizational lines, driving a more expansive view of the firm's stakeholders. For example, the business models of successful companies are now encompassing customers, suppliers, distributors and retailers within the informal boundaries of the organization – which makes them active stakeholders in the business. But stakeholders also include employees, alliance partners, co-venturers, shareholders, regulators, bankers, environmental interests groups and residents of the communities in which the firm conducts business. However defined, stakeholders must be consulted when the firm makes key decisions, or at least considered during the decision-making process.

Therefore, when considering the practical question of defining the boundaries of the firm, it makes sense to ask: Over what range of activities can we implement an enterprise-wide view of the organization? Taking an enterprise-wide view means aiming at achieving the highest level of return possible from the resources available to managers within those boundaries, as defined. This thinking raises another question. If there are resources which do not contribute to the enterprise-wide goal, should they be divested or reorganized into more efficient units? The bottom line is that there should be a compelling reason for managers to sustain any activity within the organization; otherwise the activity should be eliminated or outsourced at a lower cost.

When all is said and done, management's vision of EWRM should be consistent with its view of the organization. That enterprise-wide view might extend over the entire corporation, or it may be limited to distinct operating units (which some would argue is 'sub-enterprise-wide'). In the latter case, however, executives should have strong reasons for why it is efficient to combine these operating units under a common corporate umbrella. Imposing an enterprise-wide view (or any other common direction) over units that are left to define their own vision and business concept may be inefficient, and hence not in the best interests of shareholders. Such units may be candidates for divestiture, as they may be more valuable outside the corporate umbrella than within.

Aggregating risks and opportunities should be a priority for any efficiently organized company.

The practical view of all of this thinking is that for any efficiently organized company, devising some method of aggregating its risks and opportunities should be a priority. Aggregation for results only makes sense when the components being aggregated are resources which are directed at achieving a common purpose. If these resources cannot be directed at achieving a common purpose, then management needs to consider whether they are best maintained within the firm's formal boundaries.

ACHIEVING EWRM: THE STEPS ALONG A VISIONARY JOURNEY

We have explained what EWRM is and discussed its migration from the classic risk management model. We have also discussed the implications of an enterprise-wide view. We now turn to a description of a hypothetical journey towards achieving EWRM.

As described above, EWRM is an alignment of certain key elements of an organization, with its business model and strategies. The orientation is to optimize risk, return, growth and capital. While the journey from business risk management to EWRM is not easy, the evolution can be simplified by focusing on the individual elements.

The key components – the stepping stones – towards EWRM are as follows:

- Adopt a common language.

- Establish overall risk management goals, objectives and oversight structure.

- Implement uniform processes for assessing business risk and developing risk management strategies.

- Design and implement risk management capabilities to execute defined risk management strategies.

- Build on the above foundation to continuously improve strategies, processes and measures for individual risks.

- Aggregate multiple risk measures.

- Link aggregate measures to enterprise performance.

- Build on all of the above capabilities to formulate an enterprise-wide risk strategy, resulting in new insights which spawn new risk management capabilities.

These steps along the journey that elevates business risk management to an enterprise-wide process are illustrated in Figure 2.2. Each of the steps build the enterprise's business risk management capabilities. They are further discussed below.

Fig. 2.2 Steps along the journey to EWRM

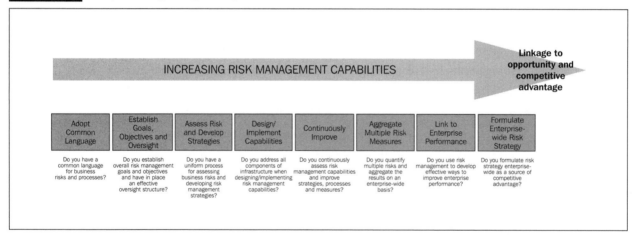

Common language

If an organization is going to co-ordinate its efforts, it has to be able to communicate. The need to develop a well understood vocabulary is essential – and this is a common theme among all companies moving towards an EWRM vision. Companies that combine a common language with a uniform risk assessment process, attest to more effective discussions at the highest levels of the organization. These discussions result in a better understanding of risk and lead to more effective risk management actions.

As Mike McLamb, CFO of MarineMax, explains: 'You do not have to call everything a "risk", but it is important to make certain that when someone talks about "customer satisfaction" or "inventory control" everyone else in the room understands what that means and what its implications are for the business.' Fernando Ruiz, Treasury Manager at Dow Chemical, takes the concept still further and says, 'There is a great deal of overlap between areas such as insurance, treasury and investment portfolio management. We want these groups to adopt a common framework and that means they have to understand one another. So yes, we are trying to develop a common language.' Microsoft's Jean-François Heitz also sees a common language as an important goal. 'We have to be able to communicate – concepts, frameworks, processes.'

In creating a common language, companies need to look at defining both their risks and their processes. The risk language includes obvious risks, but the lexicon should also consider the sources of uncertainty arising from so-called 'change events', e.g. consummating a new merger or acquisition, developing new business, implementing a new system, continuously improving a process, formulating new business strategies, introducing new products, entering new markets and other changes that are likely to spawn new risks. A process language is also useful as it breaks down the business into its operating and supporting components. Understanding processes is essential for assessing the sources or root causes of risks.

> 'We have to be able to communicate – concepts, frameworks, processes.'

Devising and implementing a common language – and a model for identifying critical risks and processes – is discussed in Chapter 3. Subsequent chapters introduce other frameworks that contribute to a common language.

Establish goals, objectives and oversight

One of the most important steps for management to take is to define the goals and objectives that they desire to accomplish with business risk management. Further, it is important to establish risk management responsibilities within the framework provided by an effective oversight structure. With these established goals and objectives, a working committee of senior managers can begin to oversee the deployment of the firm's business risk management capabilities. This vital step is outlined in Chapter 4.

Assess risk and develop strategies, and Design/implement capabilities

Another common goal of companies moving towards EWRM is the development of uniform processes and tools for identifying, sourcing and measuring risk and evaluating risk management strategies. As Mr Ruiz of Dow Chemical explains,

'Although different groups are looking at different risks, we're trying to look at all risks within one framework. In the past, treasury, operations, insurance, portfolio managers – we all ran our own shops trying to optimize one part. Over the last few years, what we are trying to do is create a framework to look at all risks from a more standard perspective.' The advantages are many, says Mr Ruiz, but foremost in his mind is the 'ability to compare apples to apples, not apples to oranges' enterprise-wide. Says Mr Ruiz, 'We are now working with the businesses trying to identify and manage exposures in a consistent fashion.'

A risk management process has common elements. We see the following tasks as vital to the identification and management of any risk:

- Assess business risks.

- Formulate risk strategies.

- Design/implement risk management capabilities to execute risk strategies by integrating the following components of infrastructure – processes, people, management reports, methodologies and systems and data.

- Monitor the performance of the process and the risk levels themselves.

- Continuously improve risk management capabilities.

Critical to all of these tasks is the collection and analysis of information for decision-making. A common set of processes provides an essential foundation ('apples to apples') for defining, organizing and reporting information that is relevant across the business units and processes and should be aggregated enterprise-wide. The execution of the various tasks of a uniform risk management process is explained in Chapters 5 and 6.

Continuously improve strategies, processes and measures

A firm's models and uniform processes for understanding its business risks and an enterprise-wide understanding of the components of risk management infrastructure provide a common language and strong foundation for continuously improving its risk management capabilities. The goal is to capitalize more effectively on organizational knowledge – and external knowledge – as it relates both to risk identification and management. As Nick Rose, Group Finance Director for Diageo, explains, 'there are enormous opportunities for pooling knowledge and sharing expertise both within and across business units.' An essential tool – the Risk Management Capability Maturity Continuum – supports staged improvements over time. It is introduced in Chapter 7, which also examines a few of the methods of identifying and sharing best practices.

Aggregate multiple risk measures, Link to enterprise performance, and Formulate enterprise-wide risk strategy

Although financial services firms clearly lead, there is a growing awareness of the importance of (a) correlating the effects of multiple risks on the business, (b) understanding the effects of comprehensive risk management strategies on enterprise performance and the firm's value creation objectives, and (c) using these more sophisticated capabilities to evaluate strategic alternatives for the enterprise as a whole. This is not a theoretical concept. Risk-adjusted performance measurement has evolved significantly at world-class financial institutions and is considered 'best practice' for managing market and credit risks. VaR and EaR (Earnings at Risk) measurement methodologies are becoming more accepted by corporate enterprises and regulators alike.

Increasingly, these tools are seen as invaluable for allocating capital and measuring performance based on the risks inherent in a business or portfolio. These and related tools can also strengthen links between performance, accountability and established risk thresholds. Regulators often view the presence of VaR type models as an indication that the enterprise has a handle on understanding its risks.

All told, these last three steps are the culmination of the journey to EWRM. They enable managers to (a) maximize the expected return and firm value for a given level of risk, (b) consider the impact of risk on capital, i.e. both the adequacy of allocated capital and its exposure to loss, and (c) achieve the firm's target leverage and desired return on allocated capital. Reviewed in Chapter 8, these final steps combined with prior steps link risk with opportunity and position business risk management as a source of competitive advantage.

Resistance and roadblocks

That there is a clear trend towards EWRM is not to say there is total support for the idea. Research for this project encountered numerous nay-sayers. Some of the roadblocks and objections include the following:

What's the value?

At the outset, EWRM may appear to some as a 'big ticket intangible'. One executive asked us, 'If I can't measure the benefits in terms of my bottom-line, why would I do anything?'

Continued ...

We agree EWRM must be measurable. And it will be as soon as measures emanating from its consistent application are well established. An example is reduced funding costs through better bond ratings for those companies able to demonstrate to rating agencies that they are applying sound risk management practices. Other examples include lower operating costs from reduced insurance and hedging transactions. The value proposition of EWRM is to help firms establish competitive advantage, improve business performance and reduce costs. This book provides insights on ways in which these benefits can be realized.

Where's the prototype?

Many managers insist there is a large gap between theory and application. 'Everyone agrees that risk aggregation and optimization makes sense,' says the finance director for a European telecommunications firm. 'But translating the theory into practice is next to impossible. Aside from a few banks, who is actually doing this?'

We agree that EWRM isn't easy to implement. But aggregating and optimizing risks begins with understanding their key drivers and focusing on the vital few. Those companies that begin the EWRM journey will be better positioned to accomplish this task than those that don't. This book provides examples of non-financial institutions that have begun that journey.

Where's the hard data?

Many managers say their systems simply do not have the information available to support any form of credible 'organization-wide' risk assessment. Without hard evidence, there is no incentive to push ahead. 'Since neither shareholders or regulators are demanding it,' explains Craig MacDonald of World Research Advisory (WRA), 'most companies haven't bothered developing it, so they do not have any information proving conclusively that it's a worthwhile goal.'

In this book, we illustrate several companies that are quite satisfied that their enterprise-wide risk assessments are not only credible, but are a vital adjunct to their business planning process.

Why get myself in hot water?

Managers hold their cards close to the chest and won't admit this openly, but the fact is some believe that EWRM is a Pandora's box. CEOs/CFOs say that their operating people don't want to admit to all the risks they really have. The CFO of a US sporting goods maker admits: 'I'm almost afraid to look.'

Ignorance is not the bliss some say it is. The directors of Barings didn't know their risks until it was too late.

Continued ...

Why damage our share valuation?

Although financial theory says Wall Street looks at risks too, the real focus is on earnings. As Rick Lawlor of WRA explains, 'If a few companies begin systematically listing their risks, their valuations could suffer pretty dramatically.' In short – the fear is that leaders could get 'stung'.

A recent UK publication on risk reporting challenges this view.[1] That publication shows that companies are already disclosing much information about their risks and recommends improved organization of that information to make risk reporting more transparent in the information age.

Why focus on saving pennies?

One potential benefit of EWRM is lower insurance costs, says David Fields of AIG Risk Finance. 'Relatively uncorrelated risks can be bundled to create better coverage at a lower premium.' But CFOs counter that insurance costs are relatively low these days, so the effort required would not warrant the savings. As the Risk Management Director at Rolls-Royce observes, 'there is no point in doing all of that pooling stuff because insurance is so cheap.' WRA's Craig MacDonald adds a related impediment: 'CFOs are in cost centres. If they go out and buy insurance products to combine financial risks with operating risks, that could thrust them into the operating budgets – and that's not something they seem anxious to put their arms around.'

Saving transaction costs is just one possible benefit of EWRM. There are many others that we illustrate in this book.

Isn't EWRM only for banks?

Financial institutions are indeed in the lead. Also, some of the leaders among commercial and industrial companies, like energy companies Dynegy and Enron, have significant trading arms that could be likened to a bank's operations. 'But make no mistake,' says Dynegy's Chief Risk Officer Glenn Labhart, 'we're an industrial company, and our enterprise-wide approach does not stop at energy trading.'

This book is focused primarily on non-financial companies, but its concepts also apply to financial institutions.

Continued ...

---

1. Institute of Chartered Accountants in England and Wales (1999) *No Surprises: The Case for Better Risk Reporting*. ICAEW.

If you can't measure it, why do it?

What gets measured, gets managed. As one executive of a US consumer products company asked us, 'How do you measure fraud risk, the risk of proprietary knowledge being compromised by hackers, earthquake risk and the risk of economic collapse in third-world countries? Without specific measures, isn't EWRM just theoretical stuff?'

Although some risks can be difficult to measure, they will not disappear if left unmeasured. Even if initial attempts at quantification can, at best, only be described as crude, they can at least lead to increased knowledge about risks and ultimately toward more refined measures.

Managers who are actually heading towards the EWRM state have little tolerance for dismissal of the concept. Says Enron Chief Risk Officer Rick Buy:

> *Every company is making bets. I've watched Enron convert from a regulated pipeline to what we are today – an industry leader in numerous segments – and it all happened because we bring this risk-focused mentality to an industrial business. We wouldn't be where we are today without this. People can dismiss it, but to my mind that's just putting your head in the sand.*

HOW FAR WILL YOU GO?

EWRM is not about making individuals better at what they already do. It is about making organizations better at managing risk through the collective and co-ordinated capabilities of individuals, functions and units. It is about building the capabilities to link risk and opportunity and position business risk management as a source of competitive advantage.

As firms create new sources of value during the twenty-first century by expanding markets, introducing new products and reconfiguring the value chain in the eyes of the customer, our premise is that they will make some fairly significant bets along the way. The fragmented risk management practices of the past are not the pathway to excellence in managing the risks associated with those bets. And don't forget: changing conditions and circumstances will inevitably spawn new risks and opportunities. The firms that are successful in managing their risks in this evergreen environment will, *over time*, maximize earnings and enjoy competitive advantage over firms that aren't. Herein lies the true value proposition of risk management to a business – wealth creation.

But how far should you go? You should recognize that the further along the journey your firm travels, the greater the alignment of strategy, processes, people, technology and knowledge, and hence the more integrated the management of risk and opportunity becomes. With each successive step, the degree of integration and sophistication increases – raising the level of complexity and the extent of commitment required. The firm's culture, the relative maturity of its risk management capabilities, the degree of centralization or decentralization, the comparability of the risk profiles relating to different product groupings and businesses within the enterprise and other factors must be considered when deciding the nature and extent of the firm's EWRM journey. We will explore these factors further in this book.

Why begin the journey? There can be many reasons (see Figure 2.3). That's why it is vital that each firm makes its own assessment of the benefits in order to determine just how far along the EWRM journey it desires to go. As a general rule, the more mature a firm's capabilities in terms of the skilled people, the processes and the supporting methodologies and technology committed to business risk management, the more steps the firm can realistically expect to take along the pathway to EWRM.

Fig. 2.3 Why begin the journey?

MOST COMMON REASONS

- Expand corporate governance
- Unexpected losses
- Implement strategic management tool
- Rapidly changing environment
- KPI shortfalls and tightened profit margins
- Manage changing business model
- Improve management of new economy assets
- Improve capital budgeting decisions

OTHER POSSIBLE REASONS

- Aggressive growth strategies, including M&A
- Improved integration desired
- Address lack of change readiness
- Incentives/rewards not aligned
- Address fragmented and narrow focus
- Reduce reactive decision-making
- More holistic approach desired

CONCLUSION

The trend towards EWRM recognizes that (a) risks are interrelated and (b) there are significant benefits that can be achieved from evaluating and managing risk on a comprehensive enterprise-wide basis. Companies are on a development continuum with respect to managing the uncertainties associated with creating value. That continuum begins with the management of discrete financial and hazard risks, broadens to encompass true business risk management and eventually evolves to an EWRM approach. EWRM is a more proactive and holistic approach to managing business risk. It is in any case superior to the *ad hoc*, reactive and fragmented activities of functions and departments operating as independent silos or to the management of business risk on an individual risk-by-risk basis.

How far a company progresses along the continuum to EWRM will be driven by its own experience and structural circumstances as well as by its desire to outperform competitors. As with any significant change, the adoption of a new perspective on risk is fundamentally a process of education, building awareness, developing buy-in and ultimately assigning accountability and accepting ownership. Firms must recognize that their risks will continue to change and evolve even as the global marketplace is changing and evolving. Therefore, developing an effective, enterprise-wide view of risk management will always be a journey, not an event. It is our premise that your company should begin that journey to transform risk management so that it is a source of competitive advantage, risk management costs are optimized and business performance is improved.

As suggested by the steps in the journey, EWRM itself is achieved in stages, beginning with the development of a common language and uniform processes, and progressing all the way to the true, aggregated and optimizing EWRM state. The ensuing chapters will now detail these stages.

How far a company progresses along the EWRM journey will be driven by its desire to outperform competitors.

3

A common language: the essential starting point

If language is not correct, then what is said is not what is meant; if what is said is not what is meant, then what must be done remains undone.

Confucius

We have to be able to communicate – concepts, frameworks, processes.

Jean-François Heitz, Treasurer, Microsoft

We have found our customized risk model a useful tool for sustaining a dialogue about our risks. I think intuitively, by being better able to understand how all our risks interrelate, we have a better understanding of our overall business process.

John Bukovski, Vice President and Chief Financial Officer, Unicom

An EWRM approach is about aligning strategy, processes, people, technology and knowledge to redefine the value proposition of risk management. Integrating these activities begins with the commitment of people to make risk management an active part of the agenda of the business. A common language supports this commitment, particularly when it is used in conjunction with an effective process that everyone understands and applies to their specific areas of responsibility.

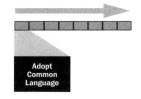

We will now outline a common language; ensuing chapters and cases show its application in practice.

A common language is a tool for facilitating and sustaining an ongoing dialogue among the firm's managers and employees about risk and the processes affected by risk. Establishing commonality is vital because each individual has a different understanding and perspective of the business. Different managers have different roles and responsibilities for managing the effects of change on the business. They also have differing biases and beliefs regarding the role of risk in managing an enterprise – some useful, some not. More likely than not, they also have their own unique functional, process or business unit lexicon. The lack of a common perspective or language inhibits communication and therefore impairs effective risk management.

The lack of a common language inhibits communication and impairs effective risk management.

Without a common language supporting a uniform process or framework, everyone starts with a 'blank sheet of paper' every time they confront the subject of risk. Imagine the implications of a new 'blank sheet' every time the organization begins or acquires a business, pursues new markets, introduces new products and services or implements initiatives to reduce its cost structure – every time the organization encounters new change. The introduction of a common risk language not only focuses the debate, it is the first step in ensuring that the organization follows a uniform process to examine its risks thoroughly and consistently.

In this chapter, we discuss the development of:

- a definition of risk consistent with the dynamic view of creating value in a business;

- a risk language consistent with the new value proposition of risk management, i.e. risk and opportunity go hand in hand, to assist companies with the identification of risk and as a framework for discussion and analysis;

- a process classification scheme that decomposes the business into its operating, management and support components.

Together, these three components lay the foundation for a common language – the essential first building block of EWRM.

Why do we need a common language?

Corporations can ill-afford miscommunication, particularly as it relates to anything as essential as the management of risks and opportunities. An effective common language is vital in that:

- *It enables communication.* Business unit or process managers speak their own unique language. So do treasury, insurance, internal audit and other risk-focused groups. As Paul Brink of Dow Chemical explains, 'two people from different parts of the company can be talking about the same things and not realize it because they use different terminology. A good example is the treasury and the insurance functions – they use similar tools, but one calls something an option while another calls it a deductible.' That's a simple example, but as Mr Brink explains, 'that's the sort of thing we have to address.' Effective communication is the building block of understanding and, ultimately, achieving effective focus, strategy and action.

- *It promotes learning.* The need to view uncertainty as having both upside and downside potential cannot be understated. Yet risk is still viewed as an absolute 'evil' in many parts of an organization. 'I'm always asked, are we "risk free" yet?' says André Marcil, General Manager – Control and Integrated Risk Management at Hydro-Quebec. His answer? 'I hope not, because if we are not taking risks we are not creating value.' Effective communication is the first step in overcoming this 'risk is downside' bias and ultimately integrating superior strategic and business risk management.

- *It facilitates aggregation.* Two or more groups may be facing identical or similar risks, but because of the lexicon, this is overlooked. Using common definitions of risk – and common valuations (see Chapter 8) – enables a firm to look at its risks from an enterprise-wide perspective. In some cases, this

Continued …

---

could lead to the identification of opportunities for offsets. 'It's too early to say, as we've just begun this process, but we're compiling everything on Lotus Notes,' says Peter Cartmell, Director of Risk Strategy at Cadbury-Schweppes plc. But at the very least, it lends itself to the development and deployment of best practices for similar risks: cross-functional, cross-business unit and cross-process co-operation is optimized. 'Cross-fertilization,' continues Mr Cartmell, 'is always a good thing.'

- *It is the fundamental building block of EWRM.* Without a common language, there can be no further progress towards EWRM. A common language 'underpins our process of risk profiling,' says Chris Valentine, Director of Risk Management of Cable & Wireless. Risk profiling, or risk mapping, is the process by which companies take the first step towards translating their risk language and risk identification activities into a risk management action plan.

Whether referred to as risk mapping (Enron and Hydro-Quebec), risk profiling (Cable & Wireless and Cadbury-Schweppes) or even risk footprinting (Diageo/Guinness), the process is a highly effective means of discussing, identifying and prioritizing risks. Though somewhat subjective, risks are plotted on a grid in terms of their likelihood and impact. The end result is a graphic portrayal of the greatest risks faced by the business. 'Without a common business risk language, without an understanding of the role of risk in a business,' explains Nick Chown of the Royal Mail, 'the process will be an empty exercise.' Ultimately, the common language is the first step towards enabling business unit and process managers to get a handle on their risks as well as generate opportunities for risk identification, aggregation, learning and knowledge sharing.

But recognize...

The reasons and the means are clear, but managers cannot lose sight of the just stated objective – the purpose of language is to communicate. As Mark Twain observed, 'In Paris they simply stared when I spoke to them in French; I never did succeed in making those people understand their language.' For this reason, there must be oversight to ensure that the rationale and hence the importance of the common language is not lost on the audience. 'This cannot be a meaningless exercise,' says Mr Valentine. Adds Rick Causey, EVP and Chief Accounting Officer of Enron, without this fundamental understanding, 'You won't get far.'

DEFINING RISK

We define *risk* as the distribution of possible outcomes in a firm's performance over a given time horizon due to changes in key underlying variables. The greater the dispersion of possible outcomes, the higher the firm's level of exposure to uncertain returns. These uncertain returns can have either positive or negative values, and hence both positive and negative changes in key variables must be viewed as sources of risk. Because of the potential for positive outcomes, risk can be a good thing.

A 'risk-free' event is one that can be expected to happen in the future with absolute certainty. Since there are very few examples of such events, we begin with the presumption that risk is inherent in virtually everything. Every business activity, every opportunity and every change in the external environment and internally within the business bears some degree of uncertainty. Indeed, uncertainty is what makes life interesting and exciting – there are no guarantees!

Because it is unclear what will actually happen in the future, there are important questions germane to risk management:

- What specific possible outcomes do we face? Are they related?
- How sensitive are our strategies, market positions, earnings, cash flow, assets (whether owned or not, and including intangibles) and other sources of value to the occurrence of future events?
- Is our achievement of critical organization objectives, e.g. quality, timeliness, safety, etc., influenced by the occurrence of many possible events? If not, which specific events could, if they occurred, affect our organization's ability to achieve its objectives and execute its strategies successfully?
- How capable are we of responding to whatever may happen in the future?
- How much potential reward is required before we are willing to accept the risks associated with the uncertainties we face?
- Finally, if we decide to accept the exposures giving rise to our risks, do we have sufficient capital to absorb significant unforeseen losses, should they occur?

Thus, the organization's sensitivity to risk is a function of three things:

1. The significance (or severity) of the enterprise's exposures, that is, the sensitivity of the company's assets and performance to the realization of different events (like competitor acts, changes in interest rates, weather conditions, changes in customer satisfaction levels, etc.);
2. The likelihood of those different events occurring; and
3. The enterprise's ability to manage the business implications of those different possible future events, should they occur.

Because of the potential for positive outcomes, risk can be a good thing.

Exposure and uncertainty

Exposure and uncertainty are important aspects of risk and provide insights as to the manner in which risk is managed:

- *Exposure* arises when any asset or source of value of the enterprise is affected by changes in key underlying variables resulting from the occurrence of a risk event. A firm is exposed to risk when a realized change in a variable within a given time horizon will result in a change in one or more of its key performance indicators (KPIs). The greater the potential realized change in performance, either positive or negative, the greater the exposure. A firm may be exposed to performance variation on account of its business model, strategies, processes, brands, customers, employee work force, market positions or other sources of earnings and cash flow. As Nick Chown, Group Risk Manager of the British Post Office, points out, 'we are here to take risks as we create new sources of value in the marketplace.' We agree. The risk taking process often creates new or increased exposures.

- *Uncertainty* arises when we do not know in advance the magnitude and direction of change in the value of a key variable, i.e. competitor behaviour, interest rates, commodity prices, technological innovation, currency price movements, human performance, regulatory actions, etc. Changes in variables create uncertainty for the enterprise only when its sources of value are exposed. Truly understanding the sources of uncertainty relating to each of the firm's exposures is a demanding but essential process. If we do not know the key variables that create uncertainty for each of our exposures, it is imperative that we identify and understand them. That exercise lays the foundation for deciding how to measure and manage risk.

  Uncertainty, as we define it, refers to any situation in which all possible outcomes are identified and the related probabilities are assessed to the best of our knowledge, but we simply do not know which event will occur. While this definition may appear to rule out circumstances where we lack understanding, it is implicit that when we list events whose cumulative probabilities add up to 100 per cent, we are assuming that there is nothing else which could happen. If the probabilities of events we list add up to less than 100 per cent, we are implicitly assuming an 'unknown' category with an implicit probability (equal to the difference between 100 per cent and the cumulative probabilities of all the other events listed).

A firm's exposure can result in either upside or downside consequences. This is seen in the way exposure and uncertainty are assessed. For example, assume

Continued ...

we list all foreseeable future outcomes, including estimates of the net cash flows relating to each possible outcome and their respective probabilities. What would the results of this exercise show us? It depicts both the upside and downside exposure because the expected future net cash flows of all foreseeable outcomes include both positive and negative results, giving rise to *performance variability*. In the situation where only negative things can happen (such as when enumerating the consequences of a hazard), we would list only downside exposures, i.e. every foreseeable outcome results in a negative net cash flow, creating a *loss exposure*.

Business risk is the level of exposure to uncertainties that the enterprise must understand and effectively manage as it creates value.

Let's take our definition of risk a step further. To provide a context for risk management in a business environment, we define *business risk* as the level of exposure to uncertainties that the enterprise must understand and effectively manage as it executes its strategies to achieve its business objectives and create value. These uncertain events are often external to a firm's normal business operations, but in many cases they represent internal process issues. Table 3.1 provides some examples of commonly recognized sources of uncertainty in a business.

Table 3.1 Commonly recognized sources of uncertainty in a business

	Examples of Sources of Uncertainty
Externally-driven (environment)	*Actions:* what will competitors, customers, regulators, governments, special interests groups, etc. do?
	Key underlying variables: what is the future value of such variables as interest rates, inflation, regulatory changes, market demand, labour supply, housing starts, production volume of competitors, customer demographics, exchange rates or commodity prices?
	Potential catastrophic events: windstorm, earthquake, war, terrorism or other catastrophic events – what if they occur and how vulnerable are we?
Internally-driven (process)	*Brands:* have we invested adequately and wisely to reduce the risk of broken brand promises to an acceptable level?
	Customers: are we fulfilling their needs as well as, if not better than, competitors?
	Suppliers: are they supporting our business model effectively?

Employees: are we winning the 'war for talent' and maximizing the value of our human capital?

Operating processes: are they performing effectively and efficiently?

Technologies: which ones are best suited to integrate into and support the processes of our business, increasing our efficiency and effectiveness?

Channels: are they functioning as intended by our business model?

Knowledge: what is the value of the firm's knowledge and are we exploiting it to our advantage?

Opportunity cost: is there unrecognized value or unexploited resources?

Potential 'stop the show' events: unethical practices, fraud, illegal acts and business control breakdowns – what if they occur and how vulnerable are we?

Decision-driven (information)

M&A: who to acquire – and why?

New markets: which ones best complement the company's business strategy, desired risk profile and risk appetite?

R&D investment: will we achieve breakthroughs that fuel future growth and get to market before our competitors?

Products and services: what mix will provide the highest possible stream of future net cash flows at the lowest risk?

The yield curve: where to borrow?

While not exhaustive, the list in Table 3.1 is indicative of the uncertainties faced by many businesses. Most of these uncertainties can impede or enhance the achievement of objectives and implementation of key business strategies. Currency risk, for example, arises from the firm's exposure to fluctuating exchange rates, yet its impact can be positive or negative. Exposure to a single brand also creates uncertainty – if the firm does all of the right things to nurture and support the brand, it will prosper; if it does not and competitors offer a superior brand promise, the results can be disastrous. Similarly, future events – shifts in the economy, the performance of distributors, regulatory actions, changing demographics – could benefit or impair future operations.

Sources of uncertainty, simply stated, can result in good or bad consequences to the business. The more extreme the potential impact and the more likely its occurrence, the greater the business risk.

A LANGUAGE FOR RISK

Now that we have defined business risk, a framework is needed to enable the organization to prioritize and collect the information relating to its exposures and sources of uncertainty. The framework must be suitably general so that all sources and classifications of risk are included. It must cast a wide net so that it is a useful tool for identifying and prioritizing risk. Virtually all companies who are developing a common risk language begin with a broad template. As an example, Arthur Andersen breaks business risk into three broad groups: Environment, Process and Information for decision-making.

> **The framework must cast a wide net so that it is a useful tool for identifying and prioritizing risk.**

■ *'Environment risk'* arises when there are external forces that can affect a firm's performance, or make its choices regarding its strategies, operations, customer and supplier relationships, organizational structure or financing obsolete or ineffective. These forces include the actions of competitors and regulators, shifts in market prices, technological innovation, changes in industry fundamentals, the availability of capital or other factors outside the company's direct ability to control.

■ *'Process risk'* arises when business processes do not achieve the objectives they were designed to achieve in supporting the firm's business model. For example, characteristics of poorly performing processes, or 'process risks', include:

  – poor alignment with enterprise-wide business objectives and strategies;

  – ineffectiveness in satisfying customers;

  – inefficient operations;

  – diluting (instead of creating or preserving) value; and

  – failing to protect significant financial, physical, customer, employee/supplier, knowledge and information assets from unacceptable losses, risk-taking, misappropriation or misuse.

■ *'Information for decision-making risk'* arises when information used to support business decisions is incomplete, out of date, inaccurate, late or simply irrelevant to the decision-making process. Our research with the Economist Intelligence Unit in 1995,[1] as updated by the *New Dimensions on Business Risk* project in the summer of 1998, indicates that a significant majority of companies (at least four out of every five) believe that their decision-support systems are far from optimal.

---

1. Economist Intelligence Unit (1995) *Managing business risk: An integrated approach*, written in co-operation with Arthur Andersen.

When the dust clears...

These three components of business risk are interrelated. The environment risks and process risks that the firm faces are driven by the external and internal realities of the business. Information for decision-making risk is directly affected by the effectiveness and reliability of information processing systems and informal 'intelligence gathering' processes for capturing relevant data, converting that data to information and providing that information to the appropriate managers in the form of written reports and oral communications. Process risk is sometimes virtually indistinguishable from information for decision-making risk because information is needed to make informed decisions. When the dust clears from this steady flow of information, decision-makers should receive the insights they need about the external environment and the performance of the firm's processes so they can manage the firm's risks effectively.

The three components of business risk that we have introduced provide a broad foundation on which more specific categories of risk can be identified and detailed. They are depicted in Figure 3.1.

Fig. 3.1 The Arthur Andersen Business Risk Model™ – an overview

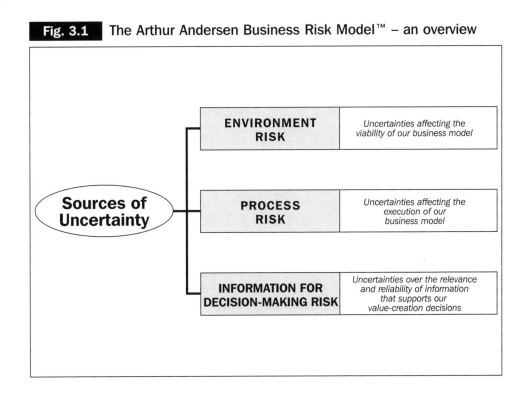

When all is said and done, a firm is defined by the choices its managers make; hence, variables that increase the uncertainty of key decisions generate additional risk. Looking at risk in a consistent way across all categories is important as it provides the basis for defining everything in common terms. A common language, therefore, makes the task of integrating risk management more straightforward, and hence facilitates communication and decision-making. A well-conceptualized model is a springboard to deeper discussions that lead to a better understanding of risk, an essential first step towards EWRM.

The use of a common risk language begins at a strategic level. Most common languages begin with a model like the one above, but then are customized to the firm's unique circumstances, business unit by business unit and process by process. As Chris Valentine, Director of Risk Management at Cable & Wireless explains, 'Our definition of risk, our language if you will, begins from the context of the most critical risks as seen by our senior management.' From there, 'individual operating units and business managers add detail as is relevant, but within the same context.' Similar practice is also taking place at organizations like the British Post Office, Hydro-Quebec and many of the other firms pursuing EWRM.

Some risk events are sources or drivers of other risk events.

As risk identification drills deeper into a company's various business units or processes, the basic risk language explodes into greater detail. Further defining the business risk language introduced above, Arthur Andersen has detailed over 75 risk categories. Each one relates to one of the three broad components of risk, and together all of them create a common risk language for business people to use in a wide variety of situations. The model shown in Figure 3.2 can be used to organize and illustrate the consequences, sources, best measures and best practices for managing each risk that a business may face.

The components and subcomponents of the model and the various risk categories included under them provide a 'risk language' to the firm and its business units. A 'risk management glossary' that provides definitions of each risk category in the model enhances its usefulness as a common language. The glossary may also include other risk management terms as well. All told, this tool is a 'living' document that is continuously updated and customized. Appendix 2 includes summary definitions of each of the risk categories in the model. It can be used as a starting point for developing a customized glossary. There is also a glossary provided in this book that includes key terms.

The model depicts the risk categories for each major source of business risk. Because risk is dynamic, these risk categories are interrelated. In other words, some risk events are, in effect, sources or drivers of other risk events. For example, information processing/technology risk is positioned at the centre of 'process risk' on the model because these risks affect virtually all other process risks in some way (as well as many environment and information for decision-making risks).

Fig. 3.2 The Arthur Andersen Business Risk Model™ © 2000 Arthur
Andersen. All rights reserved.

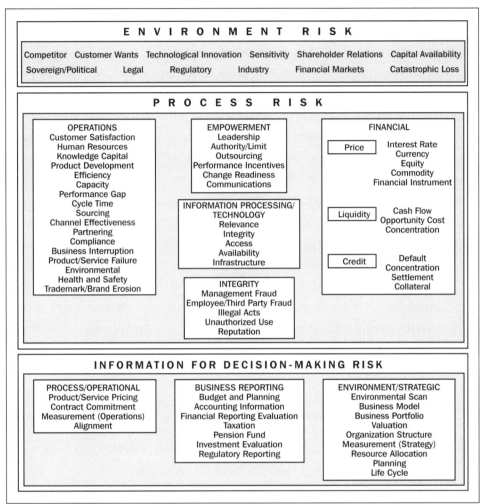

It is possible to customize this generic model by industry or by company, as the
risk categories may be modified depending on the firm's specific circumstances. In
customizing the model to many industries, Arthur Andersen has found that the
components and subcomponents remain constant, while the detailed risk
categories are subject to change. To illustrate, environment risk and operations
process risk are often modified during the customization process to reflect the
unique characteristics of a particular industry. As Jean-François Heitz of
Microsoft explains, 'we used their model *as* a model, but made many refinements
of our own, relevant to our business.'

Business: chess it's not

Business is like a game of chess. Firms make their moves, placing their bets on
research and development, new products, new markets and new businesses.
These choices create exposure to uncertainty because they commit the

Continued ...

organization to pursue opportunities that can lead to a variety of possible outcomes having positive and negative consequences. At the end of the game, the firm will either create or dilute value depending on whether its moves are superior relative to the moves of the other players.

But there is an added twist to this game in the new economy. The rules of the marketplace today are that opponents – in fact the entire universe of environment risks – make moves whenever they like, regardless of whether or not we have moved. The only way to play by these rules is to have a superior business model and strategy in place that enables us to move quickly or, better still, to set the pace of play. Otherwise, we are constantly in a reactive mode.

Managing business risk, therefore, requires continual vigilance and persistence. Peter Drucker speaks of 'windows of opportunity' that managers either ignore through inaction or choose to exploit through innovation and adjustment of the firm's business model. Drucker recommends a systematic policy to look every six to twelve months for changes that might be opportunities – so that the entire organization can learn to see change as an opportunity. He suggests that the enterprise focus on the following areas that are sources of environment and process risk:[2]

- *The organization's own unexpected successes and unexpected failures, but also the unexpected successes and unexpected failures of the organization's competitors,*
- *Incongruities, especially incongruities in the process, whether of production or distribution, or incongruities in customer behaviour,*
- *Process needs,*
- *Changes in industry and market structures,*
- *Changes in demographics,*
- *Changes in meaning and perception, and finally*
- *New knowledge.*

As Drucker points out, a change in any one of these areas raises several questions. For example, 'Is this an opportunity for us to innovate, that is, to develop different products, services, processes? Does it indicate new and different markets and/or customers? New and different technologies? New and different distribution channels?'[3] Whether the firm chooses to act or not, these dynamics are continually assaulting its risk profile. In essence, the decision to make no move may be the worst move of all.

---

2. Peter F. Drucker (1999) *Management Challenges for the 21st Century*. HarperCollins, pp. 84–5.
3. Ibid.

A PROCESS CLASSIFICATION SCHEME

A risk language is supplemented by a process classification scheme. A process consists of the activities performed by people and supported by tools and technology that are designed to achieve one or more specified business objectives. In essence, a process is what you do to transform inputs into a product or deliverable that is of value to customers (external and internal). It is an 'end-to-end' system. Understanding business processes is essential for assessing the sources or root causes of risks, because most risks are best understood and managed as close as possible to the source.

Every business can be decomposed into operating, management and support processes. A process classification scheme is a summary of a firm's processes and it becomes a useful tool when assessing the source of risks. The process scheme includes the major processes (including shared services) for each business unit of the firm. There are two general classifications of processes in any business:

Understanding business processes is essential for assessing the sources or root causes of risks.

- *Primary core processes* include the business processes that either 'touch the customer' directly today or significantly impact on how the firm will touch the customer in the future. If there is a performance failure in any of these processes, either the customer will know almost immediately (or within a very short timeframe) or the business will be playing a losing hand strategically over time until it ultimately fails. When working back from the customer to identify processes, the primary processes will always appear first (i.e. invoicing the customer, processing customer receipts, product delivery, customer service, product development, etc.).

- *Management and support processes* are required for the primary core processes to perform effectively and efficiently. These processes include information management, communications, quality planning and implementation, human resources management, capital budgeting, fixed asset management, cash management, monitoring and training. For the most part, failure in these processes will not be immediately evident to the customer (losses of critical systems that enable primary processes to function is an obvious exception). However, it will eventually cause the performance of one or more of the primary processes to significantly deteriorate or deviate from established business objectives.

These process categories are further illustrated in Figure 3.3 using Arthur Andersen's Global Best Practices™ Process Classification Scheme. These categories are further broken down into subprocesses that can be applied or customized to any business or industry. The point is that the firm must devise its own framework for organizing its process classification scheme and populate that framework over time. A process scheme is a useful tool during the risk assessment process.

Fig. 3.3 Process classification scheme

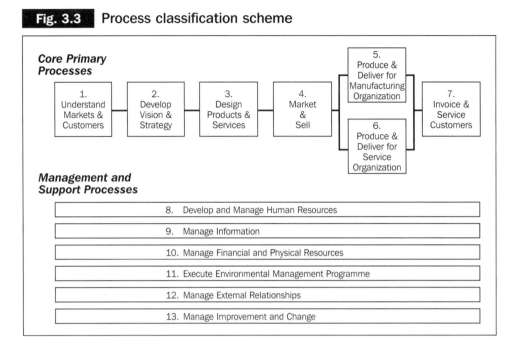

DEVELOPING A LANGUAGE

There are many methods for developing a risk and process language, with the two primary approaches being top-down and bottom-up. The top-down approach involves a small group of stakeholders that work together to customize the framework, which is then pushed down into the organization. 'We chose a top-down approach,' says Chris Valentine of Cable & Wireless, 'because this is being driven by senior management – it is a board initiative.' A 'grassroots' or bottom-up approach, as used by Unicom, is driven by key operating and functional support personnel, with the support of top management, and is a feasible alternative that takes more time to accomplish to build consensus. Ultimately, if a company hopes to achieve a true EWRM state, a consistent framework is essential. Using either approach, management should designate a multidisciplinary team to drive the developmental process.

Defining the risk language should first start with defining what 'risk' is to the firm and then developing a useful risk model consistent with that definition. The definition of business risk provided in this chapter provides a starting point for this exercise; the Business Risk Model™ is a framework that managers can customize to their business and use to identify sources of uncertainty. A risk model is also a much more effective tool if definitions are provided for each of the risks (see Appendix 2).

Development of a process classification scheme requires the input of people who are knowledgeable of the business. The process definition and Global Best Practices™ scheme we introduce in this chapter provide a useful starting point for managers to customize their own scheme to break down the business into its process components. However, there are alternative models available – Holderbank, for example, uses the well-known 'Porter model'.

A common definition of risk, a risk model and a process classification scheme lay the foundation for a common language. We provide other frameworks in this book that facilitate communication throughout the organization, e.g. the uniform process introduced in Chapter 5 and the components of infrastructure illustrated in Chapter 6. Mental models are, in effect, a part of the firm's common language *if* they are effective in simplifying and focusing communications.

CONCLUSION

To communicate effectively up and down the firm and across its units, functions and departments, managers and employees need a common language. As with anything else heavily dependent on effective communication, the absence of a language leads to miscommunications and oversights. If the appropriate people are effectively communicating information about risks and opportunities and co-ordinating business risk management activities, the firm will be better positioned to learn and adapt to its changing environment.

> Mental models are a part of the common language *if* they simplify and focus communications.

A common language adds value in that it can help business unit or process managers to more effectively identify and assess their exposures and potential sources of uncertainty and design new and better risk management capabilities. However, its real value becomes evident when it is deployed within a uniform business risk management process that is applied across the enterprise. Only then will the breakthrough benefits be realized: prioritization, sourcing, quantification, aggregation, learning, knowledge sharing and superior risk management strategy development.

You should recognize that a common language is essential, but it is only a first step in the journey to EWRM. The next chapters begin to detail the true value of a common language and of EWRM.

Holderbank: building an enterprise-wide business risk management approach

- How to assess and manage both risk and opportunity
- Integrating risk management with business planning and action
- A two-phase approach: pilots first, then enterprise-wide

If this book describes a journey, then bags at Switzerland's Holderbank are fully packed. Though highly decentralized, the world's largest cement maker has its Executive Committee's (ExCo) approval to proceed with care and haste on an enterprise-wide mission to more rigorously, consistently and proactively assess and manage its business risks. The company has so far developed a common risk language and has similarly identified a six-step strategic process: both of which have been successfully refined, and both of which are within various stages of implementation within several major business lines. Building on this approach, the company is now working out the details of integrating proactive business risk management with both strategic planning and day-to-day operations. Early successes are ratifying the approach and accordingly the company is now on track to further refine the programme for roll-out enterprise-wide.

Creating a readily replicated and consistent framework is particularly vital given the company's organization. Holderbank is a globally diverse company, active in all inhabitable continents. Its 40,000-plus employees operate within a highly decentralized management structure. Although comprising numerous legal entities, the group is primarily organized into approximately 40 principal operating companies.

Overall, the Holderbank group focuses on the production and distribution of cement, concrete and aggregates (gravel, sand and crushed stone). But in addition, companies in the firm also offer engineering, research, consulting and management services. Holderbank is a major player in developed markets, with principal competitors including France's Lafarge and Mexico's Cemex along with various local and regional competitors. Going forward, however, the group also sees great opportunity for long-term growth amid the world's developing economies.

Top management approval came swiftly following detailed presentations of the need for an enterprise-wide programme along with a broad sketch of both specific goals and the proposed process. However, before the ExCo would commit to full implementation, it was decided that the process would first be tested via a handful of pilot programmes conducted with the company's key business line. It was at this point, April 1998, that the position of Senior Vice President, Corporate Risk Management was created and accepted by Mr Roland Köhler. As 'CRO' of the organization, it is his objective to develop, roll out and oversee the programme.

THE HOLDERBANK VISION

'We live with risk every day.'

According to CEO Dr hc. Thomas Schmidheiny, 'We live with risk every day.' So for Dr Schmidheiny, a primary goal of Holderbank's business risk management (BRM) activities is to focus his organization's attention. 'We're in 60 countries worldwide, and I believe it is important that we have a consistent approach. Everyone should be thinking about, understanding, defining, identifying, measuring and managing risk.'

Accordingly, the Holderbank vision is the creation of a comprehensive, enterprise-wide risk management approach (EWRM). The vision statement asserts that business risk management is a continuous process and is in any case an integral element of corporate governance. Moreover, it also states that the company must promote efficient and effective assessment of risk, increase risk awareness and improve the management of risk throughout the group. The statement also reinforces the scope of business risk management as including the anticipation and avoidance of threats and losses as well as the identification and realization of opportunities. Says Mr Köhler, 'Our focus is also on creating value.'

Perhaps most acutely, while the vision recognizes the importance of anticipating and avoiding threats, it has an equal focus on identifying and realizing opportunities. 'This is not the elimination of risk,' says Dr Schmidheiny, 'because without risk, we are out of business.' Rather, this is a 'wake-up call to the organization. People have to have a systematic and proactive way of looking at risks and opportunities and bringing these discussions to the table.'

Finally, in accord with a decentralized organization, the Holderbank vision focuses on placing responsibility for risk identification and management in the hands of those best equipped to deal with the risks. Says Dr Schmidheiny, 'It is a strength of our organization that our people in the field are able to solve problems.' The process being implemented at Holderbank helps field managers identify their risks, but leaves it largely up to the local management teams how those risks will be dealt with. 'They can't ignore the risks,' says Mr Köhler, 'but what they do is up to them and it becomes an integral part of their business plan.'

'We are not telling them how to manage risks, we are equipping them with better tools.'

In essence, says Dr Schmidheiny, 'we are not telling them how to manage risks, but we are equipping them with better tools to make sure that risks are dealt with appropriately.' All told, the voyage is a leading-edge example of a company attempting to position risk assessment and management as a fundamental organizing and operating principle.

The drive towards a more comprehensive view of risk at Holderbank is fuelled by a handful of important factors. These include (but are by no means limited to) the following:

- *The need to manage for the long term.* Holderbank's operations are capital intensive. Cement production lines, for example, are expensive to install and operate. Consequently, each operating company needs to be keenly focused on strategic issues which impact on sales and capacity utilization – not just in the current fiscal year but over the long haul. A key goal of the EWRM implementation is to help operating managers better understand their operating environment and how to anticipate both threats and opportunities.

- *The need to 'know'.* With newspapers continually reporting examples of failed controls, it is incumbent on a senior management team to gain a clearer understanding of operational activities. Moreover, as in other parts of the world, Switzerland has recently enacted more stringent requirements in the area of corporate governance. With so many governments and shareholders demanding greater disclosure relating to company risk practices, the answer 'we're not sure' is inadequate.

  Also on the regulatory front, liability in areas such as ethics, environmental law and health and safety standards is increasing, for example in Australia. It is vital for any company to understand its risks and develop the means to ensure that it is in compliance with rules world-wide. However, says Dr Schmidheiny, 'I believe that people are often defensive about their risks: they don't want to talk about them.' Consequently, 'What we are creating here, I hope, is a process that treats discussion of these risks as a positive step so that we can bring things into the open. It's not your risks or his risks, it's our risks so what do we do about them?'

- *The need for forward-looking monitoring and risk management.* Holderbank does not have an internal audit function at the group level, although most of the big operating companies have internal audit functions using both internal and external resources. Even so, traditional audit techniques are all about the 'past'; they are not focused as much as they could be on identifying opportunities going forward. For this reason, the proactive, opportunity-minded aspects of an enterprise-wide approach to risk assessment and management have proven highly appealing to both the ExCo and operating managers. This approach recognizes that responsibility for business risk management is a line management matter. It therefore empowers process owners at all levels.

- *The need to identify and implement best practices.* An effective enterprise-wide business risk management function ensures that best practices are more widely utilized. This is particularly important in a decentralized company. Therefore, a stated goal is to find ways of making certain that acquired knowledge is fully deployed and leveraged throughout the organization. This desire is understood and shared by operating managers participating in the pilot projects. For example, Mr Calie Ehrke is Administration Manager of the Dudfield Operation, part of Alpha Ltd in South Africa (a Holderbank affiliate). Says Mr Ehrke, 'one thing we really appreciate about the BRM Process is that we are able to benchmark best practices and share knowledge. That is already starting to pay off.'

A good example of a best practice now being widely disseminated is the concept of risk mapping. This relatively subjective but flexible tool is ideal for helping management teams evaluate their strategies in terms of both risks and opportunities. But the real value of risk mapping is not the document that comes out of the discussions, but rather the thought processes behind it. Discussions of risk maps are helping managers to focus on both risks and opportunities. Says Mr Ehrke, the risk mapping process has proven invaluable, 'helping us to identify risks we had not been focusing on before.' More importantly, 'now we have managers assigned to those risks, and that's where the improvement will come from.'

Business risk: a focus on group learning

Central to Holderbank's business risk initiatives is the idea that there are lessons to be learned throughout the organization. An intended outcome is greater risk and opportunity awareness at the group, group company (business unit) and individual (employee) levels. Figure C1.1 illustrates this.

Fig. C1.1 Business risk management and faster learning

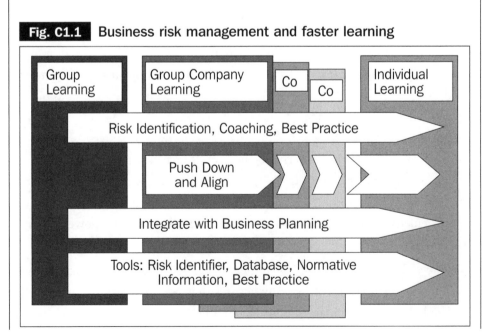

Group Learning

Group Company Learning

Co

Co

Individual Learning

Risk Identification, Coaching, Best Practice

Push Down and Align

Integrate with Business Planning

Tools: Risk Identifier, Database, Normative Information, Best Practice

Continued ...

There are four elements to this learning strategy. First is the idea that a rigorous and collaborative enterprise-wide risk programme will harness the abilities of the organization. Employees at all levels will become more conscious of risk and opportunity and their role in evaluating trade-off decisions. This will aid risk identification, encourage teamwork (and coaching) and promote the need to find and adopt best practices. Second, but closely related, the goal is to drive the importance of sound risk and opportunity management from the group company level through all operations and again all the way down to individual employees. Here the goal is to align the organization, essentially using risk and opportunity management as a fundamental organizing and operating principle.

The third step is critical. Without a specific action plan, much of the firm's initiatives could fall by the wayside. For this reason, it is absolutely essential that business risk objectives become a visible component of business planning. Similarly, there must be a means of measuring progress towards business risk objectives, and whatever metrics are designed must again relate closely to the business plan.

Finally, the company is rolling out enhancements to an existing enterprise-wide database. Using Lotus Notes as a platform, practical information relating to the company's risk initiatives is centralized then disseminated to those who need it. Similarly, communications tools, analogous to Internet newsgroups, are being established. The goal is to help Holderbank's affiliated companies and employees share knowledge relating to strategic risk assessment and management.

One challenge for the CRO is the segregation of information. Technically, each group company maintains its own database, which is connected with the generic corporate-wide database. For confidentiality reasons, the individual operating companies cannot use the technology to directly exchange detailed operating information with one another. Therefore, the database has been set up to allow each individual company to enter its own information which is available within the group company only. Additionally, corporate risk management has access to the data of all group companies in order to accelerate knowledge sharing by transforming group company-specific successful practices into generic information for dissemination across the entire group. Direct knowledge sharing and/or Q&A among group companies is also possible and is supported by the 'open' discussion platform features of the database.

SIX STEPS: THE PILOT PROCESS

The above – and additional – business needs are behind the decision to pursue an enterprise-wide vision. But the most compelling argument, says Dr Schmidheiny, is a simple one: 'It is the right thing to do.' That said, the ExCo decided to pursue a new approach enterprise-wide only with sufficient evidence that this was the right strategy. According to Mr Köhler, 'if it *is* the right thing, then we should be able to prove that. But if we are doing the wrong thing, and we introduce it enterprise-wide, we are going to have a lot of companies doing the wrong thing.' For this reason, the ExCo agreed that the approach should be implemented first on a limited or pilot basis.

Six of the group's operating companies – representing approximately 30 per cent of the group's annual revenue – were chosen for the pilot. Although an argument could be made to begin with the smallest divisions, instead the group chose to focus on some of its largest – for example, their Swiss- and US-based cement subsidiaries. These choices were made for two reasons. One, cement is the segment the company understands best, and so it would be able to ask itself the right questions. Two, cement is the most important segment to Holderbank, and therefore the most valuable area for the group to gain insights. In the end, all chosen pilot affiliates were also under the direct control of members of the ExCo. This, it was determined, would ensure commitment to the programme as well as provide direct feedback to the management committee.

With pilots chosen, it was time to begin the process. Working with a major consulting firm, Holderbank identified a common risk language and a six-step approach that showed great promise. The risk model helped the company identify its key baskets of risk, and the six-step process provided a means for translating identified risks into practical actions. However, each of these tools was customized to meet the needs of the individual pilot companies. There was never an intention to dictate 'this is how it will work'. Instead, the idea was to use the common risk language and the six-step process as points of departure. Therefore, as refinements are necessary, they are made. The goal is to develop something positive and effective, not to insist on conformance to a model.

An overview of the six-step process is presented below (see Figure C1.2). The first three steps – 1. *identify*, 2. *source* and 3. *measure* risks – were completed successfully by the six pilot operating companies and are being implemented across the global organization during 1999 and 2000. Concurrent with this roll-out, the second three steps – 4. *evaluate*, 5. *manage* and 6. *monitor* risks – are now being executed by the original six operating companies that piloted the first three steps. Following their development and implementation, the second three steps will be rolled out enterprise-wide. A more detailed discussion of each of the six steps is given below.

Fig. C1.2 The Holderbank six-step process

1. Identify	• **Identify risks** based on a Holderbank generic model • Create **risk awareness**
2. Source	• Detect and understand origin of possible threats and opportunites (**risk drivers**) • Identify **risk holders** (functional and/or divisional managers)
3. Measure	• Assess **significance and likelihood** of risks • Design **actual risk map**
4. Evaluate	• **Decide on options** for risk management strategies • Design **target risk map**
5. Manage	• Ensure that key risks are reflected in **business plan** and action is taken • **Assess value added** from improving risk/taking on opportunities
6. Monitor	• **Continuous consideration** of risk profile and control procedures • **Regular reporting** on key risks (red quartile)

The idea is to focus on risk at a highly strategic level and to generally broaden risk awareness.

Identifying, sourcing and measuring risks

1. Identify risks

The goal here is to lead the operating company through an exploration of the critical business risks for Holderbank and for cement producers at large. The simplest way to understand this process is to think of a tool such as the 'Porter model' and use it to assess competitors, suppliers, customers and new market entrants or alternative products. Each pilot company's business profile, as defined by the Porter model, provides an understanding of the critical environment and operating factors affecting the business. These factors were then defined in terms of a risk model derived by Holderbank from the Business Risk Model™ provided by the consulting firm, Arthur Andersen. The Arthur Andersen model, introduced in Chapter 3, delineates risk categories into broad groups such as 'environment' or 'process' risk. Says Mr Köhler, 'The model defines risks in broad terms and helps us to arrive at a common risk language and a common understanding of our risks.' The idea here is to focus on risk at a highly strategic level and to generally broaden risk awareness.

2. Source risks

In Step 2, the goal is to drill down to detect the universe of potential threats and opportunities. These are referred to as 'risk drivers' by the firm. To better understand the nature of a risk driver, consider *capacity risk*, the risk that a cement production line or the surrounding assets might be underutilized. Capacity risk is also the risk that the company might not have sufficient capacity to meet demand. Capacity risk might be influenced by competitor actions, import restrictions or liberalizations, current or future economic climates, maintenance scheduling and many other external and internal factors. To illustrate the firm's approach, Figure C1.3 provides a map for drivers of hiring/retaining risk.

Fig. C1.3 Example of risk drivers map

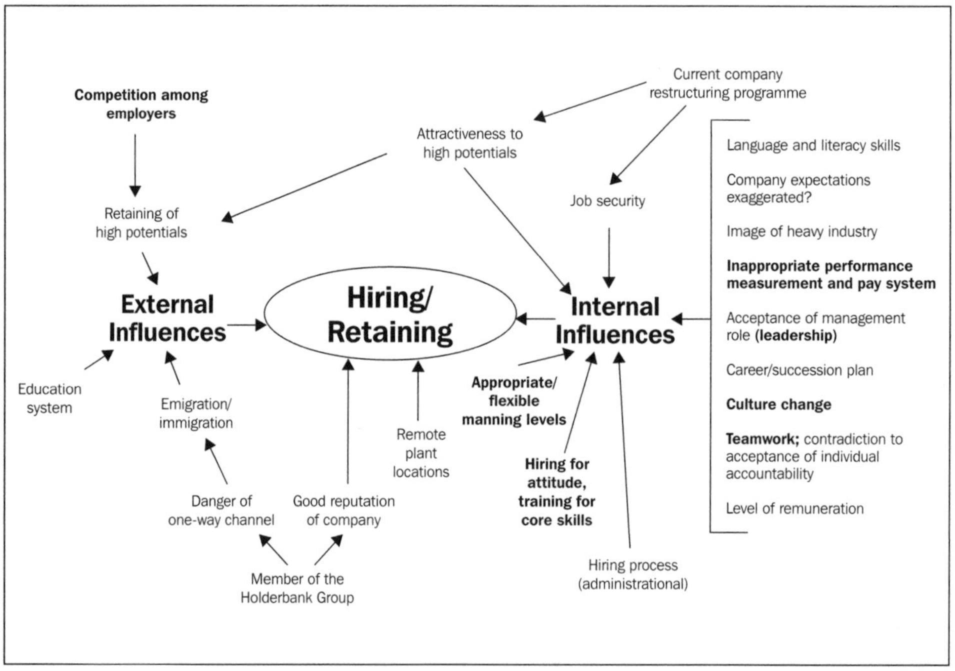

Once the sources of any risk or opportunity are understood, an executive manager is assigned who is in the best position to oversee the risk, which Holderbank refers to as a 'risk owner'. Thus, after a map is completed, the drivers that the risk owners determine are the ones having the most impact on the risk are designated in red. Referred to as 'the key drivers', these are the ones that receive attention from a measurement standpoint. This is an important distinction because under Holderbank's approach, the risk itself is not measured; rather it is the resulting impact or potential impact of the key drivers that is measured.

Here, it is vital to recognize that not all risks are functional in nature. Often, risks are housed within a cross-functional set of processes. All of this makes the identification of a risk owner, someone close to and ultimately responsible for a risk, essential.

3. Measure risks

From here, the process becomes more focused on the impact of the risk. Working with the CRO and his staff, the operating company pinpoints its most critical risks and opportunities. Here, the company utilizes the technique of risk mapping to create a comprehensive picture.

The risk mapping process utilizes a grid to segregate risks into one of four quadrants. Across the X axis, the likelihood of a risk or opportunity's emergence increases; up the Y axis its potential value (or significance) increases. The four quadrants are therefore low likelihood/low value; low likelihood/high value; high likelihood/low value; and high likelihood/high value (see Figure C1.4). Naturally, the most attention is focused on high likelihood/high value risks.

The goal is to measure the financial impact in a meaningful way whenever possible.

Fig. C1.4 Risk map of group company

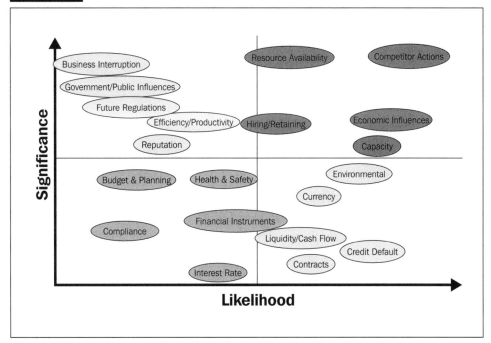

Developing the actual risk map is a relatively subjective process. Measuring risks in terms of monetary value is an inexact science, as is predicting the probability of a risk's occurrence.

However, if enough assessments are gathered from enough knowledgeable people, the estimation error is reduced. But precision is not the goal – the more important issue is order of magnitude and relative ranking.

In Step 2, the company asks: is this a significant risk, recognizing that 'significant' means it could have an impact, positive or negative. The goal of Step 3, however, is to attempt to put a value on significance. Precision is more easily obtained for some risks than for others, but in all cases, the goal is to measure the financial impact in a meaningful way whenever possible.

Ultimately, the greatest value is derived from the process itself: it is better to have identified and measured a set of risks – even if imprecisely – than to retain these risks unconsciously without knowledge or understanding. During one and a half day sessions with operating managers, extensive discussions help determine probabilities and monetary values and hence the relative positioning or ranking of each risk. Though this process is inexact, measurement in the pilot companies proceeded in a highly collaborative and interactive manner.

The process is also highly effective, says Mr Ehrke. His group was already beginning to look at various risks through an initiative known as 'Alpha 2000'. 'But when it comes to a comprehensive focus on risks, the business risk process was definitely more rigorous,' explains Mr Ehrke. In particular, 'the process helped us to focus for the first time on certain economic risks and their impact – such as the holistic effects of AIDS here in South Africa. We had previously dealt only with its impact on workforce demographics.' Unquestionably, the process enforces a discipline and is a powerful means of focusing the attention of decision-makers on the most appropriate risks and opportunities.

> 'The process helped us to focus for the first time on certain risks and their impact.'

As these sessions are facilitated, Holderbank uses its own, customized program written in Visual Basic that projects the developing risk picture in full colour providing a focus for discussions. With this software, risks or opportunities in the highest intensity quadrant assume a red colour (referred to as 'red bubbles' by participants), while all others fade to green. Using technology to conduct such discussions visually proves 'very enlightening and productive,' says Mr Köhler. The ability to debate the issues using the risk identifier and to discuss and watch 'as the bubbles move from red to green, or green to red' is a powerful means of focusing attention and thinking. 'It's not only effective, I think participants actually enjoy it,' says Mr Köhler. Furthermore, the exercise creates focus. As Mr Köhler points out, 'We need to funnel the number of risks down to the vital few so we will know where to concentrate our resources.'

Evaluating, managing and monitoring

Steps 1, 2 and 3 have been completed in the pilot companies and are presently being rolled out in other group companies. The challenge from here is to translate the knowledge gleaned into tangible and effective action. Steps 4, 5 and 6 begin the development of actual risk management strategies and tactics, their implementation as part of executing the business plan and then monitoring the results. Here the company is in most cases just beginning its journey as it tackles these steps at the six pilot operating companies. But Holderbank has a clear idea of what it hopes to accomplish.

4. Evaluate options

Working from the risk map, local management teams assess their greatest risks and opportunities. In Step 4, they begin evaluating various risk management alternatives. Once all alternatives have been identified, risk owners are in a position to choose the combination of actions that best fulfil strategic goals.

A highly useful tool in Step 4 is the target risk map. Whereas the risk map from Step 3 profiles the relative positions of all identified risks and opportunities as they exist today, the target risk map depicts the desired (and reasonably attainable) positions. For each of these 'red bubbles', explains Mr Ehrke, 'we have now assigned a risk owner whose job it is to manage that risk.'

Improved risk profiles are achieved via a variety of techniques. In some cases, the probability of a negative risk (or loss exposure) can be reduced. Alternatively, certain risks can be hedged, reducing their financial impact. In all cases, the target risk map is a depiction of the desired risk profile, achievable via the actions identified by management. But for the first time, says Mr Ehrke, 'we now have a consistent, enterprise-wide definition of risks and common processes, so now we can benchmark enterprise-wide.'

> 'If you have differing priorities in the business plan compared to the risk map, then something must be wrong.'

5. Manage risks

The above steps mean nothing if they are not translated into action, and that means incorporation into the business plan. According to Mr Ehrke, 'We are now aligning our business planning process.' Adds Mr Köhler, 'If you have differing priorities in the business plan compared to the risk map, then something, either in your planning or in your risk mapping process, must be wrong.' Beyond including specific actions in the business plan to manage priority risks and opportunities, it is also vitally important to take steps to measure the value added as a result of these actions. This step reinforces the value of the process or, alternatively, points out the need for further refinement.

6. Monitor

Business risk management cannot be a one-off exercise. A company must take steps to see if it has actually made progress in managing its risks and opportunities. At Holderbank, this is viewed as a continuous process.

An important part of this step is determining what reports are necessary and with what frequency (see Figure C1.5). The goal is not to burden risk owners with additional reporting requirements, but rather to provide them and their overseers with useful and meaningful information and controls.

Reports on the most critical risks (the 'red bubbles') will include actual and target risk maps, lists of key risk drivers and relevant key performance indicators as well as progress reports on risk management strategies. The frequency of such reporting will be contingent on the perceived needs of the individual pilot companies, but in any case will be reported to risk owners at least every six months, and to the ExCo at least annually.

Fig. C1.5 Risk reporting

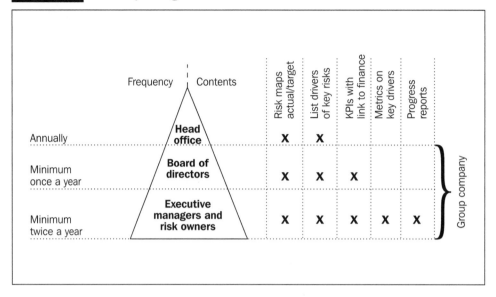

THE ORGANIZATION

The organization that puts the process into operation is vital to the programme's success. Holderbank's organization is shown in Figure C1.6.

Fig. C1.6 Holderbank corporate business risk management organization

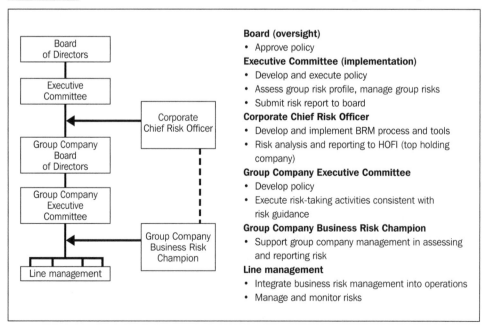

There are three important principles driving this organizational structure:

- *Executive leadership*. There are several key aspects to ensuring leadership from the top. First, the CEO or a delegated member of the ExCo owns and is committed to the business risk management process. Second, the Corporate Business Risk Management Function acts by order of the CEO/Chairman. Third, functional and/or divisional managers have responsibility for managing risks and opportunities in their respective fields. Finally, a reliable flow of information should be reported to the Group Company Executive Management and the ExCo about risk management activities.

- *BRM is a line management matter*. Responsibility cannot be transferred. This premise is fundamental to the process and realization of the Holderbank EWRM vision. Says Dr Schmidheiny, 'Risks cannot be managed from afar.'

- *Empowered process owners at all levels*. The key to empowerment is the effective leadership of the Group Company Business Risk Champion who is the co-ordination point within the group company and liaison with the Corporate Business Risk Management Function. The risk champion actively supports implementation of business risk management and continuous improvement, shares information across functions/divisions (e.g. through cross functional/divisional teams), reports to the CEO or delegated executive management member, co-ordinates business risk management activities with key functions (e.g. external audit, internal audit, insurance, business planning, etc.) and provides management with advice on best practices in business risk management.

> **Risk champions are vital to an effectively functioning risk management organization.**

Risk champions are vital to an effectively functioning risk management organization. Therefore, persons with the appropriate attributes are needed in this important role. For example, they must:

- operate effectively at all levels of the business;
- have a broad understanding of all areas of the business;
- be able to organize and motivate others (who in many cases may be in a more senior position);
- possess the authority and resources to monitor the process;
- understand the actual risk controls in place; and
- have the capability to accumulate and summarize risk reports from different functions/divisions and establish a continuous dialogue with top management.

The absence of any of the above qualities can sabotage the effectiveness of the programme.

Quickstarting the process: a CRO's advice

As Holderbank CRO, Mr Köhler has two critical pieces of advice for other managers potentially charged with launching an EWRM programme on behalf of their organizations:

1. *Get top management approval.* Without the ExCo's unqualified support, 'you are destined to fail,' says Mr Köhler. His advice: if the ExCo isn't '100% behind the programme,' do not accept the task.

2. *Use a workshop approach to create local management buy-in.* Holderbank found the use of one and a half day meetings – supported by technology – highly effective in gaining the interest, confidence and support of local managers. 'There is no faster, more effective means to jump start your risk management implementation,' says Mr Köhler. He further advises to make certain the facilitator knows the target industry inside-out. Otherwise, results will be less than stellar and credibility will be strained.

GAUGING SUCCESS

Via the above organizational structure, work is progressing rapidly in the pilot companies. In particular, the participants in the piloting process are working their way through Steps 4, 5 and 6 on their way to linking risk management strategy with business planning. The six-step process is tightly aligned with the company's three-phased business planning process, as shown in Figure C1.7.

Fig. C1.7 Links to business planning

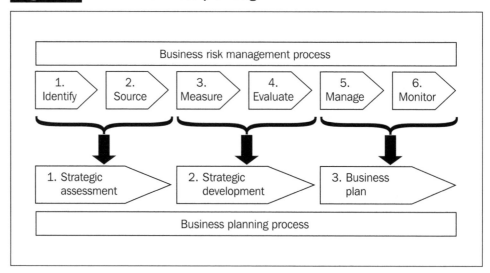

As indicated earlier, *strategic assessment* involves attaining a general understanding of the company and its environment. Steps 1 and 2 identify and source risk, contributing significantly to that vital process.

Strategic development is the identification of alternatives and the selection of appropriate strategies and organizational design improvements. Steps 3 and 4 measure and evaluate risk and opportunities and relate to the development phase because they entail the measurement of risk, the design of a target risk map, the evaluation/selection of alternatives, and the definition of a risk policy that sets forth both thresholds (tolerance) and responsibility.

Finally, the *business plan* is a comprehensive picture of the implementation of risk management capabilities which execute the strategies, including the definition of resource requirements and functional plans. Steps 5 and 6 are complementary in that they present an overview of quantitative and qualitative impacts of risks as well as the actual actions and milestones designed to steer the company towards its target risk map. In particular, Step 6 drives the development of clear and appropriate metrics and reporting standards, denoting frequency and level of detail for the ExCo, individual company and operating managers.

The company is convinced its programme will deliver many hard (tangible) and soft (human) benefits. Particularly valuable in the firm's mind is that the above processes achieve a concrete linkage of business planning to risk and opportunity management. No longer disjointed or isolated processes, business risk assessment and management 'are now integral to business planning', says Mr Ehrke, a benefit echoed by both the CEO and CRO.

The company is thus certain its business processes are in control and that its risks are being capably managed. As a consequence, the company believes it will, in time, gain recognition among investors and suppliers of capital and will eventually enjoy reduced insurance costs along with lower capital costs. If a company can show its insurance providers that it is working to improve its processes in a comprehensive, disciplined manner which should translate to a lower incidence rate, then the situation begs for lower premium costs. At the same time, adds Dr Schmidheiny, 'if you can show your shareholders the same things, they should have higher confidence in your company, and that can attract lower financing costs.' Although these latter outcomes have not yet been realized to any significant degree, the company is confident they will materialize 'over time'.

In addition to the hard (tangible) benefits, the firm also sees soft (human) benefits (see Figure C1.8). These intangible benefits include an increased awareness of risks and opportunities, improved communication, as well as a more proactive and 'change oriented' organization. For example, says Dr Schmidheiny, 'I could not put a price on it today, but it is a major achievement that people now understand that they have to live with risk in every way – if you ignore it, it doesn't go away.' As for such intangibles, Holderbank believes these have much greater value than most companies give them credit for.

Fig. C1.8 Key benefits of the Holderbank programme

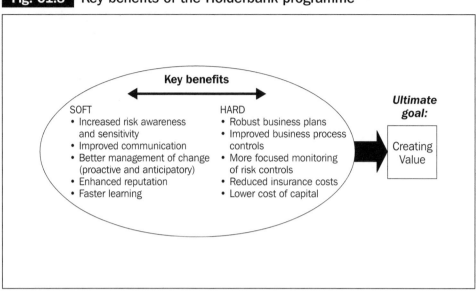

Given the above benefits, Holderbank's management committee is convinced that the firm is on the right track. 'Top management agrees that what we are doing is not a meaningless exercise but rather, it is a vital addition to our business processes,' says Mr Köhler. 'We are out to do a better job of identifying, anticipating and assessing our risks and opportunities – consciously and proactively.' The early results are highly positive, so it seems that Mr Köhler and Holderbank will continue their journey.

Applications of EWRM at mid-sized companies: the lessons go both ways

Mid-sized organizations have an advantage over larger ones. Because of their smaller size and flatter organizational structures, these companies are (a) never far from their risks and (b) tend to have a tighter business risk/opportunity focus. At larger companies, these conditions tend to apply only at middle and lower levels. But this creates a gap: senior management is always 'behind' market trends and central co-ordination is not optimized. The situation is described by Andy Grove, former CEO of Intel:

> *Middle managers, especially those who deal with the outside world, are often the first to realize that what worked before doesn't quite work anymore; that the rules are changing. They usually don't have an easy time explaining it to senior management, so the senior management in a company is sometimes late to realize that the world is changing on them – and the leader is often the last of all to know.*[1]

Through EWRM, a large organization can attain the strategic alignment and entrepreneurial zeal of a mid-sized company while simultaneously retaining and leveraging the advantages of big business. But by the same token, smaller companies can also gain competitive advantage from EWRM if for no other reasons than the achievement of acute strategic focus and the creation of a solid base for growth. The bottom line is that while small companies have much to learn about EWRM from larger companies, the larger companies have just as much to learn about risk and opportunity management from successful mid-sized companies. Two outstanding examples of mid-sized, risk-focused organizations are Eidos, a $365 million UK-based game developer, and MarineMax, a $300 million US-based recreational boat dealer.

Smaller companies can also gain competitive advantage from EWRM

EIDOS PLC: CREATING GAMES IS NO GAME

- Innovation: the heart of the Eidos business model
- Using incentives to foster innovation
- How to think like a small company

---

1. Andrew S. Grove (1996) *Only the Paranoid Survive: How to Exploit the Crisis Points that Challenge Every Company and Career*. Doubleday, pp. 21–2.

Video game maker Eidos is the second largest independent publisher of Playstation games in the US, UK, Germany and France. The company is also very close to its business risks. 'Risk is the flipside of opportunity,' says CFO Jeremy M. J. Lewis. 'Being close to risk really means thinking every minute of every day about opportunities and threats, and that's what we do.'

Eidos's management is so close to the business because they literally 'live' the business. For starters, just about every one of the company's top executives is an avid game player. Moreover, with fewer management layers, communications are apt to be more complete and interactive. When they're not themselves busy playing (call it a 'review') Tomb Raider III or Soul Reaver (two of the group's top titles), Eidos's top executives are generally brainstorming together on the organization's risks and opportunities. Creating an organization that is 'close to its risks' and that engages in 'close communication and co-ordination' are key objectives of EWRM.

As for Eidos's set of risks and opportunities, foremost of these is the creation of new and successful games. Although video games may be considered child's play by some, the target audience is actually very well informed and sophisticated creating a highly competitive market. 'With all the product reviews in gaming magazines and websites, chat rooms and word of mouth, we can't afford to put out anything that's not world-class,' explains Mr Lewis. 'Believe me, there's a lot of weak games out there and they're not selling.'

Like most companies, Eidos can ill afford to waste its scarce resources. The investment outlay for video game development is substantial, both in time and money. It takes approximately two years for a game to move from proposal to 'PlayStation', one of the leading game-playing units targeted by the company. Moreover, 'it costs around $2 million to develop a typical game that will be successful in this marketplace,' explains Mr Lewis. 'We spend over 20 per cent of our revenues on game development each year. That's serious money for us, and it goes straight to P&L.'

The principal challenge for Eidos is therefore the continual development of successful games, and in fact, this is the focus of the company's business model. The most important aspect of game development is creativity and innovation – and the company is organized to stimulate these activities. 'Innovation cannot be salaried,' says Mr Lewis. Instead, 'gifted, creative types who know how to develop original and immersive games tend to like artistic freedom. They want to be away from headquarters, they want to run their own show, and they need incentive to create – a piece of the pie if you will.' Consequently, Eidos treats all game developers as though they were outside suppliers, be they wholly owned (such as Crystal Dynamics in Palo Alto, US and Core Design in Derby, UK) or wholly external to the organization. Internal or external, 'our game developers know that if they do a great job, they're going to win big too,' explains Mr Lewis. The corollary is, 'for rubbish, they get very little,' says Mr Lewis. 'If the game wins big, only then can they afford a Maserati. But not until all of our development costs have been recovered.'

The publishing committee

With both external and internal game developers alike, Eidos senior management stays close to the investment. A key tool is a process implemented in early 1998. Every six to eight weeks, the group pulls together the executive committee of the board along with the creative directors from its major offices in Germany, Japan and the United States for a two-day 'publishing' meeting. In a room replete with monitors and audiovisual projection equipment, the development teams from each and every project 'under development' are 'paraded in one at a time to report on progress and show us their latest version of the game,' explains Mr Lewis. Participants are intensely questioned regarding all aspects of the project in what truly is a 'go/no-go' evaluation process. If the game is heading in the wrong direction, or if the original idea is not meeting expectations, 'funding can be cut off,' explains Mr Lewis.

'If you do not have the courage to take chances like this, you're not going to have any kind of breakthrough.'

Generally, a development group will be given a chance to correct shortcomings. But if the design team consistently fails to impress the publishing committee, the project is rejected. At this point, the team has two choices. It can either cease and desist with the project, or it can continue work – without Eidos funding – hoping to convince the committee of the game's merit at a future meeting. A third alternative is that the game can be shown to a third party. As Mr Lewis explains, if the committee rejects the project, developers 'can take it wherever they like for further development funding, but we're through.' Even wholly-owned development companies are free to 'shop' their unfunded games – games the developers believe have merit – to outside companies.

Eidos's greatest success to date is Lara Croft, star of Tomb Raider I, II and now III. But Eidos has approximately 40 to 45 games in development at all times, culled from 50 to 60 new game proposals per week resulting in approximately 20 to 25 new titles each year. Lara's arrival is an example of the innovation necessary for a company to achieve superior results. As the design team contemplated an 'Indiana Jones'-style character for its evolving adventure game, Eidos designers thought of the target audience (teenage males) and developed a radical departure from earlier action games: instead of a ruggedly handsome hero, why not a beautiful heroine?

Because the story line is that Lara is not only beautiful, but also intelligent (and lethal: Lara 'takes no prisoners'), she is also a success with female gamers. The overall lesson, says Mr Lewis: 'If you do not have the courage to take chances like this – there were no real starring role female heroines in video games up to this point – you're not going to have any kind of breakthrough successes.'

Meet Lara Croft: star of Tomb Raider 1–100

Few characters, live or programming code-based, achieve the fame of Lara Croft, star of Eidos's mega-hit video games Tomb Raider, Tomb Raider II and Tomb Raider III. Lara's iconic stature translates into over 16 million unit sales generating over $300 million at retail. *PC Gamer* describes her as 'the undisputed Queen of action gaming'. Looking ahead, top challenges for Eidos are (a) turning Ms Croft into a lasting franchise, and (b) creating more Lara Crofts.

The franchise

Like Rocky, James Bond or Mickey Mouse, successive releases of Lara continue to sell. In fact, each release of Tomb Raider (and for that matter, most other initially successful titles) outsells every previous release. 'We can't say with absolute precision why that is,' says Mr Lewis, 'but we're fairly certain it's because the number of game units – PlayStations, PCs, etc. – keeps growing as well.' Clearly, a strong character becomes a franchise, and Eidos is confident 'that this can be sustained,' says Mr Lewis. 'Mickey Mouse has been around for ages and James Bond is in his nineteenth movie – why not Lara?'

Because they are a franchise, Eidos protects its characters. For example, a major men's magazine was about to launch a pictorial featuring one of the live models who had portrayed Lara during publicity activities. 'We had to put the stop to that,' explains Mr Lewis. 'They can photograph this model, but she's not Lara, so they can't call her Lara.' Whether it's a photo shoot in a magazine or Lara Croft T-shirts being sold 'from the back of a van', Eidos recognizes its franchises must be protected 'like those of any other entertainment company,' says Mr Lewis.

The future

The success of Lara also explains another detail of Eidos's strategy. Instead of developing their own characters, some game makers are willing to pay royalties to utilize established characters – they pay a licensing fee to obtain a 'star' for their games. 'But when you have to borrow someone else's characters, that royalty comes right off the top,' says Mr Lewis. Moreover, 'they may charge us "X" for the first two or three years' rights. But if the game is hugely successful, the next time we go to negotiate for a second or third release, the new price could be "5X".' Concludes Mr Lewis, 'the real value is in the characters and the environment you create for them. This value is something you create and own, not something you license from others.'

Other risks...

While the need to release 'hot' innovative games tops the list of opportunities, Eidos is cognizant and proactive in the assessment and management of its other business risks as well, which include contractual risks, pricing risks and human resources risks. A good example is its approach to social/cultural risk. Like the music and movie businesses, the gaming industry has been criticized for its portrayal of violence. Eidos pays close attention to such portrayal, but takes two explicit steps to mitigate potential regulatory risk:

- First, the company has for many years included a 'rating' system on its games indicating appropriateness for various age groups. 'That is voluntary,' says Mr Lewis.

- Second, the company has standards for what is and isn't acceptable in its video games. 'If it's an Eidos game, you won't be scoring any points for shooting anyone other than a very bad or dangerous guy. You don't shoot police, you don't blow up civilians – you are an agent for good in our game environments.'

The gaming industry has been criticized for its portrayal of violence.

Telling the world

Like other UK companies, Eidos is keenly aware of the annual assessment of risk and control processes mandated by the Turnbull Report. However, this is not driving the risk and opportunity assessment practices of the company. Instead, Eidos executives have always realized that sound risk assessment and management is simply good business and vital to the company's success in creating value.

'Fast-moving companies in this multimedia sector are entrepreneurial,' says Mr Lewis. 'One thing I've observed, they tend to be driven by capable and visionary personalities whose bread and butter is thinking about risk and opportunity. That's what lies at the heart of a great business: who's coming up behind us? what's the next great innovation? how do we take advantage of the Internet? do we have the right systems to keep track of what we need to know? That's how an entrepreneurial company thinks – and that's Eidos.'

Eidos, by the way, is very well positioned to take advantage of new selling channels like the Internet. Explains Mr Lewis, 'the company had its start in video compression – and we've maintained that capability.'

Eidos is itself a case study in the value of revealing a risk-focused culture and business model to shareholders. For several years, Eidos's share price had been trading in a narrow range around $10 a share. The company – focusing on its business instead of its share price – had little time to explain its inner workings to 'Wall Street'. In September 1998, Mr Lewis joined as CFO from Flemings, the

London-based investment bank where he was involved in mergers and acquisitions. Then in February 1999, together with Charles Cornwall, Mike McGarvey and Jeremy Heath-Smith, he mounted a road show for institutional investors to explain the risk and opportunity-oriented thinking behind the Eidos organization.

The result 'has been very pleasing,' says Mr Lewis. Valuations have since climbed steadily as high as over $70 a share. 'The Turnbull Report is important and we're going to look at it closely,' says Mr Lewis. 'But the things I'm telling you about today, the things we are doing, we do them for a simple reason – they are the best way to create value from what we do. Turnbull won't change that.'

HOW MARINEMAX TURNS RISK INTO OPPORTUNITY

- How a new business model helps MarineMax prosper in both good times and bad
- Why customer satisfaction is the number one corporate priority
- Lessons from an acquisitions-minded organization

Recreational boating – the consumer segment of the marine industry – has been experiencing flat or even declining sales. Yet one group of retailers, members of the MarineMax family, has seen same-store sales growth averaging 17 per cent per year for the past five years. The company attributes its success to a business strategy that first focuses on the most critical risks faced by its industry and second turns these perceived risks into opportunities. Moreover, the company engages the entire organization in the ongoing identification, prioritization and management of these risks, creating a business model ideally suited to its industry.

Like all enterprises, MarineMax faces a handful of business risks. However, the primary emphasis is on two in particular: (1) ensuring that boating remains a popular pastime (read: delighting the customer), and (2) positioning itself for continuing success regardless of economic or legislative events.

Risk 1: 'the two best days in boating'

According to CFO Michael McLamb, the greatest risk to a boating retailer is not that a customer will turn to the competition 'three piers down' but rather that they may choose to forego boating altogether. 'You've probably heard somewhere that the two best days you own a boat are the day you buy a boat and the day you get rid of the boat,' says McLamb. 'It is our focus to end that cliché.'

MarineMax's management teams are focused on the long-term performance of the company and therefore the health – the perceptions – of the industry. In turn, they recognize that to capture the harried Baby Boomers for whom time is a precious commodity, the boating experience must be free of the breakdowns, slipshod repairs and other various 'hassles' that have characterized much of the boating experience in the past.

'We're competing for customers who want an effortless and satisfying pastime – and we're up against every other form of recreation known to man,' says McLamb. 'We have to deliver a consistently high-quality experience or risk losing the customer for keeps. We're not selling fibreglass and motors and mechanical devices, we're selling an enjoyable lifestyle choice.'

Accordingly, MarineMax focuses every element of the organization on the delivery of 'an unsurpassed' level of service in the industry. Its approach is fivefold:

- *Market premium products*. Certain consumers are price sensitive. But in general, the most profitable segment for the long term, the Baby Boomers, is willing to pay a bit more in exchange for a consistently enjoyable experience. Correspondingly, MarineMax chooses to market premium quality boats and equipment. 'A boat, inherently, is going to have problems from time to time,' says McLamb. But by selling premium quality boats, 'it gives us the highest percentage likelihood that the boats are going to work and work well.'

- *Deliver proactive, 'hassle-free' service*. The competition for recreational expenditure is as much about time as it is money. Extensive psychographic research has shown that members of MarineMax's target market place an especially high premium on their leisure time. Therefore, the company endeavours to make boat ownership and operation 'hassle free'. To accomplish this, every boat sold comes with a service agreement known as MarineMax Care. This includes two years of proactive maintenance on-site by mobile service teams. The goal, says McLamb, 'is to make sure when you're there with the coolers and the family on a Saturday morning, you turn the key and you're boating, every time.' The objective is not mere customer satisfaction but, rather, the creation of 'raving fans'.

- *Provide customer training*. A third critical element of the business risk strategy is to make boating safe and fun for all participants. This begins with the provision of in-water delivery wherever possible accompanied by immediate training for novice 'captains'. Delivery includes a review of the onboard systems as well as a demonstration of proper launching and docking techniques. In addition, MarineMax seeks to broaden involvement in the boating experience and enhance safety by providing training for any boat owner's 'significant other' known as 'Captain's Too'. There is also a programme for kids, known as 'Kids in Boating'.

- *Focus on safety and the long term*. Finally, MarineMax strives to be an active sponsor of boating safety courses wherever its products are sold. Says McLamb, 'we focus on the long term, and that means giving everyone on board a sense of involvement as well as creating a safe environment. The more we make boating a satisfying, safe, enjoyable lifestyle, the harder it's going to be for people to walk away from it – even if their net worth declines moderately.'

■ *Do the right thing*. Enterprise-wide, MarineMax understands that its strategies are long term. At every retail location, a plaque recites the firm's value statements. These include honesty, integrity, trust, loyalty, professionalism and consistency. Most importantly, says McLamb, the values say: 'Always do what is right, and always consider the long term. These are more than just words, they are at the heart of our business strategy.'

The MarineMax University

Keeping the organization focused on the above values and strategies that address business risks is an ongoing process at MarineMax. One means is through quarterly multi-day meetings with senior management at all operating subsidiaries. In attendance are the CEO, CFO and COO. While only certain stretches of these meetings address risk emphatically, 'whatever it's labelled, really the whole day addresses business risk in one form or another,' says CFO McLamb.

A second mechanism is a formal employee learning programme known as MarineMax University. The firm has spent almost 2 million dollars on training in the past year alone, so far moving in excess of 200 employees through the programme. The university is designed to teach the strategies of the company, which not only improves operations but also promotes 'buy-in' to the company's philosophies and business practices. Often, the programme is a real eye opener even for industry veterans.

'We get guys who've been in this business for 25 years saying "you're not going to be able to teach me anything,"' says McLamb. But at the end of the courses, attendees are asked to give a presentation. 'A lot of these same guys end up giving gut-wrenching talks about how much they've learned and what new strategies they're going to be taking with them and implementing in their regions.'

Even more intriguing, MarineMax does not limit attendance to current MarineMax employees – outsiders are often invited to attend. Similarly, MarineMax offers its training materials to acquisition candidates with the express intent that the knowledge be passed on to their dealerships. The rationale is twofold. First, since MarineMax is acquisition-minded, 'if we get more companies managing according to our philosophies, it will improve their fundamentals and reduce integration issues if and when we acquire them.' Second, says McLamb, 'to the extent we can get everyone in the industry focusing on the needs of the customer, we can really build this segment and keep customers in boating.' The MarineMax view: a rising tide lifts all boats.

Risk 2: managing downturns

The management teams at MarineMax are focused on prospering both in robust growth periods and economic downturns. The fact is, the company firmly believes its structure and business strategies will enable it to actually arise from any downturn even stronger than before. The boating industry is characterized by many thousands of individual boat dealers. These 'mom and pop' dealerships are neither particularly well capitalized nor necessarily manned by highly experienced business people. Consequently, many disappear rapidly during any lulls in a regional economy.

As a result, the companies in the MarineMax family tend to be hurt far less during any economic lulls. As McLamb explains, relative to pre-1991 performance, both revenues and unit sales in the boating industry declined 28 per cent after a luxury tax was enacted. However, for MarineMax, revenues declined only 16 per cent; gross profit fell to a much less degree. 'Since the time of Noah, there's an element out there that will be buying boats and getting service no matter what. So as the number of outlets declines – as the local retailers close shop – we grow market share.' This is well-evidenced by 1992 results: MarineMax revenues climbed 40 per cent.

Although it would prefer a healthy economy for all, MarineMax views economic events as less of a risk and more of an opportunity for long-term growth. The company's well-capitalized structure is a key factor in its ability to acquire new dealerships and customers thus growing market share during economic lulls. But at the same time, the company also credits its business strategies, which include the following:

> MarineMax believes its structure and business strategies will enable it to arise from any downturn even stronger than before.

- *Keep an eye on costs*. The MarineMax mantra is to manage as capably during good as in lean times. This means keeping a close eye on costs and inventories no matter the economic climate. Says McLamb, 'If we stick to our fundamentals, we'll always be in a position to expand and grow market share and emerge from any downturn stronger than when we went in.'

- *Keep an eye on inventory*. Large inventories represent an ineffective use of capital. The company manages this via two mechanisms. First, the company levies a management interest charge (currently 7.25 per cent) for actual inventory levels. Since a portion of local management salaries are based on profitability, this provides an incentive for local dealerships to strike a balance between holding large inventories (stimulating sales) and incurring the related risks and explicit holding costs. Second, the company teaches its managers to stock what sells. Via a sophisticated reporting system, internal information is mined continually. In addition, the company also tracks boating registrations religiously. 'We know how many and what types of boats are being sold,' says McLamb, and the information is factored into inventory planning and decision-making.

- *Manage model years.* A critical element in inventory management is turnover. This is particularly important as new models are about to appear. 'If a customer sees a '99 model on the lot beside a 2000, and the prices are comparable, he will want the new boat. That '99 is going to do nothing but age,' says McLamb. As a result, the company offers incentives to move older models along. For example, in addition to customary commissions, a salesperson might be offered an additional $1–5 for every day a boat has been in inventory.

- *Manage as a group.* MarineMax's business structure brings a decided advantage to traditional marine retailing. Because it has retail locations nationwide and manages product ordering and logistics centrally, it can shift inventory where needed. For example, when 'El Niño' struck the west coast of the United States in 1998, boat registrations fell approximately 30 per cent in California. But rather than endure high inventories, the firm was able to move units to retail locations in other parts of the country. Moreover, it was able to reroute scheduled California-bound shipments from manufacturers. In general, says McLamb, 'We can manage excess inventory usually with the click of a mouse. That's a big advantage.'

- *Grow.* MarineMax is an opportunistic organization seeking continual expansion into profitable markets. Although the group will never overpay for an acquisition, CFO McLamb believes 'once we've done our homework, if an acquisition is right for us, we pay a very fair multiple of earnings.'

> All elements of an organization must understand both risks and opportunities.

Beyond seeking new retailers, the group has recently moved into the boating brokerage business by acquiring one of the largest boat brokers. 'Retailers have typically viewed brokers as a competitor,' says McLamb. In accordance with its mission to completely meet the needs of customers, brokerage seemed a logical business complement for MarineMax. Not only is this a large and profitable business (pre-owned boats represent 50 per cent of industry-wide sales), providing this service improves 'liquidity' for customers. This is a particularly attractive business segment for MarineMax given its MarineMax Care programme. Says McLamb, 'On any boat we've sold, we have detailed maintenance records. We know the condition of the boat making it easier to price and to offer a warranty and continued maintenance programme.' MarineMax now includes 'an attractive folder', detailing the firm's brokerage capabilities, with the sale of every new boat.

Managing risk: an enterprise-wide imperative

An organization's ability to gauge and manage its risks defines its success. To be truly successful, McLamb insists that all elements of an organization must understand both risks and opportunities and be engaged in the attainment of corporate goals. This requires enlightenment, 'buy-in' and co-ordination – all of which are addressed by the above strategies and processes. It also requires a means of measuring success and implementing continual refinement and improvement.

The company achieves buy-in and co-ordination via its training (e.g. MarineMax University) as well as through its ongoing internal communications (e.g. weekly teleconferences). 'We believe that the future state of risk management is a model that is embraced and empowered throughout the organization at all levels. It can't be a process driven solely by the CEO or the board,' says McLamb. In this vision, those closest to the risk 'are the ones who can feed relevant information to the right places in the organization to help us take advantage of opportunities.' According to McLamb, the greatest challenge for enterprise-wide risk management is achieving the right calibre, training and beliefs of personnel, combining technical, human and cultural elements. 'If they don't believe in the risk, if they don't understand the risks appropriately, they won't be able to monitor and help to control those risks.'

> 'We believe that the future state of risk management is a model that is embraced and empowered throughout the organization at all levels.'

Measuring performance in the achievement of goals is equally critical. Here, the company uses both macro and micro indicators. On the macro side, the most important gauges include measures such as sales growth, net income, market-share growth and customer satisfaction. Says McLamb, 'If your customer satisfaction levels are high, you're probably going to see some increased sales and also profitability.' At the micro-level, the company focuses on items such as inventory turns, aged inventory and various other metrics 'we've built into our EDP system from an accounting standpoint to help measure areas that drive our risks,' explains McLamb.

Finally, a successful enterprise-wide risk approach includes continual feedback and evaluation. The company's business model achieves this through a variety of mechanisms:

- First, there are clear risk owners with compensation closely tied to performance versus risks. This creates the incentive to continually re-evaluate risks and opportunities and to be proactive.

- Second, the company relies on its management information systems and external data gathering to ensure it has the most relevant information for decision-making and strategic refinement.

- Finally, there is a culture of open and continual information exchange. Senior management has formed a partnership with local operating companies where both are focused on the same sets of long- and short-term goals.

Through these and other mechanisms, MarineMax continually improves its assessment and management of risk and therefore opportunity.

The MarineMax business model looks at the traditional shortcomings of the marine industry and turns these into growth opportunities. 'If your timeframe is the last 15 years, and you consider most of the large manufacturers and some of the other large retailers, most have either disappeared or have had to file Chapter 11 more than once.' According to McLamb:

> *What's at risk if you don't successfully monitor your business risks is, quite frankly, business failure. We understand our strengths, our customers, our competition, our mission and our industry. Maybe ours is an uncomplicated industry, but I believe what we have here is an organization that knows what it has to do to be successful, knows how to turn risks into opportunities and that's what we do here every day.*

4

Risk management goals, objectives and oversight: laying the foundation

Certainty generally is illusion, and repose is not the destiny of man.

Oliver Wendell Holmes, Jr

Just as strategic focus is a success sustainer, blind devotion to the past is a success killer.

Leonard L. Berry (Distinguished Professor, Texas A&M University)

If we can help business managers better understand the risks surrounding their opportunities, they'll make better decisions. If they make better decisions, we're a more successful company.

Nick Chown, Group Risk Manager, British Post Office

In this chapter, we focus on the steps that senior management must take to lay the foundation for establishing a business risk management process, which we will introduce in Chapter 5. This means setting risk management goals and objectives and establishing an organizational structure that provides leadership and oversight.

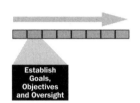

For risk management to be effective, it must also align seamlessly with a company's business strategies, processes and capabilities. It must further delineate specific tasks and reporting relationships as well as designate clear risk owners. Finally, it must specify permissible – and desirable – actions, yet at the same time, give risk owners ample room to manage day to day. In essence, it must institutionalize and facilitate EWRM. All of this begins at the top of the organization.

BUSINESS OBJECTIVES AND STRATEGIES PROVIDE THE CONTEXT

CEOs set the stage for risk taking by defining the mission of the company. That mission must be translated into specific and yet empowering business strategies and policies. Formal strategy and policy structures are developed so that risk owners and other stakeholders share a common understanding of the firm's risk-taking philosophy, risk tolerance and expected standards of conduct. Strategies address general principles that apply to all aspects of the business while policies focus on more specific guidelines for risks, products or transaction types.

The company's business objectives and strategies define its business model for creating value and drive its risk management strategies and policies. They clarify the activities the firm will undertake, how it will conduct business and where. The firm's policies articulate its strategies and lay out the vital 'rules of the road' in terms that everyone understands.

Business strategies and policies are important because they provide a powerful context for risk management. For example, a thorough understanding of a firm's business objectives and strategy (not to mention its operations) is very useful when articulating its desired risks, or the risks it chooses to accept as it creates value. A firm's strategy addresses many elements of its business model, for example:

- the products and services it provides;
- the markets it serves and channels it utilizes;
- the processes through which it converts materials and labour into products and services;
- the employees it hires, trains and retains;
- the suppliers and customers with which it does business;
- the countries and communities in which it operates; and
- the shareholders and bankers that supply its capital.

Business risks are inherent in all of these elements. Why? Because in the normal course of executing its strategy, the firm creates and increases exposures to uncertainty. Therefore, business objectives and strategies provide the context for understanding the risks the enterprise desires to take.

Just as some risks are desirable, others are undesirable. These risks should be avoided, transferred or reduced. That is why policies are needed to provide assurance to the board and executive management that the corporate tolerances for risk are effectively communicated and monitored. 'Tolerance' is the ability of a firm to accept or withstand risk from a given source or event, e.g. what is the firm's tolerance for actual results deviating from plan? In effect, risk tolerances address the question, 'What performance variability and loss exposure are we willing to accept as we pursue our objectives and execute our strategies? Policies can be a useful tool in delineating desirable from undesirable risks so that the appropriate risk management strategies can be planned.

Policies focus primarily on the 'what' and not the 'how'. In essence, they establish the guidelines needed for day-to-day decision-making which allow process and risk owners adequate flexibility to manage the business under changing conditions. As US General George S. Patton once said: 'Never tell people how to do things. Tell them what to do and they will surprise you with their ingenuity.' Chief Risk Officer Nick Chown of the British Post Office agrees: a balance must be struck 'between the need to control and co-ordinate and the need to let business people go out and do their stuff.'

RISK STRATEGY AND POLICY IN AN EWRM ENVIRONMENT

Your company undoubtedly has formal or informal risk management policies and strategies in place today. But how and why were they developed? Were they defined to satisfy legal and regulatory requirements? Were they developed in a fragmented environment with a bias toward 'risk as downside'? Were they designed with little or no focus on risk management as a source of value? As you review the five steps below, keep in mind, what would change as you evolve towards EWRM.

Articulate the risk management vision

What do you wish to accomplish through risk management? The vision provides a sense of purpose and focuses subsequent development of more specific risk management goals and strategies. An example of an EWRM-oriented vision statement is provided by Holderbank:

> *Business Risk Management is a continuous process, and an element of Corporate Governance. It promotes efficient and effective assessment of risk, increases risk awareness and improves the management of risk throughout the Group. This includes anticipating and avoiding threats and losses as well as identifying and realizing opportunities.*

Define overall risk management goals and objectives

A broad statement of goals and objectives articulates the value proposition of risk management, e.g. to establish sustainable competitive advantage, optimize the cost of managing business risk, make informed and conscious risk management choices on an enterprise-wide basis and improve overall business performance. While not intended to detract from their primary responsibilities, a company's risk managers are asked: Are you focusing on enterprise-wide objectives? How do your goals and objectives mesh with the group at large as it makes the transition to EWRM? The purpose of this enterprise-wide perspective is to encourage managers to look beyond their immediate areas of responsibility for opportunities and risks requiring group-wide attention and co-ordination. The goals and objectives must make this point clear.

The risk strategy must be consistent with other firm strategies.

Develop strategies to achieve overall goals and objectives; align risk strategies and business strategies

A sound strategy for the organization as a whole and its units and divisions provides a framework for accepting and rejecting risk as the firm seeks new sources of value in the marketplace. The risk strategy must be consistent with other firm strategies, regardless of whether it is formulated separately or integrated with existing business strategies.

If the risk strategy is formulated *after* the business strategy is developed (which is often the case, as risk is often considered intuitively when formulating business strategy), then the business strategy needs to be confirmed or adjusted when risks are fully considered. This is important as we can point to companies who determined that certain business strategies warranted an overhaul once the risks involved were fully understood.

Therefore, business and risk strategies should be developed concurrently – at least at a high level – so they are in sync with one another. They then can be defined in greater detail and subsequently realigned. That is why, in many of our case examples, the firms are integrating their business risk management with their business planning and strategic management processes.

When aligning risk management strategy with business strategy, there are many issues to consider, for example:

■ Is risk management a continuous process or a periodic activity?

■ Are certain risks more vital to our value creation strategies than others?

■ Are certain risks more common enterprise-wide than others?

■ Do our primary risk-taking activities capitalize on our core competencies?

■ How strong are our risk management capabilities relative to our competitors, particularly for mission-critical risks?

■ Who is responsible for developing risk strategies and assigning risk authorities? Who is responsible for executing those strategies and authorities?

The Holderbank case illustrates the tight linkage of the firm's risk management process with its three-phased business planning process – strategic assessment, strategic development and business planning. Similar connections are in evidence at nearly all leading EWRM-oriented companies. For example, at Guinness, 'our business strategy, our risk footprints and our Key Performance Indicator models are aligned,' explains Finance Director Ray Joy. 'Implementing a business strategy highlights new risks, so we develop KPIs that tell us what we're doing well and where we need to improve in managing those risks.'

Develop a formal risk management policy

The risk management policy assigns responsibility for performing key tasks, establishes accountability with the appropriate managers, defines boundaries and limits, and formalizes reporting channels. These elements provide the baseline for a sound policy statement.

While the actual format and details of a baseline policy structure vary from one firm to another, the following issues should be explicitly addressed:

■ the objectives of assessing, managing and monitoring business risk;

■ responsibilities of risk owners and risk oversight personnel;

- roles and responsibilities of operating managers in managing business risk at the business unit and divisional level;

- overall enterprise-wide risk tolerances linked to established business objectives and strategies (e.g. if management's goals are to earn $2.50 per share and retire $50 million in debt during the coming year, how much exposure to earnings and cash flow variability can the business withstand?);

- boundaries and limit structures linked to enterprise goals that clearly specify management's 'risk tolerance' (i.e. how much risk is the firm willing to accept?) – this includes prescribed exposure limits for authorized business activities which are potentially risky if not well managed;

- risk authorities, i.e. who is authorized to commit firm resources in conjunction with volatile and high-risk activities and execute specific business risk management strategies?

- required risk reporting and approved methodologies for measuring risk.

The policy is most effective if it addresses risks that must be managed on a day-to-day basis and defines the primary business risk management strategies that management has selected. This additional specificity comes later after the strategies are developed (see Chapter 5). Once the specific strategies have been selected, the policy structure is expanded to address:

- a description of the business risks that management has determined are 'mission-critical'; and

- strategies for managing different types of risks, including acceptable or preferred risk management techniques and prescribed tools, products and practices.

In an EWRM environment, the firm's policy structure is further expanded depending on the capabilities that management decides to adopt, for example:

- It explains why an enterprise-wide view is appropriate and the scope of its application, e.g. it emphasizes the importance of individual units aligned with group-wide risk management objectives and encourages managers to ask: 'If this is a good decision for my group, is it also the best decision for the enterprise as a whole?' (see Chapter 2).

- It describes the value of evaluating business risk using a common language and according to uniform processes to enable enterprise-wide aggregation, analysis and knowledge sharing (see Chapters 3 and 5).

- It summarizes the overall process for building and improving risk management capabilities to be applied by the enterprise and each of its business units (see Chapters 5 and 6).

- It articulates the components of infrastructure that define risk management capabilities and acknowledges that there are varying levels of capability that are appropriate, given the nature of the risks and their criticality to the business (see Chapters 6 and 7).

- It provides a framework for vertical and cross-functional communications and knowledge sharing to make business risk management truly an enterprise-wide effort (see Chapter 7).

- It frames the approved guidance on the use of risk families or pools as a portfolio for risk management purposes. (*Note:* A family or 'pool' is a natural grouping of risks sharing fundamental characteristics, e.g. common drivers, positive or negative correlations, etc. These categorizations assist managers in understanding the interrelationships between risks for purposes of selecting the appropriate measurement methodologies and management solutions.)

- It institutionalizes the measures of success by which risk management will be evaluated.

- It integrates risk management with strategic management and business planning (for more on the above three points, see Chapter 8).

- It defines the value proposition of risk management in the organization (see Chapter 9).

All told, the policy in an EWRM environment is a broad one that is consistent with the organization's structure and culture.

Policies should be well documented to avoid ambiguity. Manuals should be as brief as possible and 'user-friendly'. The nature and level of detail of the policy documentation is a function of management's operating philosophy, the complexity of the business and the nature of its risks.

Obtain approvals, communicate widely and periodically evaluate

The risk management vision, goals and objectives, strategy and policy, and any changes to them are (a) approved by the board of directors, (b) implemented under the direction and co-ordination of a senior executive and/or a chartered risk management executive committee reporting directly to the CEO, and (c) widely communicated throughout the firm.

Executive management should periodically evaluate the firm's risk management goals and objectives in co-operation with the board, key executive and operating managers and process/activity and risk owners. A feedback and re-evaluation process can be executed via facilitated meetings, task forces, focus groups and through the ongoing activities of existing executive and risk management committees.

ORGANIZATIONAL OVERSIGHT STRUCTURE

Once overall risk management goals and objectives are defined, executive management must ensure that the organizational structure in place is adequate to oversee risk management. An effective oversight structure often includes senior management working committees, a senior executive responsible for EWRM, formal charters and job descriptions, clear authorization levels and effective reporting lines.

An effectively functioning oversight structure ensures that risk owners are designated on a timely basis, communication plans are both coherent and capably executed, resources allocated to risk management and staffing are sufficient, incentives for desired behaviours are in place and hiring, retention and training practices work as intended. It ensures that managers at all levels are active participants in the risk management process. It also delineates the specific roles and responsibilities of risk-taking versus risk monitoring.

To perform the many tasks relevant to risk management in a co-ordinated fashion and implement an EWRM process, everyone in the organization from top to bottom plays a role (see Figure 4.1). Note that the reporting relationships in Figure 4.1 are for illustration purposes only. For example, in practice the reporting relationship of the chief risk officer varies. Furthermore, the executive committee often designates a working *risk management executive committee* (RMEC) to oversee risk management on its behalf, so the RMEC may or may not report directly to the CEO. There are, therefore, variations in practice.

In general, the board of directors provides an oversight role, understanding the critical risks, approving EWRM policies and strategies and determining that risks are managed effectively. The CEO is the 'comprehensive risk executive' and is ultimately responsible for EWRM priorities, including strategies, tolerances and policies. The CEO acts as the final enforcer on such matters.

The RMEC co-ordinates decision-making. For example, it recommends EWRM risk tolerances and profiles to the CEO and board. It evaluates measurement methodologies. It establishes capital allocation frameworks. It develops enterprise-wide and specific-risk policies. It assigns owners of significant risks. And it evaluates the effectiveness of the infrastructure in place for managing specific risks. Executives serving on the RMEC may include those noted in Figure 4.1.

The chief risk officer (CRO) is a member of the RMEC and reports either to the CEO or to a ranking senior executive. The CRO oversees the business risk management function and is the ultimate champion of the corporate business risk management process. The CRO may also have authority for managing selected risks.

An effectively functioning oversight structure ensures that managers at all levels are active participants in the risk management process.

Fig. 4.1 Organizational oversight structure

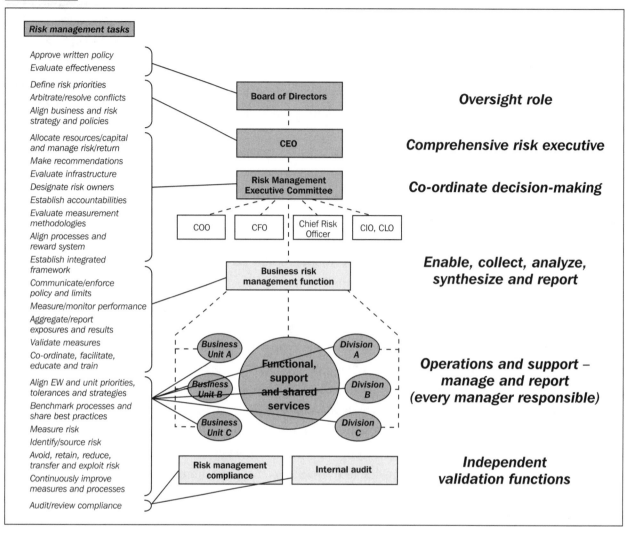

Operating and support management include line operations as well as treasury and insurable risk managers. They manage risk and report results. For example, they assess risks and processes and provide input on enterprise-wide risk priorities and strategies. They formulate unit strategies consistent with enterprise-wide strategies. They target business and product development activities to create new sources of value consistent with enterprise-wide tolerances. They set unit risk thresholds consistent with enterprise-wide policies. They assign risk management responsibilities and accountabilities within their respective units. They also report on the overall quality of business risk management processes. Success in EWRM ultimately is determined by the extent to which line and functional managers participate in the process with an integrated approach and are held accountable for enterprise-wide results.

To bring the top of the organization and the activities of its business units together, a *business risk management function* (BRMF) provides 'enabling frameworks'. These tools, such as a common risk language (and others that will

Success in EWRM ultimately is determined by the extent to which managers participate in the process and are held accountable.

be introduced in this book), facilitate the collection, analysis and synthesis of data. They support the reporting of exposures and results of the process on an aggregate enterprise-wide basis. The BRMF usually reports to a senior executive (i.e. a CRO) or to the RMEC. Its charter is approved by the RMEC.

Finally, there is the validation role of *risk management compliance* and *internal audit*. In some organizations, these groups may be one and the same. They perform audits and periodic or continuous reviews to provide assurances to the RMEC and the board that critical processes are performing effectively, key measures and reports are reliable and established policies are in an ongoing state of compliance.

All of these people, functions and different levels of the firm play a vital role within the organization in making the EWRM process work. The RMEC and CRO provide the vital oversight.

When evaluating the organizational oversight structure for risk management, there are many alternative models to consider. While difficult to generalize, the distinctions between them can be summarized in terms of several design principles relating to the roles and authorities at various levels of the firm, as expressed by the questions below:

- What is the role of the board of directors and the CEO?

- Is there an RMEC? If so, what is its composition, role and responsibilities? (*Note:* The RMEC in practice is named differently from firm to firm. It may be a functioning committee of the board or a committee consisting of senior executives and key operating unit managers reporting to the firm's executive committee or to the CEO.)

- Does the firm designate a single officer to assume responsibility for risk management, i.e. a CRO? Is this officer independent of operations, i.e. does he or she report to the CEO or to the RMEC? If there is no single risk officer, is there a committee (or equivalent group) with similar responsibilities?

- With respect to the CRO (or equivalent committee):
  - What is the nature of the risks integrated under the officer's (or committee's) charter?
  - What are the roles and responsibilities as summarized in the charter?
  - Is the role consultative (assess and recommend) or authoritarian (approve) or both?
  - Is there an adequate support staff?

- What are the roles and responsibilities of business unit and divisional management?

- What independent validation and compliance functions are there? To whom do these functions report? Examples of such functions include internal audit, risk management oversight/compliance and value at risk review.

- How is accountability for managing risk determined? Who 'owns' the responsibility for managing specific risks and through what channels do they report results?

Depending on the answers to these and other questions, an oversight structure is designed to serve as both the 'referee' and the sponsor for moving the organization forward to an EWRM environment.

To illustrate, the following models present alternatives to the design of a risk management oversight structure. In all of these models, the CRO (or other equivalent executive) is a senior executive reporting directly to the CEO, is a member of the RMEC and is supported by a business risk management function (BRMF).

Process champion model

This model (see Figure 4.2) establishes a senior executive, i.e. a CRO, as the champion of the business risk management process (BRMP) as it is applied at all units and levels of the enterprise. As process champion, the CRO:

- does not directly own responsibility for managing specific risks, but operates in a consultative and collaborative role, with power vested by the RMEC;

- works with others to establish, maintain and continuously improve business risk management processes enterprise-wide;

- supports the board (and its committees), the executive committee, the RMEC and key operating and functional managers; and

- directs the BRMF (a) in the collection, aggregation, summarization and assessment of data obtained from business and functional units regarding risk exposures and performance, and (b) in the assembly of business risk reports.

While this model can be sketched out in many ways, the consultative and collaborative process champion approach is the one that non-financial institutions are generally adopting in practice, primarily because of cultural constraints. The primary variant in practice is whether the CRO reports to the CEO or to a senior executive, i.e. the CFO.

Fig. 4.2 Process champion model

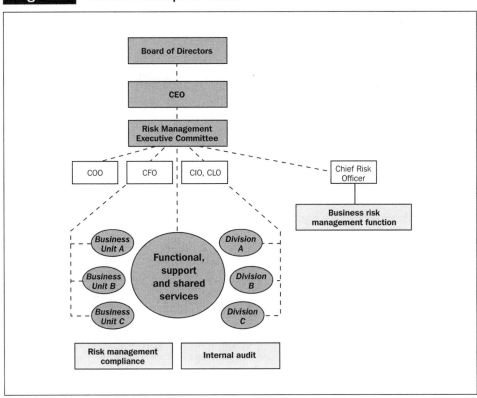

Comprehensive risks model and focused risks model

Under these two approaches, a senior executive (a CRO) and/or an RMEC own the responsibility for integrating the management of either (a) all significant business risks or (b) certain specifically designated risks. Their authority is vested by the CEO and the firm's executive committee.

To illustrate the comprehensive risks model in a financial institution, the CRO and/or RMEC would oversee and co-ordinate the management of market, credit and operational risks. They also would be responsible for overseeing one or more of such functions as back office, legal, information technology and insurable risk management. The objective is to consolidate as many risk management activities as possible so that they can be effectively integrated and co-ordinated. Under the comprehensive approach, a single unit defines the integrating risk management framework and executes analysis and reporting functions across all business units. This oversight model may be applied in many ways. While the approach is obviously enterprise-wide in scope, it may not be feasible for all organizations.[1]

---

1. 'Organizing a financial institution to deliver enterprise-wide risk management,' Michael Haubenstock, *The Journal of Lending and Credit Risk Management*, February 1999.

Alternatively, in a financial institution under a focused risks model (as shown in Figure 4.3), the CRO and/or RMEC oversee the management of market and credit risks. Back-office activities, legal, information technology, insurable risk management as well as internal audit are directed by other executives. Operational risks are managed by operations and other functional groups.

Fig. 4.3 Focused risks model

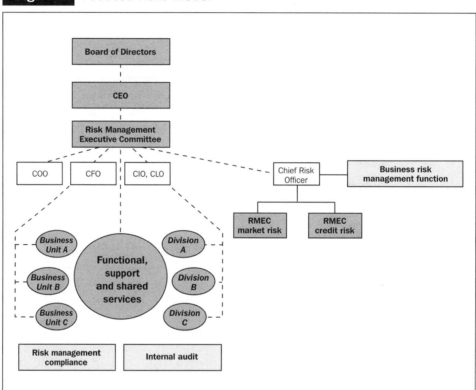

Expanded corporate governance model

Any risk management organizational oversight structure is, by definition, a 'corporate governance model'. This specific model (see Figure 4.4), however, is a variation of any of the other three models (process champion, comprehensive risks or focused risks). It incorporates the added feature of certain designated functional groups reporting directly to the CRO or RMEC responsible for risk management to enhance the co-ordination of corporate governance activities. These groups will vary depending on how the board and CEO define the accountability of the RMEC or CRO for the governance process. They may include internal audit, risk management oversight/compliance, legal and regulatory compliance, and value at risk review.

Fig. 4.4 Expanded corporate governance model

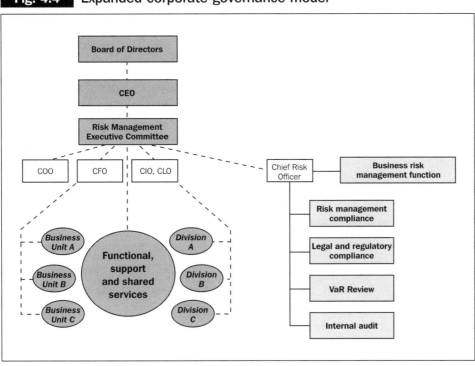

There are *many* possible approaches for organizing risk management in an organization. We have just covered a few of them. We see the application of the 'comprehensive risks model' and 'focused risks model' primarily in the financial services industry (banks, insurance and investment companies). These models may be difficult to implement in other industries because the organizational culture is likely to resist what some may view as an authoritarian approach. Therefore, we expect to see the emergence of more consultative and collaborative approaches in non-financial services industries. For example, Holderbank has adopted the 'process champion model'. What makes this model effective is the authority vested in the responsible individuals by the executive committee and the board of directors.

Whatever organizational model is used, it must have teeth. That is why direct reporting to the CEO or to another senior executive is vital. Furthermore, responsibility for risk-taking activities must always be delineated from risk monitoring and oversight activities.

SUMMARY

Defining business risk management goals and objectives and establishing an effective organizational oversight structure for risk management is the logical way for senior managers to lead the transition to EWRM from the top. This vital step provides a framework within which a working group of senior executives deploy a common language and execute the process for building and improving risk management capabilities. Simply stated, it lays a strong foundation for business risk management in the organization. The next chapter introduces a uniform process for managing risk that is built on that foundation.

The British Post Office: delivering the EWRM message

- A new organization focused on evolving opportunities
- Mating risk mapping to an existing set of processes
- Keeping things simple: risk management is not 'rocket science'

The British Post Office is undergoing massive transformation. Responding to competitive threats and opportunities, the £7 billion group is increasing the number of business units from the current five. The objective is to create a dynamic, 'market facing' organization. At the same time, somewhat opportunistically, the group is also rolling out a new 'business risk management model'. Its objective is to improve risk management capabilities and assist business units in achieving their performance goals. Under the auspices of Group Treasury Director Roger Durrant and Group Risk Manager Nick Chown, the risk model includes such familiar EWRM elements as a common risk language and a uniform process featuring risk mapping and risk control self-assessment.

Both tasks – the broader reorganization and the implementation of the risk model – are enormous undertakings. Nonetheless, both the restructuring and the deployment of risk profiling are to be completed by the end of April 2000 with the remainder of the risk model to be fully deployed by the end of 2001. 'We've already done a great deal with regard to both the reorganization and the deployment of the risk model – but we are not complacent and there is certainly a lot more to do,' says Mr Chown. 'But this restructuring is a great opportunity to simultaneously embed risk management awareness and capability throughout the processes of the group better than before.'

> The objective is to improve risk management capabilities and assist business units in achieving their performance goals.

THE REORGANIZATION

Restructuring on a massive scale, the Post Office is responding to a changing world. Traditional mail faces new competitors such as Federal Express, TNT and UPS. There are also new channels for the exchange of information the potential of which is only now reaching fruition, such as the Internet, intranets and extranets. Finally, the group is looking to enhance its business model by extracting the greatest potential value from its existing assets, for example the provision of banking and governmental services from its extensive network of Post Office counters (the network of physical branches).

All told, the group has done a great deal of work to identify its existing and potential customers, markets and competitors. Recognizing the need for flexibility and focus, the reorganization is intended to 'enable our business units to become more "market facing" better able to respond to new opportunities and threats and create new sources of value,' says Mr Chown.

Traditionally, the Post Office operated through five 'legacy' business units:

- The Royal Mail (the traditional letter distribution activities);
- Parcelforce Worldwide (its parcel services);
- Subscription Services Ltd (customer management services including call centres);
- Post Office Counters (the network of post offices); and
- Post Office Services Group (internal audit, legal, accounting, IT services, etc.).

After the reorganization, there will be 16 business units:

- twelve 'market facing' units (linked closely with customers and target markets) – these include new services such as ViaCode (focusing on products for securing e-business using strong encryption and digital signatures) and Network Banking (providing banking services across the counters);
- two exclusively service delivery operations looking after the mail and retail financial services 'pipelines' (various of the marketing units are vertically integrated operations providing service delivery as well as marketing, e.g. Packages & Express will control the parcels pipeline);
- Post Office Services Group and Post Office Property Holdings (which, as its name suggests, 'owns' and manages the Post Office's property portfolio).

The Post Office is confident this reorganization will enable the business units to more capably identify and act on increasingly complex opportunities as they emerge. For example, is the Internet a threat or an opportunity? At least initially, 'we're finding that the arrival of the Internet is creating even greater volumes of parcels and mail,' says Mr Chown. 'If you're buying goods online, or ordering catalogues, someone has to deliver them.' The future is less certain, however, and will need to be opportunistically monitored by divisions focused on specific business niches targeted to end users. At the same time, the reorganization itself creates new risks. 'Will the business units be able to sort out all the various new boundaries between themselves?' asks Mr Chown. 'Will the batons be passed properly?'

THE RISK MODEL

The Post Office is taking advantage of the broader reorganization to simultaneously launch a series of processes it refers to as its 'business risk management model'. The risk model comprises a handful of familiar EWRM elements such as risk mapping, contingency planning and control risks self-assessment.

> The risk model comprises familiar EWRM elements such as risk mapping, contingency planning and self-assessment.

The key pegs of the risk model include the following:

Risk mapping

Capital outlays and new ventures have always been assessed via traditional techniques such as internal rate of return (IRR) and sensitivity analysis. But as part of the roll-out for 2001, risk mapping (or profiling in Post Office parlance) is required for all key activities.

Mr Chown is confident that risk profiling will enable the Post Office to identify correlations between business units. 'Although we have deployed risk profiling for about three years now, we've never before undertaken anything so systematic in this area,' he explains. Collecting the risk profiles on a Lotus Notes database 'will help us tease out opportunities to reduce costs or absorb risks, given an offsetting risk somewhere else.' In particular, risk profiling will help the Post Office identify strengths and weaknesses in the newly reorganizing business units. There are all sorts of emerging interdependencies, for example a marketing unit using services from a delivery unit. Says Mr Chown, 'we will use the risk profiles to add value to the various inter-business agreements we are setting up. Group risk management will add value in this area by acting as the conduit between the units.'

Mating risk maps to existing business processes

Worth noting is the way the Post Office is improving the effectiveness of risk mapping by mating it to an existing framework already in use by the group. This accelerates acceptance of the risk mapping process, and provides a basis for communication through an established common business language.

But they are also taking the opportunity of incorporating some new 'technology' where it will add real value. For example, they will be feeding risk profiling output back to the business units using a new, very visual risk matrix as well as the 'traditional' risk map after trialling a variant on the traditional high/low risk matrix with a unit whose Finance Director responded by saying: 'This picture says it all to a senior person with minimal time.'

The quality model

The Post Office runs its business in accordance with the European Foundation for Quality Management model (EFQM) which it has now customized into a Post Office Management Model (POMM) to set the way of working going forward. The risk profiling approach follows this model closely, achieving three explicit ends:

Continued ...

- First, 'it says to all line management that risk management is actually very linked to our quality approach. If they didn't see that link, they might suspect we're not clued in to what the Post Office is all about,' explains Mr Chown.

- Second, 'it enables us to score our risks based on the impact to our stakeholders: staff, customers, central government, and so on. Its focus isn't limited to financial risks.'

- Finally, the linkage enables the organization to 'drill down more effectively into areas such as information security or project management,' says Mr Chown.

The common language

Although not an explicit objective, the use of the above familiar framework benefits the development of a common business risk language. The Post Office is a massive organization comprising 190,000 people. 'A common business language is not mentioned as such in the model,' says Mr Chown. 'But we've realized, if we're all speaking different languages, we're going to have difficulty communicating.' POMM is, or soon will be, known to every manager in the business, and a link to this enhances communication. 'What we're doing is overlaying discussions of risk onto an already familiar model,' explains Mr Chown.

'Keep the number of risks to a reasonable level.'

Risk control action plans

The value of a risk profile is diminished if the output is not properly managed and linked to business planning. For this reason, the Post Office business risk management model includes 'Risk Control Action Plans'. These RCAPs become an integral component of the business plan. 'If the risk profiling says "yes, that's something that could hurt us or help us", then we expect to see it addressed,' says Mr Chown. 'So where a key risk action needs to be taken, we link that to business planning, the needed resources are provided, and we de-risk that area.'

As part of the risk management programme, the Post Office Executive Board has set a minimum requirement that each business unit will link its top five risks to business planning. 'If they want to do more, that's their choice,' says Mr Chown. 'But we advise them to keep the number of risks they focus on to a reasonable level so as not to spread resources too thinly. Five may not be enough, but 25 is going to be too many. Ten to twelve would be appropriate.'

There is no direct linkage of compensation to risk management action planning. Senior level pay *is* affected by achievement of targets, 'and to the extent that those targets can be affected by risk, you can say risk is also taken into account in determining their remuneration, at least indirectly,' says Mr Chown. But currently, there is no explicit link. 'That's an area we'll re-evaluate after we've gone through a few cycles – if we need a change to get the behaviours and results we want, we would consider doing it.'

'Invariably, something may go seriously wrong at some point.'

Control risk self-assessment

Internal audit at the Post Office oversees a self-assessment process originally designed to look primarily at financial controls but which now looks at the full range of risks in line with the Turnbull Committee guidance. For example, the company must ensure compliance with European competition law. Should one of the former Royal Mail divisions have been found in breach of these regulations, the fine could have been up to 10 per cent of the entire group's turnover. Self-assessment, in concert with risk-profiling and a specifically targeted control programme ('Competing Fairly'), will help the group address such risks. The group wants to implement an improved set of self-assessment processes by the end of the year 2001 to which end internal audit and risk management are reviewing the current CRSA processes to achieve a focus on the really key risks. They are also seeking to move the audit 'universe' closer towards the organization's overall risk profile.

Business continuity planning

The next peg of the programme is a call for explicit evaluations of potential business catastrophes and action plans delineating what to do when something goes wrong. 'Invariably, even in the best regulated societies, something may go seriously wrong at some point,' says Mr Chown, and so a goal of the risk model is for every business unit to have specific and flexible contingency plans 'rehearsed and ready' for an unexpected event that affects critical processes.

Insurance

This may not be the most interesting subject to many people but the Post Office has a policy of arranging insurance against catastrophe risks which it currently defines as any single event costing it £5 million or more. The risk model initiative includes the development and maintenance of a group-wide insurance risk profile as well as the processes by which operating units will notify group risk management of claims and provide data for developing insurance strategy and maintaining the insurance portfolio.

Contract risk assessment

Finally, the risk model will look closely at the assessment of liability in all commercial contracts. In particular, care needs to be paid to such areas as transfer of liability – when is the Post Office actually responsible for various goods? 'It's not that we haven't been managing this all along,' says Mr Chown. 'But it is identified as an area where we need to improve, so it's included in the model.' The Post Office has just finalized guidelines on liability within purchasing contracts. 'This is not just about the downside but about making a balanced decision having regard to both the risks involved and the competitive advantage we may get through taking on more liability than our competitors are prepared to take. It is about negotiating with a clear understanding of the risks and the opportunities.'

Advice for implementation

Implementing a new risk management model, the Post Office has three recommendations. First, obtain senior management support; second, downplay the image of risk management as 'rocket science'; third, use an appropriately 'light touch'.

■ *Senior management approval: don't leave home without it.* The risk management team at the Post Office is fortunate in that it is implementing its risk model at the same time that its operating units are undergoing restructuring. 'That's been a real plus,' says Mr Chown. 'It's all seen as part of one initiative and, crucially, as a wonderful opportunity.' That said, the importance of top management buy-in cannot be understated – an idea clearly appreciated by the executive board. For this reason, 'there is a senior director from each business unit who has been given accountability for implementing the model,' explains Mr Chown. 'By making senior people specifically accountable, the board believes we'll achieve our mission. Without board approval, we would get almost nowhere – I don't believe we could proceed without it.'

■ *Risk management: it's not rocket science.* It is also vital that the above initiative be accomplished in ways that are relevant to business managers. The great thing about techniques such as risk mapping, says Mr Chown, 'is that it's easy to deploy and so it actually gets deployed. If it were rocket science – if it is presented as rocket science – they would probably just pay lip service to it.' Risk profiling should not be presented as an entirely new way of looking at the world but merely as a more systematic and rational approach to looking at risk as part of 'business as usual'.

Continued ...

- *Control versus empowerment: use a 'light touch'*. It is a dichotomy, but in an age of autonomy, there also needs to be a higher degree of accountability and central direction. 'A common approach is essential,' says Mr Chown, 'but this cannot be allowed to become a bureaucracy, or an industry – we have to realize we're here to assist the business units and to co-ordinate the various activities, not constrain them or fit them with a straitjacket.' Consequently, all of the above is being undertaken 'with an appropriately light touch' and designed to assist the business units in meeting their objectives and targets.

'We're in business to take risks.'

THE POST OFFICE: HERE TO TAKE RISKS

Like any commercial organization, 'we're in business to take risks,' says Mr Chown. But the risks must be systematically and proactively managed. So the intended outcome of the new risk management model is to help business units strike a balance between risk-taking and value creation as they reorganize. 'It's not about putting difficulties in the way of taking risks,' explains Mr Chown. 'It's about establishing the fact that we are here to take risks as we create new sources of value in the marketplace and then providing the tools and techniques to enable line management to better assess the risks around the competitive decisions they're evaluating.'

Business managers 'know their competition and their customers and their opportunities,' says Mr Chown, 'If we can help them to better understand the risks surrounding their decision-making, they'll make better decisions. If they make better decisions, we're a more successful company.' Ultimately, the Post Office may consider still more EWRM strategies such as full risk aggregation. 'We won't be ignoring those ideas,' says Mr Chown, but for now, 'our immediate goals are stretching enough.'

The intent of the new model is to help business units strike a balance between risk-taking and value creation.

5

Uniform processes: assessing risks and developing strategies

A danger foreseen is half avoided.

Thomas Fuller

Those who trust to chance must abide by the results of chance.

Calvin Coolidge

Right from the start, we've been keen to ensure consistency in both processes and output.

Nick Rose, Finance Director, Diageo

We know what business risk is and recognize that a common language is the first step towards implementing a uniform process to examine an organization's risks thoroughly and consistently. We have also established high level goals and objectives, developed a policy statement and put an effective oversight structure in place. Now senior management is ready to get on with the job of identifying, sourcing and measuring business risk, formulating business risk management strategies and designing and implementing capabilities to carry out those strategies. In this chapter, we will define the processes needed, at a high level, to ensure a comprehensive, well controlled, consistent and yet effective approach to business risk assessment and management.

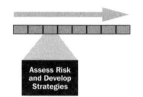

Assess Risk and Develop Strategies

A well managed organization is comprised of business processes and clearly identifiable process owners. The development and adoption of uniform business risk management processes better equips these process owners to identify the exposures, sources of uncertainty and opportunities in their path as they manage the business to create value. While senior management and board members attain greater confidence that their risks are being capably managed and controlled, at the same time, process owners – and designated risk owners – are given power tools to craft superior strategies, tactics and, ultimately, performance. It remains their judgement – they are still empowered – but their will and acumen is exercised within the context of a well defined process. In turn, a common process view of business risk management across an organization facilitates communication and leverages its capabilities.

A PROCESS VIEW OF BUSINESS RISK MANAGEMENT

Risk management cuts across units, divisions and functions – it is an element of all business activities. For this reason, there is an acute need to assist process owners in the identification, quantification and management of business risks. This is not the hijacking of the process, but rather the provision of new assessment and management tools for process owners to integrate with their existing activities. As Nick Chown, Group Risk Manager of The British Post Office which has received market recognition for its excellence in risk management, explains, 'there can be dismay at first, but before long, as understanding sets in, the business managers recognize that, as opposed to more management interference in their work, something genuinely good and relevant is underway.'

Process owners need a framework, and as process owners, they will appreciate a process-oriented approach. If a company does not have a deliberate process for managing risk, just like they have one for paying bills, then risk management won't happen. Although the specific process itself may vary somewhat from company to company, the illustration in Figure 5.1 captures the fundamental elements of an effective risk management process.

Fig. 5.1 Arthur Andersen business risk management process

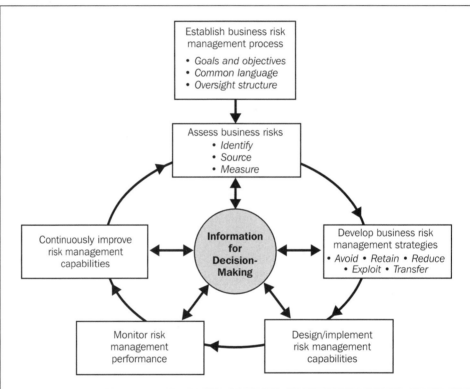

> **The BRMP is systematic process for building and improving risk management capabilities.**

Effectively implemented, the business risk management process (BRMP) in Figure 5.1 achieves two ends. First, it equips designated process and risk-owners with a useful framework for defining the essential tasks of risk management. Second, it is a systematic process for building and improving comprehensive risk management capabilities which, as they evolve enterprise-wide, provide the launchpad for a true EWRM environment. Effective business risk management is neither accidental nor incidental.

The first task of the above process – *Establish business risk management process* – is essential to all that follows. Its key elements, the development of a common language and the establishment of goals, objectives and oversight structure, were discussed in Chapters 3 and 4. This task is the proper starting point so that a working committee of senior managers, with overall goals and objectives in mind, can oversee the deployment of the remaining BRMP tasks. We address the next two tasks – *Assess business risks* and *Develop business risk management strategies* – in this chapter. (The remaining BRMP tasks are discussed in Chapter 6 where we show how risk management capabilities are designed and implemented.)

ASSESS BUSINESS RISKS

Chapter 3's common language provided examples of environment, process and information for decision-making risks that businesses face as they create value. Managers assess these risks through the following activities:

- *Identify* the risks that must be managed to assure success of the firm's business model. For example, what are the risks inherent in the firm's normal operations and in the pursuit of new growth and profit opportunities? What are the risks that can change the fundamentals driving the business model or divert senior management's agenda to focus on reactive damage control? Risk maps, described below, are useful when identifying and prioritizing risks.

- *Source* why, how and where the risks originate, either outside the organization or within its processes or activities. The more rigorous this assessment, the better positioned the firm will be to manage the risks. Risk driver analyses for key risks, process mapping for key processes and environment assessment techniques (such as industry analysis, market research and competitor analysis) increase the effectiveness of the sourcing process.

- *Measure* the severity, likelihood and financial impact of risk. There are many methodologies from which to choose depending on the degree of precision necessary. We explore some of these methodologies in this chapter.

When assessing risk, executive management primarily focuses on significant changes in competitors, markets, customers, regulations and other environment risk factors. Process/activity owners, on the other hand, focus their risk assessment on the processes and activities that they manage. If the assessments by process/activity owners identify significant enterprise-wide issues, the resulting information can be communicated upward to senior management.

Risk assessment addresses critical questions that must be answered for purposes of formulating the appropriate risk strategy (see Figure 5.2).

Fig. 5.2 Assess business risks

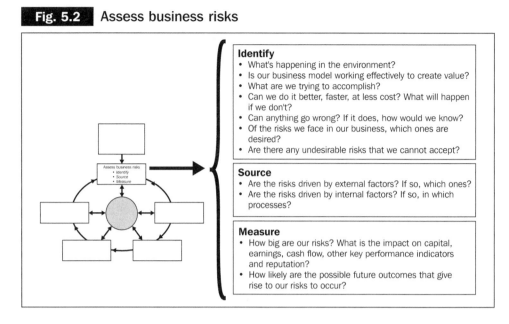

Identify
- What's happening in the environment?
- Is our business model working effectively to create value?
- What are we trying to accomplish?
- Can we do it better, faster, at less cost? What will happen if we don't?
- Can anything go wrong? If it does, how would we know?
- Of the risks we face in our business, which ones are desired?
- Are there any undesirable risks that we cannot accept?

Source
- Are the risks driven by external factors? If so, which ones?
- Are the risks driven by internal factors? If so, in which processes?

Measure
- How big are our risks? What is the impact on capital, earnings, cash flow, other key performance indicators and reputation?
- How likely are the possible future outcomes that give rise to our risks to occur?

When you *identify* risk, greater structure is introduced via the common language and a uniform process. The uniform process ensures that (a) risks are defined within the context of the company's critical processes, (b) key risks are not overlooked, and (c) risks are organized using the common language. As we illustrate later in Chapter 6, uniformity across the enterprise is powerful as it enables creative applications of technology. These applications aggregate data in meaningful ways and facilitate analysis leading to better information for decision-making and knowledge sharing.

We will now focus on risk-mapping, which is a uniform process which deploys approaches ranging from subjectively qualitative ('back of the envelope') to rigorously quantitative.

> **Risk mapping is by far the most useful and widely deployed tool for risk identification and prioritization.**

RISK MAPPING – A FUNDAMENTAL TOOL

Most unit managers and process owners – when asked – will invariably say they already know their risks. But those who have 'humoured' senior management by participating in exercises such as risk mapping far more often than not emerge as converts to this dynamic interactive process. Initially, participants are sceptical, according to Mike McLamb, CFO of MarineMax. But at the end of his company's risk-focused sessions, attendees give what Mr McLamb refers to as 'gut-wrenching talks' about the learning they have experienced and the new strategies they intend to implement.

Risk mapping is by far the most useful and widely deployed tool for risk identification and prioritization. Whether referred to as risk mapping (Holderbank, Enron and Hydro-Quebec), risk profiling (The Royal Mail) or risk footprinting (Diageo/Guinness) (see the corresponding cases), the basic technique is simple to understand. Process owners and business managers assess their risks using pre-determined criteria. Their assessments can be built from a set of risks identified as critical by senior management. Alternatively, they can be based on frameworks the participants are familiar with. For example, the British Post Office's risk profiling discussed in Case 3 is based on the European Foundation for Quality Management model already in use by the business managers.

In drilling down to the process level, companies also rely on a wider risk universe, such as the Business Risk Model™, to identify risks germane to the business. Once well-defined risks are identified, they are plotted on a grid or map in terms of their severity to the business and likelihood of occurrence:

- *Severity*. Managers rate the significance of the risk to the business using criteria they understand and accept. For example, what is the potential financial impact of each defined risk? What is the impact on achieving business objectives and the successful execution of key strategies? What is the potential cost to the business in terms of capital, earnings and cash flow? Could the occurrence of the potential future event damage reputation or brand equity, diminish investment in research and development or limit the anticipated economic benefits of planned acquisitions or process improvements?

  Whatever the criteria for rating severity, time horizon is also a factor that must be clearly defined. The short-term cost of a capacity shortage, for instance, can be quite severe to a manufacturing company. However, capacity is less of an issue over the long term because management has more flexibility to make adjustments. Therefore, separate risk maps are appropriate for risk events over the short, medium or long term.

- *Likelihood*. Using the same time horizon as that for determining severity, managers assess the likelihood that the identified risk event will occur. When estimating likelihood, be sure to consider the quality of the assessment itself. Just how likely is the risky event? If statistical methods are not used, then how do you know that the selected probabilities or likelihoods are reasonable? While we are not advocating statistics at this early stage in the process, we are suggesting that the most knowledgeable people should prioritize the risks. At this stage, we are looking for an order of magnitude estimate (as opposed to a precise number). There are techniques available to apply the judgement of an expert jury to accomplish this assessment.

Risk mapping can be applied in many ways. Its versatility is self-evident as risk maps may be developed by unit, by process, by key performance indicator (KPI) or even by major risk category (in which different types of hypothetical risk events are rated). Many organizations deploy risk mapping in a facilitated workshop or seminar environment involving multidisciplinary teams. Here, managers interact, debate and share information until a facilitator brings the process to a consensus.

Of course, on some matters, consensus is not possible, but that result is also meaningful because it indicates there are concerns as to the magnitude of the exposure and/or the extent of the uncertainty.

Some companies use low-tech nominal group techniques using whiteboards and Post-it notes; others use more sophisticated processes such as Web-enabled self-assessments, risk surveys and industry- or process-specific analytical techniques, with support from specialists in risk assessment and specific risk areas. Anonymous interactive voting software used in conjunction with facilitated meetings or web-polling is another proven method in cataloguing, sorting and prioritizing risks. When using facilitation techniques, Roland Köhler of Holderbank advises that, to be accepted by the participating executives, the facilitator must know the company's industry well. Such discussions require advance preparation and a structured approach to maximize chances of success.

The involvement of knowledgeable people in an open interactive environment is vital.

Risk-mapping – particularly when executed utilizing a common risk language – provides numerous benefits to process-owners, managers and the organization at large. For example, it:

- focuses attention on the most vital risks to source and measure with more rigorous techniques;
- serves as a focal point for developing risk strategies;
- aligns the achievement of business objectives with the management of risks;
- reduces the chances that important risks or opportunities are overlooked;
- highlights opportunities for knowledge sharing of best practices for managing risks that are common across business units and processes;
- provides a template for aggregation of risks across the enterprise.

The most effective risk mapping exercises begin with the firm's strategic objectives firmly in mind. For example, the Guinness risk map (illustrated in Case 4) was constructed using the following criteria: the company would 'grow, maximize value creation, motivate and retain exceptional people, as well as develop distinctive brands.' These underlying strategies are all a part of parent Diageo's objectives for Guinness: triple EPS over a five-year period.

However executed, there is often a great deal of subjectivity in the process, as is to be expected with any top-down approach. Absolute precision is not as vital as the exercise itself. As Nick Rose, Finance Director of Diageo explains, 'the act of developing the risk map leads business managers to recognize the significance of what they are doing.' Agrees Rick Buy, Chief Risk Officer of Enron, who explains, 'We succeed when people are in a room, sitting down, thinking and arguing not about their hurdle rate but about the things that could make [something] a grand slam or a flop.' The involvement of knowledgeable people in an open interactive environment is vital.

Risk mapping: a cascading process

Risk mapping is a powerful tool. One of its most useful features is that it can be applied at any level of any business. As Chris Wasden, Managing Director of Azurix explains, 'You can map the risks of your company overall, you can map those of a business unit, or of a process. You can drill down as far as you need to – you could even do risk maps for individual members of your team or company. The concept is durable and useful.'

Under EWRM, risk-taking activities of individual business units and processes are aligned with enterprise-wide goals. In that regard, an effective risk mapping process uses a cascading approach. The flow begins with the objectives of senior management. Next comes business unit maps which are aligned with unit management's priorities that have been developed in conjunction with the business plan presented to and approved by senior management and the board. From there, the individual process/activity owners that comprise each business unit develop their own maps, again driven by the priorities identified by the respective unit maps. All of this activity is executed in an iterative and ongoing process of refinement as conditions change.

An excellent example of 'cascading' risk maps is provided by Marconi where the BRMP is managed through a hierarchy of Business Audit Committees (BACs) (see Figure 5.3). Every month, Marconi's BACs at the business group and unit levels update their respective risk maps and risk management action plans based upon reports and input received from business management and internal and external auditors. Every quarter, the Marconi CEO and CFO review the risk maps and risk management action plans for the overall group based upon input from the various business groups. The Marconi approach also provides guidance to the business groups in the form of a 'Reportable Risk Threshold' that is linked to potential ongoing earnings impact.

While other companies and other functions may scale back the timing of their iterations (as an alternative to a monthly process), the concept is clear: at Marconi, risk maps are built from the top down in an environment of continual re-evaluation and refinement.

Fig. 5.3 Cascading risk mapping approach at Marconi

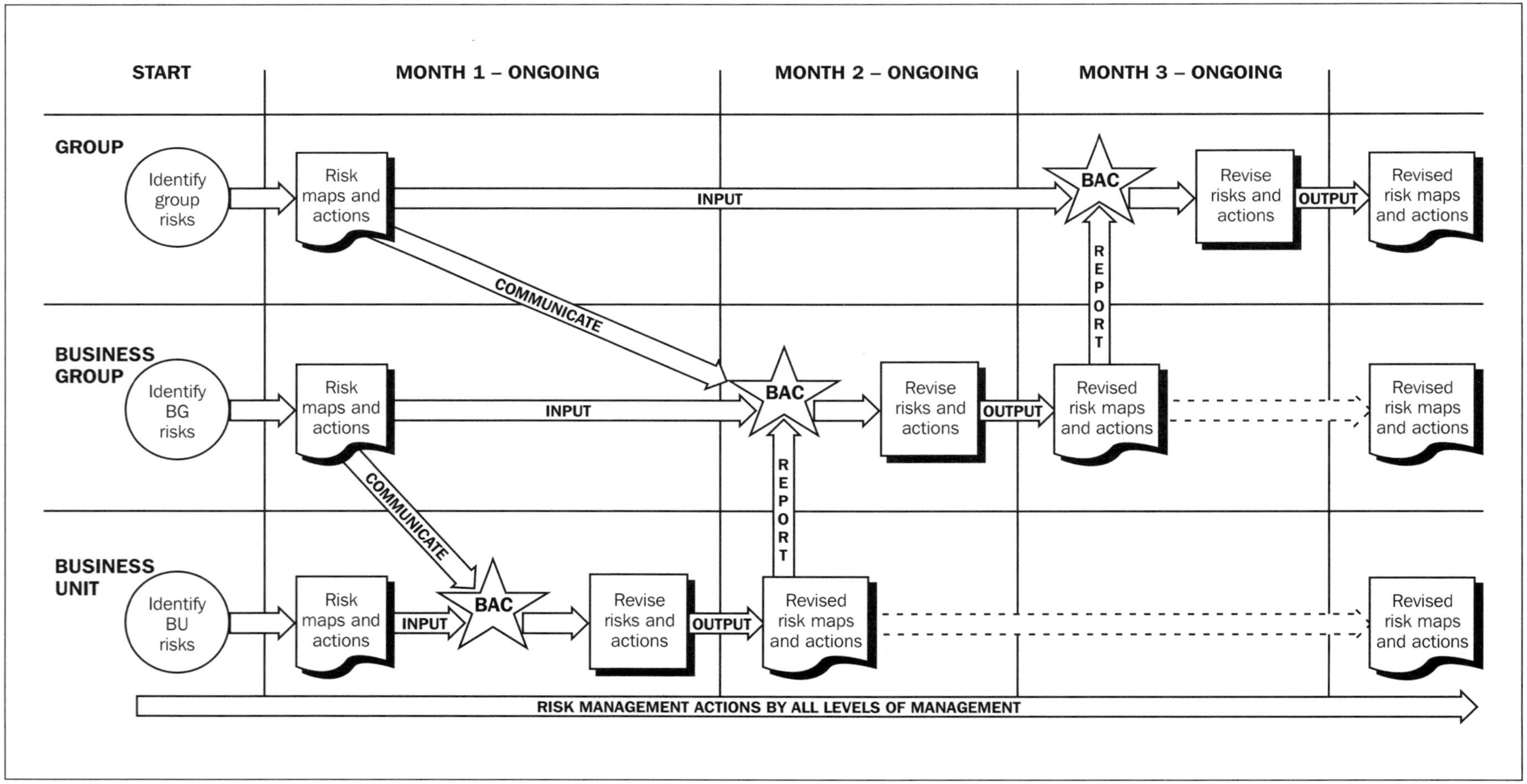

RIGOROUS ASSESSMENT: WHEN RISKS ARE VITAL

While risk mapping is relatively subjective, it paves the way for prioritizing the key risks. For example, the Holderbank case shows how the risk maps result in a more focused analysis by targeting the risks that may require the most attention from a risk management standpoint. The question is, are we sure we understand what we need to know about our risks? At this point, we must consider whether to use appropriately robust techniques to source the high priority risks to their root causes and key drivers and measure their potential impact on the business.

High priority risks should be sourced and measured using appropriately robust techniques.

When a company cannot afford to be wrong, the assessment must be more methodical. New York University professor and author of *Risk Taking: A Managerial Perspective*, Zur Shapira, agrees that risk mapping provides value. Says Dr Shapira, 'Some degree of focus is better than none – be as subjective as you have to be.' But for mission critical risks, he advises, 'you had better make sure the assessment is supported by as much hard, quantitative facts as you can find. Bring your data.' Without facts, opinions prevail; when opinions rule, the reliability of the process is reduced.

When *sourcing* risk, the company focuses on understanding the underlying causes, or 'drivers', of the risk. Risk sourcing requires an effective analysis of the external environment and the firm's internal processes and conditions. While risk identification focuses on *what* risk incidents can happen, risk sourcing is the evaluation of *why*, *how* and *where* they can happen. For example, if a manufacturing firm is concerned about the amount of time required to bring a completed product to market, then the firm's management would need to thoroughly understand a number of business processes. In particular, they need to look for unnecessary or redundant activities that clearly do not add value to the process in achieving the 'speed to market' objective. This exercise could even entail looking upstream to the firm's suppliers' processes as well as downstream to its distribution channels.

Risk sourcing has an important additional benefit. It helps risk managers understand the type and availability of relevant risk data that will influence (a) how the risk can be measured, and (b) the selection of strategies for managing the risk. Approached on a systematic basis through analyzing risk drivers (as illustated in the Holderbank case) or mapping and analyzing business processes, risk sourcing can identify risky situations that managers may decide to fix immediately with appropriate risk controls.

Root causes or sources of risk stem from a variety of factors, including:

- changes in one or more external environment factors;
- anomalies or deficiencies in one or more business processes or systems;
- poor management of interfaces between processes and activities;

- inadvertent or deliberate errors;

- breakdowns in the flow of information supporting a process (the 'flow of information' is the sequence of activities that capture and record business data, process that data into information and ultimately report information to management and outsiders);

- facilities or equipment that malfunction or are not suited for the job they are put in place to accomplish; and

- internally driven events that result from management actions or inactions, i.e. poor communications, lack of leadership, inappropriate performance expectations and incentives, etc.

Environment risks are sourced using such analytical techniques as industry analysis, competitor analysis, market analysis, country analysis, benchmarking and the analysis of other relevant external data. For process risks, process and risk owners should understand the processes first (through process mapping), then source the root causes. For all risks – environment, process and information for decision-making – risk drivers analyses are useful for sourcing.

Once risks are identified and sourced, it is time to *measure* them. Measurement methodologies enable managers to make more informed decisions about the severity of their risks and the formulation of strategies for managing those risks. Through risk measurement methodologies, managers can:

- aggregate measures of an individual risk or a group of related risks across the firm to present an enterprise-wide view;

- link the risks taken with capital, earnings and cash flow at risk and the firm's objectives and strategies, so that risk/reward trade-offs can be evaluated and capital allocated to absorb potential losses;

- set risk parameters and limits and ensure that risks taken remain within established boundaries;

- evaluate the effectiveness of alternative risk management strategies;

- better analyze performance across different risks, investments, products and units;

- plan for contingencies given possible uncertain outcomes; and

- support disclosures required by the capital markets and regulators in different countries.

As we explore risk measurement, we wish to make one point clear: *there is no need to measure all risks to the same degree or utilizing similarly rigorous techniques.* We believe there is value to roughly approximating some risks and then focusing on the cost of managing those risks. Why spend significant time and money trying to precisely quantify a risk, when the better answer may be to just get on with the task of 'fixing it'?

A Canadian process manufacturer, for example, identified two stair steps that were not sufficiently visible at night, creating a potential hazard in spite of ample outdoor lighting and guardrails. The risk was that someone would not see the stairs, trip over them and fall 40 feet to their death or serious injury. Instead of rationalizing the issue and wasting time calculating the odds, the firm focused on finding a solution. It looked at re-engineering the stairway, reducing the slope of the gradient, repositioning the lighting and other possibilities. Ultimately, the cost to mitigate an extreme safety risk proved negligible: the stair steps were painted with a $2.49 can of fluorescent paint!

Ideally, the focus of a measurement methodology should be on the key drivers which apply to individual risks or aggregated groups of related risks. But this isn't always feasible. In practice, for example, one firm measures price risk while another firm measures a driver of price risk (say, load demand), while still another firm measures a driver of load demand (say, weather). The point is that risk managers and process/activity owners must agree on the type and nature of the risks and the drivers to be measured in order to determine the appropriate measurement objectives and methodology.

As Rick Buy, EVP and CRO of Enron points out, 'One of the most important issues in risk management is narrowing the number of variables down to the vital few that really make the difference.' We agree. The challenge is figuring out what to measure at the appropriate level of decomposition.

Some of the measurement methodologies available include the following:

- *Risk indicator analysis.* This technique utilizes decision aids to help users identify and evaluate qualitative risk indicators. Decision aids typically provide a summary of questions that, depending on the response, suggest possible symptoms, warning signs or so-called 'red flags' that indicate there may be an issue warranting further analysis, e.g. a new risk to source and measure. The risk indicators may also be tied to changes in key variables available from external sources to provide an early warning that risks may be increasing or decreasing.

    The questions may be weighted based on experience so that users can understand their relative impact on the risk assessment. Managers can also use risk diagnostics to obtain additional data that will either validate or refute the ratings on a preliminary risk map developed using facilitated sessions or web-enabled polls.

- *Exposure measurement.* An important determinant of risk exposures are often associated with the gross or notional amounts at risk. However, a more sophisticated view incorporates the contingent nature of all exposures, that is it incorporates their real option values: what is the cost or benefit of the exposure after all likely transfer mitigation and exploitation cards have been played? Traditional examples of exposures include gross accounts receivable, the notional amount of currency exposure (e.g. based on specific foreign

'One of the most important issues in risk management is narrowing the number of variables down to the vital few that really make the difference.'

currency contractual commitments and operating exposures measured in terms of annual expected revenues and net profits), total fixed and floating rate debt, the gross value of commodity holdings and total physical assets (inventories, plant and equipment).

Exposures in the new economy, however, extend beyond financial and physical assets. They include all of the enterprise's sources of value, e.g. the revenue streams and profits arising from its specific brands, channels and customer relationships, the resiliency and skill level of its work force and the quality, cost and time performance of its processes relative to competitors.

Position reports are used to capture exposures and differentiate them using relevant criteria such as nature, location, duration (short- versus long-term) and type (contractual versus operational). Incorporating thinking about the contingent nature of exposures recognizes potential costs or benefits resulting from specific circumstances, e.g. realization of valid insurance claims from independent, creditworthy underwriters.

- *Risk measurement.* Uncertainty is another determinant of risk. Whereas exposure is a gross measure (total accounts receivable or revenue streams), uncertainty is a measure of the performance variability associated with returns from that gross measure. In technical terms, this is often described by looking at the shape of the distribution of possible outcomes relating to a key variable, e.g. foreign exchange, accounts receivable collections, etc. Under normal circumstances, one associates the risk with the variance (or volatility) of the variable. For example, a foreign exchange exposure might be £10 million, while the risk would be defined as the volatility of exchange rates applied to the gross value of the exposure. Therefore, risk reports apply relevant factors to identified exposures to obtain a measure of risk. Such factors include things like volatility, default probability, occurrence probability, etc.

  The objective is to take the assessment beyond risk mapping by sizing the magnitude of the potential financial impact (the 'earnings hit' for example). To illustrate for physical assets, the absolute size of loss is often measured in terms of 'maximum possible loss', 'maximum foreseeable loss' and 'normal loss'. Occurrence probabilities are often estimated for different possible outcomes – a 100 per cent loss of plant and facilities from a hurricane, a 50 per cent loss, a 10 per cent loss, etc.

- *Risk rating or scoring.* A systematic and transparent approach for 'rating' or 'scoring' the level of risk, this method uses analytical templates and systems based on the application of predefined criteria. It increases speed and consistency in terms of the facts gathered to support a decision and the criteria applied when evaluating those facts. Risk scoring has many possible applications. It is often used to consistently rate customer credit risk and support and monitor credit decisions, both by multiple executives making similar decisions across the enterprise and by individual executives evaluating multiple customers.

■ *Performance measurement.* Risk exists because of the exposure to uncertainty that lies in the future. Risk measures should, therefore, be forward looking. However, when this isn't possible, performance measures, e.g. measures of cost, quality and time performance, are often useful as surrogates.

To illustrate, it may be impossible to directly measure customer satisfaction risk, the risk that the firm's processes do not consistently meet or exceed customer expectations because of a lack of customer focus. The consequences of dissatisfied customers can be severe – permanent loss of repeat business and loss of market share – but direct measurement of this risk, considering such factors as the customer's state of mind and the likelihood of new replacement business in future periods, may be extremely difficult. However, as a surrogate, the firm can integrate internal operating statistics, customer feedback and other external information. By doing so, it can evaluate customer satisfaction measures and gain insights as to how well it is managing its customers.

■ *Risk models and analytics.* Rigorous assessment is supported by models and analytics that come in a myriad of varieties and degrees of complexity. There are models of individual risks, of groups of related risks and of a firm's aggregate risk profile. There are even models of the firm's business environment, including – in addition to its risks – other environment factors. Such factors include competitive and industry dynamics, political trends, customer demand, suppliers, technological innovation and broader market conditions (such as the market for capital, the market dynamics affecting the firm's raw material inputs or the interplay between demand and load on price sensitive energy portfolios). Other kinds of quantification include statistical analysis, distributional estimation, creating time series for specific risks, establishing correlation matrices, forward curve development, regression analysis and other analytic techniques.

Models are approximations of what is happening in the real world. It is therefore essential to understand the assumptions built into a model and how they affect its output. If a model is not well-suited for extreme events, like market crashes (for instance, the 1998 Asian currency crisis), risk managers must compensate for this shortcoming with other kinds of analyses, such as scenario analysis, sometimes referred to as 'what-if' simulation. These analytical tools take a forward-looking approach to simulating the effects of changes in market and other environment factors selected by management. The purpose is to quantify the implications of changes in key variables to the firm's business under different scenarios.

Building a model (or models) is just a first step. The real work is in using them to support risk management decisions through skilful and thoughtful implementation, including the evaluation of the susceptibility of a model's parameters to estimation error and the choice of time horizon and confidence level. That is why models must be appraised in terms of their predictability, their fit, how appropriate they are given the circumstances and the decisions that are based on their output, and, of course, the reasonableness of the assumptions used in their construction. As Ghislain Giroux-Dufort, Chief Risk Officer of Hydro-Quebec International explains, 'I'm very quantitative, and I believe in analytical tools. But you cannot run a business based solely on machines and automated systems. In the end, the human mind has to synthesize the issues and make a decision. We advocate having all the tools you need, but never abdicating the human mind.'

In general, the rigour and sophistication of the measurement methodology needed is driven by (a) the complexity of the environment (for instance the number of risks and the extent of interrelationships between risks), (b) the extent of volatility, and (c) the level of capability desired by management (such as the extent of aggregation and linkage to performance enterprise-wide). Of course, implementation costs and the availability of relevant data (with some level of implementation possible even with sparse or 'noisy' data) are also considerations. All these factors are illustrated in Figure 5.4.

Fig. 5.4 Relative sophistication of risk measurement methodologies employed and the factors impacting upon their selection in practice

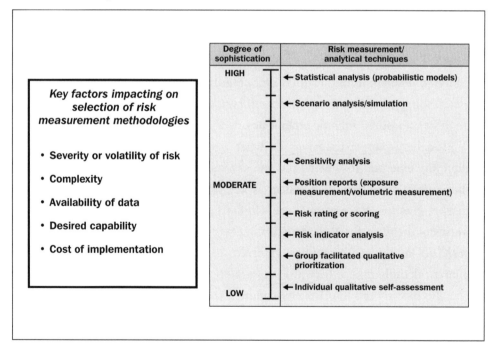

For example, large, complex portfolios of highly volatile commodities (or other financial assets) that substantially impact on earnings may require more sophisticated techniques including both statistical models and scenario analysis. Simulation-based models, for instance, can be useful for capturing the interaction of rate, price or other factors when dealing with complex portfolio or risk positions. Sensitivity analysis, or so-called stress tests, measure the potential impact of extreme market movements on the value of the portfolio.

DEVELOP BUSINESS RISK MANAGEMENT STRATEGIES

Senior management decides the goals of the enterprise. Business unit managers translate these objectives into unit strategies. Finally, process owners design and implement the processes to execute those strategies. The risk mapping process, as refined by the application of rigorous sourcing and measurement methodologies, highlights the risks inherent in the firm's *business* strategies and processes. It is now time to develop specific *risk*-related strategies. These specific strategies are then defined through specific policies that amend and update the overall policies developed, as described in Chapter 4.

The basic strategies

Though tactical choices are nearly endless, fundamentally, there are only a handful of broad risk management strategies. As noted in Figure 5.5, companies can avoid, retain, reduce, transfer and exploit their risks.

While the various risk management options presented in Figure 5.5 are, for the most part, self-explanatory, a few clarifying comments are appropriate:

- The firm first decides whether to accept or reject a risk based on an assessment of whether it is desirable or undesirable. A desirable risk is one that is inherent in the firm's business model and normal future operations. If the risk is undesirable, e.g. it is off-strategy, offers unattractive rewards relative to the risk undertaken or the firm doesn't have the capability to manage it, then the risk is rejected and the *avoid* options are appropriate. Risk avoidance is usually directed at exposures. Some options discontinue existing exposures (divest, prohibit, stop and eliminate), while other options steer clear of them altogether (prohibit, target and screen).

- If the firm accepts a risk, it has several options available. First, it can *retain* the risk at its present level, which raises the question as to how to fund losses, should any occur. Second, it can *reduce* the severity of the risk and/or its likelihood of occurrence. Risk control processes reduce the likelihood of occurrence. Geographic dispersion of assets reduces the impact of the occurrence of a single risk event on the company, i.e. the gross exposure is unchanged, but the risk is less on the whole. Third, the firm can *exploit* the risk by increasing the company's exposure to it. Finally, it can *transfer* the risk so long as a financially capable, independent counterparty is involved under a legally enforceable contract.

Fig. 5.5 Basic risk management strategies

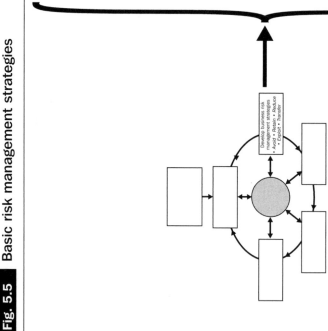

AVOID
- **DIVEST** by exiting a market or geographic area, or by selling, liquidating or spinning-off a product group or business
- **PROHIBIT** unacceptably high risk activities, transactions, financial losses and asset exposures through appropriate limit structures and corporate standards
- **STOP** specific activities by redefining objectives, refocusing strategies or redirecting resources
- **TARGET** business development and market expansion to avoid pursuit of 'off-strategy' opportunities
- **SCREEN** alternative capital projects and investments to avoid low-return, off-strategy and unacceptably high-risk projects
- **ELIMINATE** at the source by designing and implementing internal preventive processes

RETAIN
- **ACCEPT** risk at its present level taking no further action
- **REPRICE** products/services by including an explicit premium in the pricing, market conditions permitting, to compensate for risk undertaken
- **SELF-INSURE** risk through:
  — internal charges to P&L (pay as you go)
  — borrowed funds (from external sources should a risk event occur)
  — reserving losses (under accepted accounting principles)
  — using a pure captive insurance company
  — participation in a group or an industry captive
- **OFFSET** risk against others within a well defined pool
- **PLAN** for well defined contingencies by documenting a responsive plan and empowering people to make decisions and periodically test and, if necessary, execute the plan

REDUCE
- **DISPERSE** financial, physical or information assets geographically to reduce risk of unacceptable catastrophic losses
- **CONTROL** risk through internal processes or actions that reduce the likelihood of undesirable events occurring to an acceptable level (as defined by management's risk threshold)

TRANSFER
- **INSURE** through cost-effective contract with independent, financially capable, party under a well defined risk strategy
- **REINSURE** to reduce portfolio exposure through contracts with other insurers, when such arrangements are available
- **HEDGE** risk by entering into the capital markets, making feasible changes in operations or executing new borrowings
- **SECURITIZE** risk by accessing the capital markets and structuring deals with potential investors through efficient pricing mechanisms
- **SHARE** risk/rewards of investing in new markets and products by entering into alliances or joint ventures
- **OUTSOURCE** non-core processes (a viable risk transfer option only when risk is contractually transferred)
- **INDEMNIFY** risk by entering into contractual risk-sharing arrangements with independent financially capable parties

EXPLOIT
- **ALLOCATE** capital internally within the firm using robust methods to finance the risks taken and generate desired returns
- **DIVERSIFY** financial, physical, customer, employee/supplier and organizational asset holdings used by firm's business model
- **EXPAND** business portfolio by investing in new industries, geographic areas and/or customer groups
- **CREATE** new value-adding products, services and channels
- **REDESIGN** the firm's business model, i.e. its unique combination of assets and technologies for creating value
- **REORGANIZE** processes through restructuring, vertical integration, outsourcing, re-engineering and relocation
- **PRICE** to influence customer choice toward products that suit the firm's risk profile
- **ARBITRAGE** price discrepancies by purchasing securities or other assets in one market for immediate resale in another
- **RENEGOTIATE** existing contractual agreements to reshape risk profile, i.e. transfer, reduce or take risk differently
- **INFLUENCE** regulators, public opinion and standards setters through focused lobbying, political activism, public relations, etc.

Develop business risk management strategies • Avoid • Retain • Reduce • Exploit • Transfer

■ As *transfer* options, both insurance and hedging provide a form of contingent capital. In fact, more risks are becoming commercially insured. While premiums and fees do reduce earnings, the risk transfer that insurance and hedging contracts make possible enables the firm to operate with a lower level of economic capital than it would otherwise need to cover its exposures. Of course, managers should evaluate pricing of these contracts in the context of the actuarial value of the cover or fair value of the derivative.

When evaluating insurable risks, some companies measure and monitor the total cost of risk, with the objective of reducing that cost over time. These costs ordinarily include (a) the cost of insurance premiums, (b) the actual and estimated costs of processing and settling claims (for retained losses) and (c) estimated fees, commissions and administrative costs. If the costs of internal risk control activities are also included, the resulting cost of risk is a powerful measure of success for purposes of managing insurable risk; however, this is not usually done due to the difficulty in reliably estimating the costs of internal processes. Those firms that quantify the cost of risk often use it to benchmark their performance with other companies.

■ As a *transfer strategy*, securitization warrants further discussion. Securitization is often targeted to operational risks, such as with weather-related derivatives (options contracts, for instance), or preferred stock with payouts indexed to the incidence of some operational risk. The securitization process is complex. It involves a sponsor, e.g. a corporation or an insurer, which works with an investment banker, attorneys and third-party experts and advisors. Once the feasibility of the transaction is determined, rating agencies get involved and, of course, potential investors complete the deal. Like insurance, the objective is often to protect shareholder value by transferring the exposure of unwanted risk to a third party.

However, whereas traditional insurance is driven by market conditions, involves relationships with brokers, relies on judgment and underwriting expertise and is often tolerant of poor exposure data, securitization is quite different. In particular, investors buying operational risk-linked securities cannot directly observe the internal affairs of the company and do not have an ongoing relationship with the firm. Hence, both the nature of risks which can be transferred, as well as the data concerning those risks, will tend to be different from that which is possible with insurance. The advantage, however, may be a net lower cost of transferring the risk, depending on the type of risk and the degree of maturity in the market. Securitizations are also fully collateralized, which may be appealing to corporates searching for an alternative to large insurers with credit ratings lower than their own.

According to Paul VanderMarck, SVP of Risk Management Solutions (RMS), 'in a securitization, there is much more direct correlation between the risk analysis and the pricing of the transaction. Participants in a transaction also need assurance that uncertainty and basis risk is explicitly evaluated and that data quality is beyond question.' RMS has provided risk analysis for a number of catastrophe securitizations, including the first-ever securitization of weather risk by Koch Industries in November 1999. Quality of data is especially vital to the success of these transactions. According to Mr VanderMarck, 'the securitization process has little tolerance for exposure data that is incomplete, out-of-date, unreliable or lacking in sufficient detail.' Especially with operational risks, the data relating to such securities must be transparent, readily available and unambiguous in the sense that it can never be the case that the company and the outside investor have disagreements over the value of the underlying data.

As a cutting-edge tool, securitization isn't for everybody. This, of course, may change with the passage of time. Also, the total cost is not always less compared to commercial insurance, resulting in some companies aborting the process. Investors expect to be compensated for the risks they assume; therefore, they want a thorough analysis of the risk embedded in the transaction and assurances that the returns they will receive are closely tied to the calculated level of risk. To gain those assurances, the risk assessment (using sophisticated models) must make the risk sufficiently transparent so that the sensitivity to changes in key underlying variables on the security can be fairly evaluated. Therefore, Mr VanderMarck says, 'the process places the burden of risk quantification on the party seeking coverage from the capital markets rather than on the risk assessment knowledge and tools of insurers and reinsurers.'

- As a *reduce* option, risk control processes consist of pervasive management controls and specific risk controls. Management controls set direction, define boundaries and limits, organize activities, select and develop quality people, assign accountability and measure performance. Specific risk controls are focused on (a) specific business risks and (b) information and information processes. Risk control processes also include monitoring activities that provide reasonable assurance that the control processes in place are performing as intended. For a further discussion of these different types of risk controls, see Appendix 3.

- The four options – *avoid*, *retain*, *reduce* and *transfer* – address actions that are often applied to individual risks. These options are also applied to a group of related risks sharing fundamental characteristics, e.g. common drivers, positive or negative correlations, etc. For instance, if several risks are correlated with oil price exposure, the action of reducing these pooled risks means a reduction in the firm's net exposure to oil prices. All told, pooling of risks assists managers in understanding the interrelationships, or lack thereof, between individual risks for the purpose of selecting the appropriate measurement methodologies and management solutions.

■ Risk taking is fundamental to decision-making. The fifth option, *exploit*, focuses on management actions to take risks inherent in the firm's choices to enter new markets, introduce new products, merge with or acquire another firm or exploit other market opportunities, all of which result in reshaping or reconfiguring the firm's risk profile. Managers can also exploit existing risks by increasing the company's exposure to them. As Thomas Stewart points out, 'The point of risk management isn't to eliminate [risk]; that would eliminate reward. The point is to manage it – that is, to choose where to place bets, where to hedge bets and where to avoid betting altogether.'[2] Risk exploitation is the result of a proactive and conscious decision to take on new risks or increase existing risks, resulting in a different risk profile that is better suited to the firm's appetite for risk.

> **When taking on or increasing their risks, firms must understand their core competencies very well.**

When taking on or increasing their risks, firms must understand their core competencies very well. Each firm has areas where it excels relative to its competitors (for instance, a substantially lower average cost of managing a particular risk or executing a core process compared to that of competitors). The most successful firms exploit these advantages to maximum effect in the pursuit of superior returns. In leveraging these advantages, executives seek those opportunities and increase those risks that the firm is best suited to manage, whether that is because the risk matches the rest of the company's risk profile, is inherent in its business strategy or is effectively managed by its core competencies. Conversely, strongly focused managers *avoid* exposure to those areas which are not consistent with the firm's competencies or which management considers 'off-strategy'.

A risk profile can mean many things. It can apply to an individual risk, to a group of related risks, to one or more business units, to a geographic area or to a product group. To 'shape' a risk profile, managers must first understand the most important drivers that affect the risks included in the pool and whether those drivers are positively or negatively correlated (or not correlated at all). Obviously, the broader the risk pool – i.e. the more risks it includes – the more complex and difficult this task. Based on this understanding, managers then develop methodologies for performing scenario analysis to evaluate the effects of alternative strategies on the aggregate risk profile. Enron's use of RAROC is an example.

There are myriad ways to 'shape' a risk profile. For a simple example, the purchase of insurance to pass downside risks on to an external party at an acceptable cost is a *transfer* strategy that shapes the firm's risk profile differently. The gross exposure is unchanged, but the net exposure has been reduced because the firm doesn't incur the full cost of a loss event, should such an outcome occur.

---

2. Thomas A. Stewart (2000) 'Managing risk in the 21st century', *Fortune*, 7 February, pp. 202–6.

133

Examples of *exploit* strategies that shape a risk profile include:

- allocate resources to the best prospects for higher returns with acceptable risk or comparable returns at less risk;

- exploit diversification opportunities to reduce volatility;

- expand into new markets to fuel new revenue streams while balancing aggregate currency exposure;

- offer promising new products and services to fuel top-line growth and simultaneously discontinue unprofitable products and services from the firm's portfolio;

- implement improved processes to eliminate root causes of inefficiencies, errors and defects, while simultaneously increasing the likelihood of superior performance;

- influence public opinion and regulators through focused ads and other targeted media communications.

Formulating risk strategies is an iterative, fluent process driven by the available facts, measures and analyses.

Formulating risk strategies is an iterative, fluent process driven by the available facts, measures and analyses. It is not necessarily a matter of selecting one option over another. The best choice may be a combination of options. For example, when managing workplace safety, the firm may choose to (a) implement appropriate risk controls to reduce health and safety risk as much as possible, (b) obtain adequate workers compensation insurance to transfer catastrophic risk, (c) retain the remaining residual risk through deductibles to optimize transfer costs, and (d) when superior safety performance is clearly evident relative to peers, report that performance to exploit the firm's achievement so its reputation will be enhanced.

Strategic building blocks: Azurix's 'risk bits'

Azurix is devoted to the provision of water and water services. The company's business goals are to (1) build the infrastructure necessary to make water more widely available physically and less risky financially and (2) improve the efficiency of water management. According to Managing Director Chris Wasden, 'We're in the business to create water trading, expand access to conveyance systems and storage systems, and build underground storage systems. What we're trying to create is an environment where we can play all the dimensions of water risk: location, quality, time, weather and price.'

Strategy and risk

According to Mr Wasden, risk is the fundamental organizing principle at Azurix. 'Strategy is nothing more than disciplined risk management: discover

Continued ...

the capabilities you have, determine the capabilities you need in order to create value for your customers.' From there, he explains, 'you manage the risks appropriately to create superior value without creating exposure to undue losses or losses in excess of some expected level.'

Mr Wasden breaks business down into what he calls 'risk bits'. Risk bits are the risks associated with any endeavour, analogous to those that might be uncovered in a rigorous risk mapping exercise. With risk bits identified, a company has to ask itself, 'are we the most qualified to manage this, that or another specific risk, and if not, who is?' says Mr Wasden.

To build an effective business, 'you inventory the needs of customers and then the risk bits needed to provide a total solution. Those pieces of business where you can do an effective job of managing the risks you keep. Those pieces where your capabilities fall short you get rid of them, perhaps with insurance, derivatives or outsourcing.'

Where others fear to tread

The concept of risk bits, says Mr Wasden, is a key driver behind the importance of EWRM. 'As you become more risk focused, you begin to realize that your business is a collection of risks. You start to manage your business the same way an investment bank manages its business. You have people that own specific risk books, you have others whose responsibility it is to assemble those capabilities to create unique offerings to help people solve problems. So where you once had companies that looked like conglomerates, the successful companies of today look and act more like trading companies.'

Mr Wasden also believes that the world rewards capable risk takers. 'Prudent risk takers are people who understand their risks exceptionally well. They are able to create value and make money because to someone whose command of the risk is so great – the risks just don't seem as high as they do to others.'

> 'As you become more risk focused, you begin to realize that your business is a collection of risks.'

RISK STRATEGIES: TRANSLATING RISK ASSESSMENT INTO ACTION

Well-defined strategies ensure that risk ownership and accountability are sufficiently focused so that the appropriate risk management and control processes are designed and implemented. Using risk maps as a context, the natural tendency for managers is to focus on the 'high severity/high likelihood' risks as summarized in Quadrant 1 in Figure 5.6, and the 'high severity/low likelihood' risks included in Quadrant 2.

Fig. 5.6 **Using a risk map to provide a strategic context**

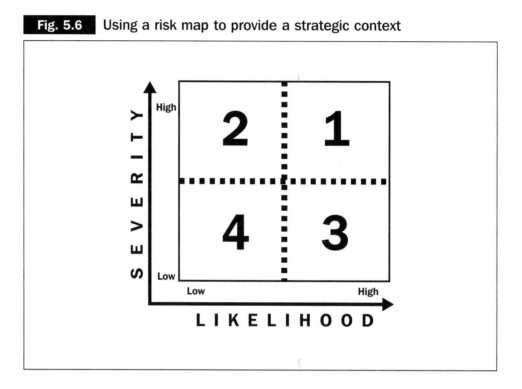

Quadrant 1 risks are in the 'red zone' because no business can survive accepting these risks at this critical level over the long term. Therefore, the firm's management of them is a strategic imperative. The strategy should be evidenced by specific action plans for which clearly designated risk owners are accountable. For these risks, *all risk management options may apply* depending on their nature and management's risk appetite and desired approach. However, if the firm cannot manage these risks effectively over the long term, avoidance strategies (divest, prohibit, stop, etc.) should be considered.

The risks in Quadrant 2, while not as critical as those in Quadrant 1, warrant close attention because they include extraordinary events, such as hurricanes, earthquakes, political events and other incidents, which can severely affect the business. These are 'yellow zone' risks. Again, *all risk management options apply, although control options are limited* because many of these risks are driven by environmental forces beyond management's control. That is why contingency planning, while appropriate for many risks, is especially vital to the management of these risks. Johnson & Johnson's world class reaction to the Tylenol crisis, for example, is a tribute to its mission statement and crisis management process. A well-defined risk scenario arising from the risk assessment process provides the basis for formulating a contingency plan that specifically identifies the individuals responsible for its execution and empowers them with decision-making authority. These plans should be tested periodically.

Quadrant 3 risks ('low severity/high likelihood') often relate to day-to-day operations and compliance issues. They are also part of the 'yellow zone' because the expected value of these risks, i.e. their potential severity times the likelihood of occurrence, can be as great as risks in Quadrant 2. If left unmanaged, the aggregate impact of these risk events, particularly if they are recurring, can approach unacceptable levels – compromising operating effectiveness and efficiency and compliance with legal and regulatory requirements. Thus, cost-effective steps should be taken to reduce their likelihood of occurrence to an acceptable level.

Managers often choose between *preventive* and *detective* risk controls to mitigate these Quadrant 3 risks. If prevention at the source is too costly or not feasible, detective risk controls are used to 'inspect and correct' at a control point downstream in the process from the actual source of risk. If detective risk controls are inefficient because they result in costly rework in the production process or excessive re-entry of data for reprocessing, preventive risk controls should be considered as best practice (see Appendix 3).

Risk incidents that are virtually certain to occur, but considered to be of little or no consequence to the business, should be monitored for changing conditions. Alternatives like outsourcing can often be useful in these (as well as in other) circumstances when the related activities are considered non-core.

The 'green zone' risks in Quadrant 4 ('low severity/low likelihood') are not significant enough to warrant allocation of significant resources because they are either irrelevant or insignificant and are usually acceptable at their present level. They present opportunities for eliminating irrelevant and redundant risk controls to reduce costs and allocate resources to manage more significant risks. They may also present opportunities for outsourcing. The factors that drive decisions to retain these risks should be monitored over time to determine whether conditions have changed.

In practice, risk maps and strategies mean nothing if they are not translated into action, and that means incorporation into the business plan. According to Roland Köhler, Chief Risk Officer at cement maker Holderbank, 'We align our risk assessment – the risk mapping – and strategy development with our business planning process. Beyond including specific risk and opportunity actions in the business plan it is also vitally important to take steps to measure the value-added as a result of these actions. This step, says Mr Köhler, either validates the actions planned or alternatively points out the need for further refinement.

Some risks are unavoidable – after all, risk-taking is the genesis of value creation. Whatever risk actions are selected, best practice is to include a discussion of the risk map and the actions to be taken in the business plan. The focus on the action plan, of course, takes the process to the next vital task, i.e. designing and implementing risk management capabilities.

Risk maps and strategies mean nothing if they are not translated into action.

Factors to consider when selecting risk strategy

There are many factors to consider when evaluating alternative risk strategies. Not surprisingly, the factors used to determine priority risks will also be useful when the time comes to develop management solutions. There are two groups of factors to consider when formulating strategic responses to the firm's business risks. The first group includes factors relating to the effects of management's broader business decisions on risk strategy.

- *Objectives and strategies*. Driven by senior and operating unit management, objectives and strategies clarify the what, where, when, who and how regarding the operations of the business. They are expressed in terms of short-term tactics, medium-term strategies and long-term business objectives, and incorporate short-, medium- and long-term constraints. Both risk mapping and the resulting risk strategies must consider these objectives and constraints.

- *Capability*. Are the risk management objectives realistic given the firm's capabilities? If not, can management assemble the capabilities needed so that they can be deployed within the firm's selected planning horizon?

- *Time horizon*. The period of time we are concerned with significantly impacts our approach to assessing and managing risk. A short-term risk, for example, confronts the firm immediately, e.g. the company's exposure to uncertainty caused by variations in the cost of its raw material or energy purchases (price risk). Long-term risks, by contrast, are more enduring and represent issues on which the firm has relatively little ability to impact over the short term, but can realistically expect to manage over the longer term, e.g. the firm's reputation, customer satisfaction, new manufacturing capabilities or technology. The key point is that any mismatch between the duration of the exposure and the length of time that management needs to implement a risk management solution presents a risk to the firm. For example, when evaluating its metals price risks, Rio Tinto plc concluded that derivatives are not an effective tool for a mine that will be in operation for 30 years. The firm's response is to pool its metals risks to exploit its diversified holdings.

- *Financing*. Risk financing is the means by which a firm pays for the outcomes of an unfavourable risk incident, whether through risk transfer or retention. External financing is a transfer to an independent, financially capable counterparty through insurance, hedging or other forms of contracting. Internal financing of risk is accomplished through a firm's own

Continued ...

financial resources, e.g. various forms of self-insurance, insurance deductibles and accounting reserves. Many risks are internally financed, but not all are explicitly recognized. A firm retains all of its risks unless it does something about them. Unless risks are considered too insignificant to warrant further analysis, unplanned retention is not risk management.

If insurance that protects the firm from catastrophic events is inexpensive relative to the potential loss, planned retention needs to be based on rational common sense. As one executive points out, 'If it costs two basis points to insure an $800 million building, how much of that risk do you really want to assume? Do you want to be the one who explains to the board that a $100 million loss could have been insured for $20,000?'[3]

- *Residual (basis) risk*. Perfect risk management solutions are rare – there will always be some residual risk. Managers should therefore seek practical solutions, not perfect ones: hold risk to tolerable levels; seek reasonable, not absolute assurance. Often, the tools used to manage a risk, such as when placing a hedge with a futures, swap or options contract, will not fully cover the underlying exposure presented by the risk. Any differential between the coverage provided by the risk management alternative and the exposure itself provides basis risk; that is, some residual risk remains with the company.

  Basis risk can occur either because the alternative does not cover all aspects of the exposure, or it covers too much. An example of the former is a grain elevator holding grain of different product specifications than that specified in a standard futures contract. An example of the latter is a company hedging a two-month energy exposure with a three-month options contract. In general, any mismatch between the coverage provided by the risk management alternative and the exposure itself will present new or continued risk to the company.

- *Manageability*. As management directs its efforts towards managing its priority risks, it should differentiate those risks where immediate improvements are more easily obtainable. While not intended as a suggestion to ignore the tough issues, a focus on manageability can lead to early successes by reaching for the 'low hanging fruit'.

The second group of factors address the nature of the risk and its effect on risk strategy.

Continued ...

---

3. Russ Banham (1999) 'Kit and Caboodle: Understanding the skepticism about enterprise risk management', *CFO Magazine*, April, pp. 63–70.

- *Scenarios*. What can happen in the future and why, how and where can it happen? What is the impact on the business? Effective risk assessment addresses these questions, providing significant input to the strategy selection process.

- *Environment*. Most environment risks are beyond the control of management; therefore, the firm must manage such risks through its strategic response. Business units *must* develop long-term strategies as well as learn to anticipate and adjust opportunistically to changes in the external environment.

- *Operational versus contractual*. Every risk management solution has to be matched with the nature and duration of the risk it addresses. For example, as noted above, when evaluating its metals price risks, Rio Tinto plc recognized that its metals risk exposure from a mine that is expected to operate for 30 years is an operational risk; therefore, its response is to pool its metals risks to exploit its diversified holdings rather than use a contractual response in the form of derivatives.

  To illustrate further, if a company's foreign exchange arises from a contract with a foreign customer, currency derivatives that align the term of the hedge with that of the contract are effective in safeguarding against adverse moves in exchange rates. By contrast, if the company has ongoing operations in the foreign country, there is no currency hedge whose size, duration and terms exactly match the company's business activities. Therefore, managers must examine the nature and duration of the risk to devise an operational response. Of course, some companies may dispute this example in situations where management is able to conclude that net income from a foreign source is reasonably predictable; when such assertions are credible, those firms may argue that hedging is effective in such circumstances.

- *Interfaces*. A major source of process risk lies in the interfaces between processes – so called 'hand-offs' between functional areas. Interfaces that are not under the control of a process-owner present a significant risk of errors and omissions. Risk controls must be designed at or as close as possible to these interface points to reduce process risk to an acceptable level.

- *Orientation*. Risk management strategies differ depending on whether the firm is managing an *existing exposure*, whether it is pre-empting an *anticipated exposure*, or whether it is strategically positioning itself by exploiting a *desired exposure*.

- *Compliance*. Situations involving compliance issues, such as laws and regulations, authorizations and approvals, hazardous materials handling,

Continued ...

Every solution has to be matched with the nature and duration of the risk it addresses.

shopfloor safety and nuclear power plant operations, have one thing in common – compliance with rigid standards is the established norm. These environments and circumstances require appropriate risk controls that reduce the likelihood of non-conformance to an acceptable level, as defined by management's thresholds.

- *Pervasiveness.* Is the exposure or uncertainty isolated or does it have multiple effects? Often, companies find certain risks affecting them similarly throughout the organization: regulatory risks, political risk and litigation, for example.

- *Frequency.* Does the exposure or uncertainty arise from infrequent events or regularly recurring events? One-time events that cannot be anticipated are difficult to measure and virtually impossible to control, but the firm can prepare contingency plans. By contrast, recurring risk events, e.g. product defects, must be carefully examined and appropriate responses developed.

- *Data availability.* Some risks have more data available than others to assist managers in measuring and analyzing them. Where data is available, the firm can use it in designing its response, but the apparent lack of data does not mean a risk shouldn't be managed.

While the above summary is not exhaustive, it provides an insight into some of the issues to consider when formulating risk strategies.

SUMMARY

In this chapter, we have discussed the importance of a uniform process that deploys the common language we introduced in Chapter 3. We have now addressed the first three tasks of that process in this and the previous chapters. In the next chapter, we address the remaining tasks of the BRMP that, in effect, build and improve the capabilities for executing established risk management strategies.

Infrastructure essentials: designing and implementing risk management capabilities

Whatever is worth doing at all, is worth doing well.

Philip Dormer Stanhope, former British Secretary of State

Risk owners, necessarily, must take the lead in determining how best to manage a given risk.

Timo Helle, VP and Director, Management Assurance,
Sonera (formerly Finland Telecom)

'Managing risk is everyone's job' is a quote that could be attributed to well over a dozen senior managers or companies in this research. But the only way to achieve such elegance is via the clear definition and alignment of the six elements of risk management infrastructure. These elements and their alignment are discussed in this chapter as we complete the discussion of the tasks of the business risk management process (BRMP). The next steps include: design and implement risk management capabilities, monitor performance and, finally, continuously improve.

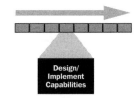

DESIGN/IMPLEMENT RISK MANAGEMENT CAPABILITIES

Once strategies for managing individual risks and groups of related risks have been determined, the appropriate risk owners are designated and each owner designs and implements the capabilities needed to execute the specific strategy for which he or she is responsible. Risk management capabilities include the processes, people, reports, methodologies and technologies (systems and data) needed to implement a particular strategy. We refer to these six elements (which include strategies and policies) as 'components of infrastructure'.

When managers begin to organize and align the firm's infrastructure for managing an individual risk or an aggregate group of related risks, they send a clear signal that they are serious about risk management. Infrastructure comprises the components shown in Figure 6.1.

The individual components are themselves important, but equally critical are the interrelationships between the components. Without alignment, comprehensive and value-driven risk management capabilities are difficult to attain.

If any one component of infrastructure is deficient, the effectiveness of other components can be significantly diminished. For example, if relevant and reliable data is not available, the value of reports to management is reduced (and may even be misleading). If reports do not provide appropriate information, risk owners cannot execute the processes for which they are accountable. Consequently, related processes fail to achieve the risk management strategy. The effect, therefore, is cumulative. As Rick Causey, Chief Accounting Officer of Enron, maintains, 'if the controls aren't there, if the information coming out of

> When managers begin to organize and align infrastructure, they send a clear signal that they are serious about risk management.

the businesses isn't complete or accurate, if the organization isn't aligned, then you can throw this whole EWRM concept out the window.'

Fig. 6.1 Six infrastructure components comprising risk management capabilities

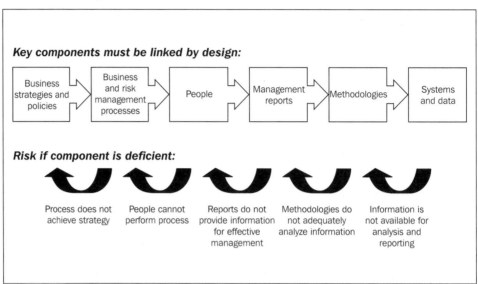

While not necessarily intended as a strictly linear process, the above components are generally designed from left to right (when viewing Figure 6.1). For example, strategies drive the design of processes, processes dictate the organization of people and skills needed, etc. Thus, use of this structure helps organize the otherwise complex network of risk management activities into a comprehensive and consistent framework. In particular, it ensures that all key components are appropriately considered. For example, by adequately developing processes and human capabilities *first*, the common problem of placing undue emphasis on models and systems is avoided. Models and systems, therefore, support processes and people.

To further illustrate what we mean by infrastructure, Figure 6.2 provides examples of integrated infrastructure components for managing sourcing risk (specifically procurement), credit risk and the hiring/retention aspects of human resources risk.

The components of infrastructure are intertwined with the multiple tasks of the BRMP. In fact, infrastructure represents the tangible tools and techniques used by businesses on a daily basis to manage risk and operationalize the BRMP. For example, (a) risk management processes are integrated with business processes, (b) management reports comprise the information for the decision-making 'centrepiece' of the BRMP and (c) methodologies provide the basis for sourcing and measuring risk and monitoring risk.

> Risk management capabilities include the processes, people, reports, methodologies and technologies needed to implement a particular strategy.

Fig. 6.2 Examples of integrated infrastructure components

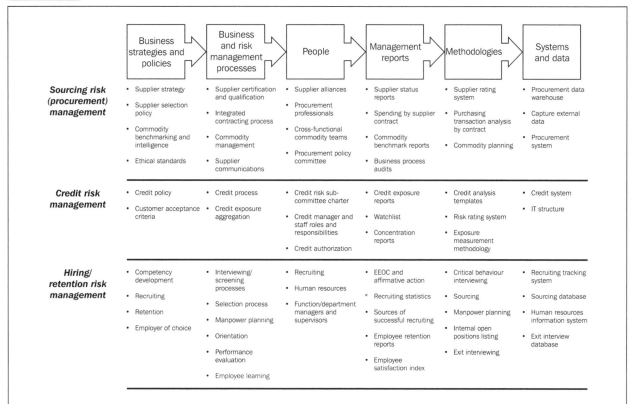

If EWRM is the alignment of strategy, processes, people, technology and knowledge, an effectively designed infrastructure enables this alignment. Synchronized with the remaining elements of the BRMP process, infrastructure becomes the 'engine' that drives EWRM-oriented organizations to a higher level of performance in managing individual risks or groups of related risks. As Chris Valentine of Cable & Wireless explains, 'a risk-focused strategic framework and business infrastructure creates enormous value relative to traditional approaches. I believe that going forward, it will prove a key differentiator between winners and also-rans.'

Risks and resources: how Cable & Wireless achieves balance

One of the realizations of EWRM is that not every risk requires the same degree of rigour and resources to manage. The UK's Cable & Wireless is addressing the need for balance by using a risk mapping process that flows from the top down, leaving 'risk-related' resource allocation decisions to operating managers. According to Director of Risk Management Chris Valentine, risk 'belongs' to the business units. Risk assessment – both upside and downside potential – are part of the business plans of operating units. Consequently, 'it is up to them to decide, in conjunction with our CEO, the degree of action and resources required to achieve the desired results,' he explains.

Continued ...

An adjunct process

Fundamentally, the £20 billion communications company is endeavouring to 'embed risk assessment and management into existing processes,' says Mr Valentine. 'What we've created is not an entirely new process, what some might call more paperwork, but rather an adjunct to the Annual Operating Plan process.' Each business unit develops its respective AOP, including key deliverables (sales, production volumes, etc.). The deliverables become the focus for detailed risk mapping.

'We ask, "What are the threats to that business plan, and how can we manage those threats or just as critically, how can we maximize upside potential?"' says Mr Valentine. 'We are looking for the uncertainties inherent in the various plans and how we can best manage them to maximize our chances to be successful.'

In this way, risk mapping 'cascades risk awareness all the way to the bottom of the organization,' says Mr Valentine. The business plan is essentially a 'contract' with the group's CEO and shareholders. 'It is up to the operating units to make certain they achieve their plan,' says Mr Valentine. 'They decide the resources and activity necessary to manage the associated risks: Do we have the right strategy? Do we have the right resources engaged? Do we have the right structures in place? Given a particular risk, do we have the right people with the right skills doing the right things?'

Of course, the appropriateness of the response is evaluated in conjunction with the parent's expectations. Moreover, there is a monthly review to gauge how the business units are performing relative to the AOP and the associated risks.

Responding to the Turnbull Report

All of this means Cable & Wireless is addressing its risks more proactively and systematically. One driver for this shift is the Turnbull Report. Released in the summer of 1999, the Turnbull Report provides guidance for complying with the UK's Combined Code – legislation requiring a review, at least annually, of the effectiveness of financial, operational and compliance controls and risk management for UK-registered companies.

But a more important impetus is the need to deliver improved company performance through a more focused approach on the management of risk in the business. This has required broadening the concept of risk management to incorporate operational and commercial risk and better align different functional areas dealing with different aspects of risk. Explains Mr Valentine, 'These are the pieces of the organization that are available to help the business units improve their capabilities to manage their identified risks.'

'EWRM is going to be, increasingly, a fundamental differentiator between successful and not-so-successful companies.'

Continued ...

All told, though the group recognizes these are just the first steps in its EWRM journey, the direction is sound. 'Perhaps Turnbull causes us to be an early-adopter,' says Mr Valentine. But whatever the reason, he is convinced 'EWRM is going to be, increasingly, a fundamental differentiator between successful and not-so-successful companies.' We agree: EWRM provides the process for managing business risk in a manner that creates value for the business rather than being merely a tool to ensure compliance.

THE COMPONENTS OF INFRASTRUCTURE

Infrastructure is vital to the achievement of risk management capabilities. Below is a discussion of each of the six components.

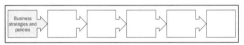 ### Business strategies and policies

The policy framework articulates the selected risk strategy so that risk owners will understand what the risk management capabilities are intended to accomplish. The policy is a statement of general principles that guide management and risk owners toward achieving specific risk management goals, implementing specific risk strategies, designing specific processes, using designated products, executing specific transaction types and complying with specific risk tolerances and expected standards of conduct. The process of framing a policy helps senior executives and the board clarify their understanding of the risks, the related impact on the business and the risk management strategy selected.

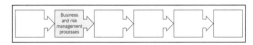 ### Business and risk management processes

Business processes are the primary means of executing business strategies and policies. Risk management activities are integrated within business processes; therefore, any incremental activities addressing risk management objectives, including risk controls, should be designed as an integral part of the firm's existing processes. This principle is important because risks are best managed and controlled as close as possible to the source. Operational risk controls should therefore be *built into* day-to-day processes as integral tasks rather than *built onto* those processes as separate appendages.

When designing processes to achieve the desired risk management objectives, the risk owners should describe precisely the sequence of activities and tasks that must be performed. These definitions include:

- the inputs;

- the desired outputs (in terms of expected quality, cost and time requirements);

- the major activities and tasks;

- the interaction and the information and decision flows between related functional units;

- the skills required;

- the desired time frame; and

- the procedures for handling exceptions and incidents.

Work flows, process maps and procedures manuals document the process design. With well defined processes, risk owners have a clearer understanding of the activities requiring the most attention from a risk management and control standpoint; thus, they are able to ensure that business processes and risk management processes are effectively integrated.

Best practice standards are provided to risk owners to guide them in the design and implementation of risk management and control processes. Best practices may be drawn externally from the experiences of other companies, industries or studies, or internally by identifying and institutionalizing the best practices of individual operating units, divisions or functional areas. For example, Motorola developed risk control standards based on its benchmarking activities with over 80 companies. These standards continue to be communicated to all process owners. A word of caution, however: a best practice for one firm may not be ideal for another.

Often, a designated executive or risk management executive committee oversees the design and implementation of new or improved processes and measures consistent with established risk strategies and tolerances. At Finland's Sonera, Timo Helle leads a group that acts as an internal consultant 'guiding the risk-mapping processes and helping with the development of appropriate actions.' Periodic status reports submitted by risk owners are the first line of assurance that objectives are being met. But as Mr Helle explains, 'if management wants further assurance, this becomes a task for internal audit.' This oversight provides assurance that risk management and control processes are being designed and implemented as planned.

 **People**

People execute processes. Overall responsibility for developing and implementing improved risk management capabilities should rest with one or more qualified individuals having the requisite knowledge, expertise and experience. Risk owners are the managers within the firm who are accountable for losses experienced when undesirable risk incidents occur. These individuals understand the risks, why they are taken, what is being done about them and the firm's policies that set

'Someone has to take ownership, so we know that the actions are in fact going to be taken.'

boundaries and limits within which they are empowered to operate. Moreover, their success is inextricably linked to the successful management of the risks for which they are accountable.

Without clear risk ownership, the process will be fragmented and ineffective. Explains Holderbank's Roland Köhler, 'Someone has to take ownership, so we know that the actions we identify are in fact going to be taken.'

As people take on new risk management responsibilities, their roles, accountability and relationships with other risk owners should be clearly defined. As with policy documentation, the nature and extent of 'user friendly' procedures manuals vary substantially from firm to firm. In part, this is often a matter of style, as procedural documentation for risk management should be consistent with documentation in other areas.

The bottom line is that risk owners should be satisfied that everyone's job is clearly spelled out so that they can hold people – both within and outside the enterprise – accountable against established business objectives and performance goals. The roles and responsibilities of risk-taking versus risk-monitoring functions should also be clearly delineated.

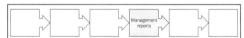 ## Management reports

Management reports are designed according to the information needs of people who are responsible for executing processes in accordance with the risk strategy. Reports are constrained by the supporting methodologies and systems as well as the availability of data. The risk reporting process is intended to provide management with knowledge about risks, including the level of exposures versus limits, 'what-if' scenarios, trends in risk drivers, risk diversification and concentrations, limits violations and other information. Personnel with risk management responsibilities use reports to monitor achievement of objectives, execution of strategies and compliance with policies.

> **Reports should be actionable, easy to use and linked to well-defined accountabilities.**

Reports should be actionable, easy to use and linked to well-defined accountabilities. They should succinctly capture and highlight key information to support more informed decisions. Internal reporting to executive management is typically more detailed than board reporting and includes some (or all) of the options listed below:

■ *P&L attribution.* How did we make or lose money? From what factors?

■ *Risks versus limits.* What are our risk levels versus policy-based limits and guidelines? It is always meaningful to report trends, e.g. how close are we to established tolerance levels and do we have more, less or the same amount of risk, individually and in the aggregate?

■ *Exceptions and 'near misses'.* What exceptions versus policy or established limits have we encountered? Are there any significant breakdowns, errors, accidents, defects, lost opportunities, losses incurred or 'close calls'?

- *Scenario analyses.* What is the impact on our earnings, cash flow and capital of changes in factors beyond our control? Such factors include interest rates, exchange rates, inflation, weather, competitor acts, supplier performance levels and other variables. Depending on the circumstances, these analyses are presented by line of business, by geographic area and/or by product/service group. For example, an overview presents a summary level analysis of significant individual and aggregate exposures, including an analysis of current risk management strategies using a 'base case' derived from a range of likely outcomes (probabilistic) or, less desirably, the most likely outcome (deterministic) and, if appropriate, supplemented by stress tests. As indicated in Case 5, the board of directors of Enron is presented with a detailed probabilistic risk strategy review on a quarterly basis.

- *Special reports.* These studies or targeted analyses explain or analyze something specific, usually in response to certain events or anticipated concerns. For example, if a specific region is encountering economic instability, a study might address, 'What is our Russia exposure?' Such analyses can be valuable because exposures are not always direct. As with the 1998 Russian debt repayment crisis, sometimes the vulnerability of a company's position can depend on newly formed perceptions of investors and lenders. The effects of market changes can also be systemic, spreading to other countries and regions.

- *Audit reports.* Are we in compliance with established policies? Are our risk controls performing as intended or are our measures reliable? Are we operating in accordance with internal limits and external and statutory requirements? Business process audits and policy reviews focus on these and other issues.

Reporting on risk is as integral to a firm's success in the new economy as reporting on quality, cost and time.

- *Key performance indicators.* KPIs used to manage the business are sometimes used to manage operating risks. An approach that is emerging in practice is the alignment of risk measures and indicators with the broader customer, employee/supplier, innovation, financial and other KPI categories relevant to a firm's business model. Reporting on risk is as integral to a firm's success in the new economy as reporting on quality, cost and time. For example, Diageo/Guinness integrates its reporting of commodity price, hiring/retention and economic risk drivers with its balanced scorecard of key performance indicators.

- *High level profile of the firm's critical exposures and drivers.* For example, one company uses a profile of its business units which includes risks affected by common drivers. This profile summarizes the environment (strategic) and process (tactical) exposures created by the firm's operating units and divisions, the key drivers of those exposures and the various strategies for managing those drivers. Holderbank, for example, uses 'current' *and* 'target' risk maps for reporting to senior management. These maps summarize the firm's risks ranked by severity and likelihood, with an analysis of key drivers provided for each significant risk. A 'risk drivers map' supports the firm's selection of key drivers.

■ *Status of improvement initiatives.* Listing this reporting option last is not intended to suggest a lack of importance. Monitoring the status of current and projected improvement efforts establishes accountability and discipline.

Management reports include position reports, transaction reports, management and board reports, valuation/scenario analyses and comprehensive risk reports (earnings at risk, value at risk, cash flow at risk). However, the nature, extent and timing of reporting vary by recipient and by type of risk.

When addressing the level of detail, it is important for managers to relate the reports they receive to the risk management goals, objectives and thresholds for which they are accountable. That exercise will help them answer the question, 'What do I do with it?' For example, executive management and the board typically do not have the time – and often do not have the expertise – to undertake in-depth reviews of detailed risk management data. By designing reports at a basic conceptual level for communicating with top management, risk managers are motivated to clarify their own thinking about the relationships between risk management and the core activities of the business. This, in turn, increases the confidence level of executive management and the board of directors in the risk management process.

With respect to reporting frequency, there are no hard and fast rules. A number of factors to consider include the volatility or severity of the risk, the needs of the user (e.g. quarterly board meetings) and the dynamics of the underlying business activities. For example, in an active treasury, exposures and performance relating to trading activities are reported on a daily basis. For less active treasuries, exposures and performance are reported on a weekly basis. By contrast, the underlying business exposures giving rise to the need to trade in derivatives are ordinarily not reported more frequently than monthly or, if they are reasonably stable, quarterly.

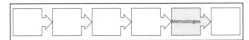 **Methodologies**

The robustness of management reports is enhanced or constrained by the methodologies supporting them. Methodologies organize key tasks and a working body of knowledge within a logical structured framework. They include the theorems, the decision rules and the hypotheses and assumptions that make the process of managing risk more rigorous and systematic. For example, effective methodologies help managers identify and prioritize risk, source risk to their root causes and key drivers and quantify risk. They also support analysis of risk/reward trade-offs, portfolio diversification, evaluation of the cost effectiveness of risk mitigation alternatives, allocation of capital to absorb potential losses, pricing of products and services to compensate adequately for risks undertaken and contingency planning given uncertain outcomes.

Methodologies are therefore needed to support decision-making. When we discussed risk assessment, we introduced several methodologies, e.g. risk mapping, risk indicator analysis, exposure measurement, risk measurement, risk rating or scoring, performance measurement and risk modelling and analytics. Other methodologies include:

- *Valuation.* Valuing individual assets and liabilities and portfolios of assets and liabilities, e.g. applying mark-to-market techniques to an investment portfolio.

- *Capital allocation.* Allocating capital (either equity or regulatory capital) to major sources of risks with the objective of optimizing the balance among three objectives – grow the business, earn sufficient returns and preserve capital, e.g. the use of RAROC as a process for allocating capital to attractive risk–return opportunities, as illustrated in the Enron case (see Case 5).

- *External and internal data correlation.* Collecting and correlating relevant external data with internal company statistics corroborates the use of internal data for management purposes, e.g. Federal Express validates its methodology for measuring service effectiveness on a daily basis by periodically correlating the trends in its internal service effectiveness index with trends in customer satisfaction derived from external surveys direct from customers.

- *Systematic loss exposure assessment.* Systematically identifying and evaluating scenarios resulting in unacceptable losses results in a rigorously determined ranking of 'downside' risks using criteria selected by management, such as severity, likelihood, and costs (to avoid, control or transfer).[1]

- *Other.* Forecasting tools and statistical process control.

These methodologies are provided as examples and are not necessarily applicable to every risk. The descriptions, documentation and underlying assumptions inherent in a firm's methodologies must be clearly specified and understood. Whenever possible, models and risk metrics should be standardized in order to provide a common denominator for comparing different strategy alternatives.

> New technologies are leading to more refined measures and are making it easier to identify and understand risks, risk drivers and the impact they have on the company.

Systems and data

Information systems support the modelling and reporting that are integral to risk management capabilities. They provide relevant, accurate and on-time information. New technologies are leading to more refined measures and are making it easier to identify and understand risks, risk drivers and the impact they have on the company. All told, systems and data should meet the company's business requirements, and be flexible enough to allow for future enhancement, scalability and integration with other systems.

---

1. Vernon L. Grose (1987) *Managing Risk: Systematic Loss Prevention for Executives.* Omega Systems Group, pp. 182–322.

Why are systems and data so important? If the necessary data is not available for analysis and reporting, and the requisite systems are not in place to process that data, then the selected methodologies will not serve their intended purpose. Therefore, systems and data are, in combination, a vital component of infrastructure. They include:

- transaction systems, e.g. deal capture systems, portfolio accounting systems, treasury systems, money market and securities trading, equity derivatives trading and risk management, etc.;
- analytical software that collects risk data as an integral part of normal business routines, e.g. risk analysis systems;
- systems that identify and capture risk drivers and other 'feeder data';
- integrated systems and databases which warehouse key data elements relating to specific BRMP tasks performed across the firm (to support risk communications and knowledge sharing, as discussed further below);
- special purpose systems that quantify individual risks and aggregate portfolios of risks;
- database systems that support the management of individual risks and risk portfolios, i.e. portfolio and market databases; and
- risk analytics programmed into decision support systems.

There are many important factors in developing risk management systems that are well beyond the scope of this book, but we point out several below.

- First, it is vital to actively engage users responsible for risk management in the definition of the required systems and data specifications. The system supports the process; the process should not be driven or constrained by the functionality of an arbitrarily selected system.
- Second, considerable thought should be given to (a) the requirements of individual units and divisions for risk management transaction and special purpose systems, and (b) the summary level needs of management and the board. The objective is to design the best way to collect, analyze and report data that best meets these requirements. For example, reporting on trade-related currency exposures is dependent on whether they are managed globally, regionally or at the business unit level. A global firm which delegates the management of currency risk to a regional treasury may only need to know the net exposures at the end of each month. By contrast, a firm which has centralized its management of currency risk as part of a global currency diversification strategy will need transaction level data on exposures, with net exposures reported to the board and management on a currency-by-currency basis.

■ Finally, systems functionality, e.g. the need for complex modelling tools, requires careful consideration as there may be many options available. For example, the choice of software tools for quantifying risk is driven by, among other things, the selected risk strategy, installation and licensing costs, performance requirements, vendor reputation, front- versus back-office needs, availability of critical data, existing legacy systems and the level of sophistication desired by operating and executive management.

EWRM: technology as the integrator

Technology is playing a critical role in the evolution of EWRM. E-mails and the Web are stimulating communication. Powerful programs are enabling analysis with data warehouses providing vast and customizable information for planning and decision-making. The fact is, without these advances in technology, EWRM would not be practical or perhaps even possible. Corporate intranets in particular are being utilized to develop databases and tools that promote an EWRM environment – and in this regard an excellent example comes from US-based Charles Schwab & Co.

Charles Schwab: INFORM

Since late 1997, Charles Schwab has been focusing on the improvement of risk communication and management throughout the company. Step one was to develop a common language, and progress here has been significant says Internal Audit Director, Dante Robinson. Now, using the common language, the company is systematically documenting the process flows of its organization. The information is being collected and made available group-wide via a web-based intranet known as INFORM.

More than half of the trades executed by brokerage giant Charles Schwab are initiated via eSchwab, making it the online trading industry's leading provider. So it comes as no surprise that the company is relying heavily on web technology to forward its EWRM vision. INFORM began life as an internal audit tool intended to document controls and procedures. However, it is now multifunctional: INFORM is actually a 'suite' of tools, providing a handful of risk management capabilities. The five principal elements are:

■ *Process Diagnostics/Procedural Documentation*. This area of INFORM provides annotated process maps: the tool helps the company decompose operational and technology processes at many levels of detail. Process owners populate INFORM with both qualitative descriptions of policies, procedures and controls and detailed process maps relating to work flow.

Continued ...

- *KPIs and Metrics*. This is a group of risk models used to quantify credit, market and operational risks.

- *Process Transformation/Automated Workflow*. This tool is used to help business units automate their control environments.

- *Filtering/Messaging*. This module helps the business units develop automated alerts. Based on pre-defined triggers or 'thresholds', the system uses 'push' technology or 'narrow casting' to warn risk owners of the potential need for action. For example, says Mr Robinson, 'if trading volume picks up substantially, INFORM will contact everyone potentially affected and provide an alert.'

- *Inter-Departmental Relationships/Life-Cycle Tracking*. This module provides detailed process and technical maps of shared or 'interdepartmental' processes. In particular it highlights the functionalities required to enable related corporate initiatives such as knowledge management or employee self-service (see below).

Using INFORM, business units are able to accomplish three critical goals. First, says Mr Robinson, 'is that they can achieve a better understanding of how their work relates to the organization at large.' Most organizations today feature competent communication upwards and downwards. INFORM, however, enables cross-business unit information-sharing and communication. As Mr Robinson explains, managers using this system 'can see the handoffs, the upstream and downstream impacts of their work. They can also better understand how other units exercise and control their business plans. It's very powerful.'

Second, INFORM becomes a powerful tool for internal benchmarking. Since the group is using a common risk language, operating units can examine how other units measure and control their risks. Business units, Mr Robinson explains, 'can compare their performance to that of other business units and therefore focus improvement efforts.' Internal Audit can compare its assessment of processes, controls and procedures to that of any given operating unit to identify potential gaps. Both of these capabilities are vitally important to the company because control self-assessment 'is an important initiative around here,' says Mr Robinson.

Third, INFORM offers a bevy on ancillary benefits and functionality. For example, INFORM provides risk models, useful for quantification. Also not to be underestimated is its value as a training tool. Instead of handing volumes of procedural manuals to new hires, 'they can use INFORM to see our controls and work flow – and get a real understanding of the work they will

Continued ...

be doing,' says Mr Robinson. Another anticipated benefit is the ability to offer 'self-service' to employees. As Mr Robinson explains, 'there are many things that employees will be able to do for themselves here' as opposed to relying on a service function such as human resources.

A vast repository

Enrolment in the INFORM project is voluntary, but more business units are participating 'all the time,' says Mr Robinson. 'They see the value. It's a common language tool, a training tool, an operations tool. Overall, it's a repository of a vast amount of very useful information and it is accessible to anyone who needs it.' During the roll-out phase of INFORM, access to employees is limited. But according to Mr Robinson, ultimately the tool will be available to all eyes via the company's intranet. Some areas may be password protected or available on a read-only basis, but the vision, says Mr Robinson, is to provide an 'equal opportunity tool'. All told, intranets are a powerful tool for enabling an EWRM environment.

 **Summary**

Summarizing the process of designing and implementing capabilities, an effective infrastructure provides the processes, skills, specific methodologies and other risk management tools needed to execute business risk management strategies. The infrastructure itself is developed one link at a time, each component driven by the previous one. These risk management capabilities operationalize the remaining tasks of the BRMP, as discussed further in subsequent sections of this chapter.

While many firms will not have processes that they formally recognize as the 'business risk management process' *per se*, all successful firms execute processes that fall within the BRMP's scope. As illustrated in Figure 6.3, its activities are analogous to the well known 'Plan–Do–Check–Act' cycle. For example, establishing goals, objectives and oversight, assessing risk and developing risk management strategies is 'planning', designing and implementing risk management capabilities is 'doing', monitoring performance is 'checking' and continuous improvement based on checking of results is 'acting'. The centrepiece of the process, information for decision-making, facilitates all of the other tasks and is equivalent to 'managing by fact'.

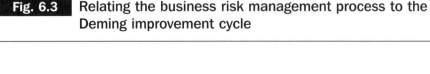

Fig. 6.3 Relating the business risk management process to the Deming improvement cycle

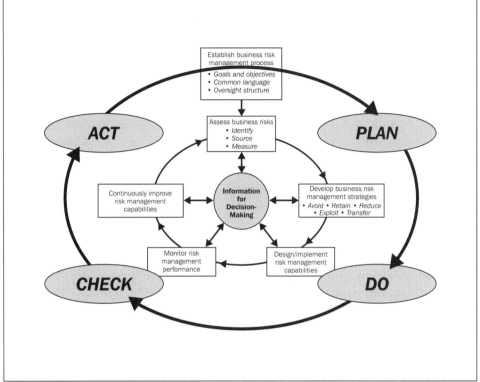

The BRMP framework, or a derivative thereof (customized to the enterprise), is an essential building block if a true EWRM environment is to be attained. It is only one model, yet it can be applied to the management of an individual risk or to an aggregate group of related risks. It can be used as a tool for benchmarking risk management practices, achieving a sharper focus on improvement opportunities and increasing risk awareness and sensitivity.

MONITOR RISK MANAGEMENT PERFORMANCE

It is not enough to put risk assessment methodologies into practice, formulate a risk strategy, and design and implement risk management capabilities to execute that strategy. The effectiveness of the processes, people, methodologies and technology specifically designated to execute the selected risk management strategy must be monitored on an ongoing basis. Monitoring consists of both formal and informal processes applied by executive/senior management, process/activity owners, risk owners and internal auditors. While the people who are most knowledgeable of the process (the 'owners') have primary responsibility for self-assessing its performance, it is necessary for executives who are independent of the process to also monitor its performance.

EWRM broadens the perspective for the role of monitoring in providing assurances.

EWRM broadens the perspective for the role of monitoring in providing assurances to the board and to executive management. Monitoring is applied to the following:

- *Existing priority risks.* Stress testing, simulations and scenario analysis are examples of techniques that managers use in conjunction with established limit structures to determine whether changes in the firm's risk profile have occurred. Firms like Enron execute stress testing not only on trading portfolios and incremental investments but also on the overall business.

- *New emerging risks.* Changing conditions and circumstances externally (environment risks) and internally within the business (process risks) should be identified on a timely basis. Significant changes warrant additional assessment so the appropriate risk management options can be evaluated and risk management ownership clearly defined. The Royal Mail applies this discipline to its business.

- *Risk management performance.* Metrics assist executive management and risk owners in assessing whether established risk control processes are performing as intended and in taking timely corrective action when appropriate. At Diageo, Finance Director Nick Rose explains, increasingly, 'our metrics apply to key performance indicators which we are continuously refining.' Aligning risk management performance with the firm's balanced scorecard may yet prove to be an emerging best practice.

- *Specific measures, policies and procedures.* Auditing provides assurance that risk measures are reliable, risk management processes are performing as intended, and established policies and procedures are being complied with. Most of our case companies apply this form of monitoring.

Monitoring addresses key 'How do we know ...' questions that every responsible person needs to ask, as illustrated in Figure 6.4.

Aligning risk management performance with the balanced scorecard may emerge as best practice.

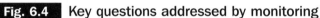

Fig. 6.4 Key questions addressed by monitoring

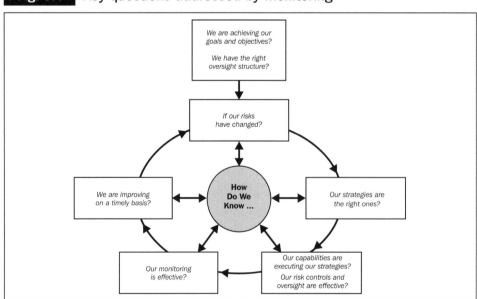

In summary, monitoring consists of a combination of metrics, regular communications and periodic audits and evaluations by independent executives and functions at appropriate levels of the firm. It provides vital assurances to directors and senior managers as the organization manages change.

CONTINUOUSLY IMPROVE RISK MANAGEMENT CAPABILITIES

The need for improvements to processes, people, reports, methodologies and systems that are identified through monitoring should be evaluated and implemented, as appropriate, consistent with a continuous improvement philosophy. Continuous improvement applies to business risk management as it does to any other process. We see three enablers of such a philosophy:

- benchmarking performance to identify best practices;
- four-way interactive communications and knowledge sharing; and
- integrating the firm's risk language and process into its employee learning programmes.

These enablers of continuous improvement of risk strategies, processes and measures are discussed in Chapter 7.

> Continuous improvement applies to business risk management as it does to any other process.

INFORMATION FOR DECISION-MAKING

When we discussed the design and implementation of risk management capabilities, we indicated that management reports, methodologies and systems and data are vital components of infrastructure. These infrastructure components lay the foundation for information for decision-making.

An enterprise-wide view ultimately leads the firm to integrating its business risk management information for decision-making with other information used in the business. The firm measures and reports what matters – this means *all* of its critical information relating to quality, cost, time *and* risk should be integrated on its balanced scorecard. Admittedly, this is easier said than done, but companies committed to EWRM work to make it happen. This vital linkage to enterprise performance is discussed in Chapter 8.

One increasingly important component of risk management systems is the ability to leverage risk management through the communications capabilities of the firm's networks. We see companies deploying intranet-based technology solutions to:

- support implementation of an integrated, enterprise-wide approach to business risk assessment and management;

- manage organizational risk knowledge; and

- stimulate continuous improvement of risk management capabilities.

In addition to using Internet technologies to create their own intranet applications, companies are also using the Internet to build connections with other entities and data sources. Web-enabled risk management systems organize information and data about risks and risk management for extraction and analysis. They automate and accelerate the risk reporting process and provide real-time information on risk exposures, losses and incidents through polling methodologies that engage process/activity owners and risk owners throughout the enterprise.

Many types of data are relevant to risk managers, including the historical, transaction, positional and calculated. Not only do databases maintain these data, they also support risk management at all levels of the enterprise by providing a framework for identifying, capturing and organizing risk data elements from external and internal sources that are made readily available to risk owners. Examples of data elements supporting all of the BRMP tasks and standardizing terminology, definitions and measures are presented in Figure 6.5.

Fig. 6.5 **Examples of data elements supporting a risk management system**

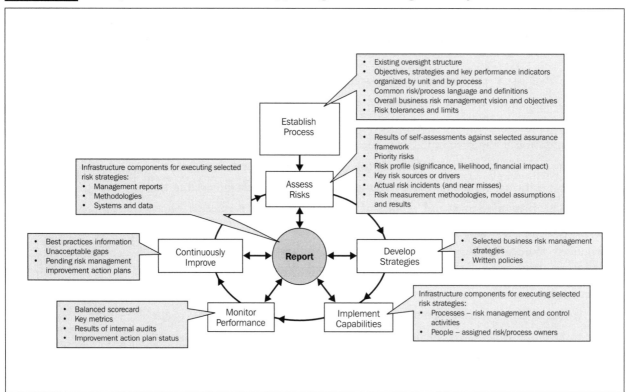

How is this facility used? A central Business Risk Management Function (BRMF) uses it to warehouse the data elements that link operating units, processes and functions. Risk and process owners throughout the organization input data about business processes, risks, risk management processes and risk controls. Once populated, the database provides tabular summaries of information regarding the firm's enterprise-wide capabilities. For example:

- it supports management's documentation and communication of a common risk and process language, the firm's critical processes and risks and the key business and process objectives, strategies and performance indicators;

- it provides the vehicle for managers and risk owners to document risk data at the organization, operating unit, process and sub-process levels using predetermined frameworks;

- it provides templates for managers and risk owners to document risk ratings, risk tolerances and residual risk; and

- it enables process/activity owners and risk owners to document their self-assessments of the effectiveness of the business risk management process and key risk controls, summarize risk management strategies and activities for priority risks and document gaps in risk management performance.

The system enables data mining in which analytical software or a central group, such as a BRMF, extracts data for analysis to create relevant information and a wealth of different reports. Extraction and analysis can be used:

- to identify trends that warrant management attention;

- to assist senior management in supporting the firm's assertion that it is complying with established frameworks, e.g. COSO in the US, CoCo in Canada, Turnbull in the UK, KonTraG in Germany, Standards Australia, etc.;

- to capture improvement opportunities identified by management, process and risk owners and internal audit;

- to stimulate the development of improvement action plans and support monitoring of the status of open action items;

- to support identification of best practice for sharing elsewhere in the firm; and

- to provide a foundation for developing a BRMP scorecard for the enterprise as a whole, for specific operating units and divisions, for specific processes and for specific risks.

Web-enabled networks are playing an ever-increasing role in the 'cutting-edge' risk manager's process (see discussion of Pioneer International below). As it evolves as a reporting, monitoring and reference tool, the risk management system creates value for the firm that its competitors cannot easily replicate. For example, the ability to 'roll up' information using common data elements can lead to the creation of 'scorecard reporting' of the business risk profile and risk management performance at all levels of the enterprise. Depending on the circumstances, this information is summarized on an enterprise-wide, a business unit, a geographic and a product basis, and enables decision-makers to evaluate trends monthly, weekly, daily or even real-time. From there, other applications are developed, e.g. internal benchmarking, knowledge sharing, early warning techniques, scenario assessment and risk aggregation. This four-way 'down, cross-functional and up' information flow supported by a risk management system is what we envision as EWRM environments evolve.

There are, of course, issues that must be considered to ensure effective management of the availability, security, integrity and relevance of data feeds and the information processing and technology systems supporting risk management. Reliable systems are the foundation of an effective infrastructure; they support the methodologies and reporting that provide relevant information to appropriate decision-makers on a timely basis. These systems must be flexible enough to accommodate upgrades over time as circumstances and the firm's risk management objectives change.

> **The risk management system creates value for the firm that its competitors cannot easily replicate.**

Pioneer International: risk databases

As this book was heading to press, Australian-based Pioneer International, a $2 billion global manufacturer, distributor and retailer of industrial products, was heading into a friendly merger with the UK's £3 billion Hanson plc. Together, the two form the world's new leading producer of aggregates and enhances the combined companies' positions in several related categories.

Though their future is now uncertain, Pioneer International's EWRM initiatives are nonetheless noteworthy. With the support of the audit committee and senior management, Pioneer was in the midst of implementing a proprietary risk management approach across the world. 'Our focus is on all of our key business risks,' says Joel Williams, IA Managing Director. Moreover, the focus is on business objectives, not controls.

Pioneer's approach is based on several design principles, including 'top-down' direction, 'bottom-up' validation (to confirm the identified risks, assessment of risk issues and risk management practices in place), consistent application of COSO (including senior management involvement during risk management design and implementation) and periodic risk reviews and issues resolution.

Aiding these initiatives are a series of sophisticated databases and online tools. Mr Williams explains:

Continued ...

Our intent is to use technology to show the consequences and likelihood of our risks enterprise-wide and by region, show the potential impact of those risks on the company and the effectiveness of the specific risk management techniques that are addressing those risks. We want a tool that assists managers at all levels of the company all the way up to the audit committee. So this capability will facilitate knowledge sharing about our risks and the way we manage them.

Pioneer's technology includes:

■ *Business unit risk profiles*. This tool compares the degree of residual risk between business units in the Pioneer group and ranks the residual risk against funds employed and the desired risk profile for any given level of funds employed. 'Residual risk' is determined by a weighting of key risks and risk management activities, developed with the use of the additional IT tools cited below.

■ *Risk assessment cube*. Known as the 'RAC' this 'is a value chain model that defines the key activities of our organization,' explains Mr Williams. To identify all potential activities, the business is decomposed into processes using a standard process classification scheme. These activities encompass all key business activities, for example sales pricing, information technology development, product and service quality, strategy and business development, health and safety, and management information. 'The RAC graphically displays activities in order of priority using the COSO framework,' says Mr Williams. 'It helps us gauge the effectiveness with which we manage the risks associated with those activities.'

■ *Risk management reports*. An 'RMR' is prepared for each key activity. These reports document objectives, consequences if the objectives are not met, a consequence rating, existing risk management processes, assessments of the processes and an overall assessment of whether the objectives are achieved.

■ *Risk issue reports*. Risk issues and their consequence ratings are recorded in the same database as RMRs along with the respective action plans developed by management.

■ *Audit reviews, assessment and testing*. Internal Audit independently assesses the information in the RACs, RMRs and RIRs.

Reliable systems are the foundation of an effective infrastructure.

Continued ...

This framework and its accompanying databases were successfully piloted in the group's Hong Kong operations in the summer of 1999. Prior to the merger with Hanson plc, the intent was to implement the approach throughout the rest of the organization. Whether or not that will happen remains to be seen, but the lesson remains. As Mr Williams explains, 'It was worth the time and effort because now we have an approach that fits our culture because it is written in management's language.'

SUMMARY

The preceding chapter built on Chapters 3, 4 and 5 to show how to put flesh on the bones of a skeletal BRMP. It has emphasized the importance of developing appropriate capabilities for managing specific business risks. It has outlined the linkage of the components of the infrastructure flowing from strategies and policies through processes, people, management reports and methodologies all the way to needed systems and data. It has illustrated the essentials of monitoring risk and the performance of risk management capabilities and creating an environment for continuous improvement. In Chapter 7, we will further address the need for continuously improving risk management capabilities and the means by which that task is accomplished.

Diageo plc: laying the foundation to integrate risk management with enterprise performance

- Risk mapping as a springboard for focused risk management
- Integrating risk management with key performance indicators (KPIs)
- Aggregation: the next step to an enterprise-wide risk strategy

Pillsbury, Burger King, United Distillers & Vintners, Guinness – these are cornerstones of Diageo, the $30 billion food and beverage giant created by the merger of Grand Metropolitan and Guinness. A 'branded' organization, its stable includes 'The Whopper', the Pillsbury Doughboy, Haagen-Dazs, Guinness Stout, Harp Lager, Tanqueray Gin and Johnny Walker Scotch Whisky.

Diageo is also one of the pioneers of EWRM. The group recognizes that risk and opportunity are intertwined and takes a systematic approach to risk identification and management. With methodologies applied consistently across the organization, the group is in the best possible position to identify commonly held risks, apply best practices and ultimately, manage risks on an aggregate enterprise-wide basis.

STRATEGY FIRST

The primary tenet at Diageo is that risk management should be linked to strategy. Linkage is vital, says Diageo Finance Director Nick Rose, because for risk management to seem relevant to business units, it must add value. 'Very quickly you have to get the organization to realize that this is not something driven by finance or insurance, this is something business managers should want to take on and own – it's for their benefit.'

Diageo, therefore, has stressed the benefits of EWRM in terms of its divisions' ability to achieve their performance goals. 'We want to help you minimize the chances of being blown off course and, frankly, increase your chances of getting paid out in your compensation plans,' explains Mr Rose. 'We also have tools and people who can help. Why work tremendously hard only to see things wiped out by something that could have been foreseen and managed?'

Diageo's EWRM approach is elegant yet comprehensive. Strategy for each division is developed in conjunction with the parent. Using a five-year strategic plan as the baseline, each business unit constructs a risk map, all using a uniform

'Why work hard only to see things wiped out by something that could have been foreseen and managed?'

risk language and methodology. From here, the group refines KPIs (key performance indicators) designed to measure progress versus plan as well as, increasingly, to track and control performance relative to risks. As a final step, the group measures its risks on an enterprise-wide basis and is now poised to begin managing risks on an aggregated basis. That next step, says Mr Rose, 'is something we're looking into aggressively.'

RISK FOOTPRINTS

Risk is evaluated as uncertainties that the firm must manage.

The first leg of the programme is risk-mapping, and at Diageo this relates directly to performance goals. Each Diageo division develops a consolidated risk 'footprint' that indicates a risk is green (low risk – not a dire situation), amber (medium risk – pay attention) or red (high-risk – manage actively). The map in Figure C4.1 illustrates the concept (specific risk rankings and references have been removed for confidentiality).

Fig. C4.1 Guinness business risk profile

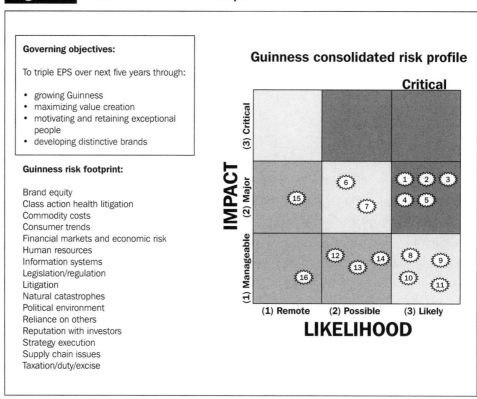

Governing objectives:

To triple EPS over next five years through:

- growing Guinness
- maximizing value creation
- motivating and retaining exceptional people
- developing distinctive brands

Guinness risk footprint:

Brand equity
Class action health litigation
Commodity costs
Consumer trends
Financial markets and economic risk
Human resources
Information systems
Legislation/regulation
Litigation
Natural catastrophes
Political environment
Reliance on others
Reputation with investors
Strategy execution
Supply chain issues
Taxation/duty/excise

Guinness consolidated risk profile

This 'traffic light' analogy is already familiar to operating managers. The risk map in Figure C4.1 assesses impact on specific business objectives. Risk is evaluated as uncertainties that the firm must manage as it grows, creates value, manages its people and develops its brands. As Mr Rose explains, 'it's the same system we use for highlighting KPI performance – are we on track, falling behind or in the red?' (see box below).

Each division develops its own assessment of its risks, which are reported to the group. At the group level, Mr Rose and his team consolidate the risk footprints looking for synergies and possible oversights. Here, consistency is vital. 'One of the things we are doing as these arrive is compare them across businesses,' explains Mr Rose. In some cases, for example, a particular risk might arise in three divisions' risk maps but not in the fourth. When that happens, 'We ask, "is that logical or did something slip through the cracks?"' says Mr Rose. 'Right from the start, we've been keen to ensure consistency in both processes and output – so whether it's from Pillsbury, UDV, Guinness or Burger King, all the footprints are developed and look the same.'

It is also vital to ask division managers to expose their gross risk impacts and likelihoods. Explains Mr Rose, 'We found the potential if not tendency for business managers to say "well yes, that is a risk, but we've already got techniques in place to manage it, so its likelihood of occurrence and its potential impact on the business are negligible."' The problem with this approach is that risks are not recorded, senior management may be unaware the risk exists at all, and opportunities for knowledge sharing (for example, the sharing of risk management strategy and control best practices) and risk aggregation are obstructed. Moreover, explains Mr Rose, 'the mere fact that it is a significant gross risk means it requires a management response. So our position is that the board needs to know about gross risks so they can be in a position to ensure the appropriate management of that risk is in place.' The bottom line is that, because the net risk never makes management's screen, a net approach may result in failure to allocate the capital and resources needed to maintain the critical processes and controls that keep a 'high gross' risk at a 'low net' risk position on the risk map.

PEELING THE ONION

As risk assessment drills deeper into the organization, greater detail emerges. As Ray Joy, Finance Director of Diageo affiliate Guinness explains, 'The whole thing cascades; you peel back more layers of the onion to reveal more focused risk footprints and KPIs.' For example, the overall Guinness risk map shows 'supply chain issues' as an important risk (see Figure C4.1). However, a Guinness brewery in Dublin might further dissect 'supply chain risk', perhaps detailing 'total delivered economic costs' into sub-categories of labour, raw materials and engineering. 'Whatever is driving the risk at that level would show up on their risk footprint and they would develop appropriate KPIs and establish targets,'

The linkage between strategy, risk maps and KPIs is essential.

explains Mr Joy. In this way, the risk footprinting is a way of helping the businesses recognize what is important and what can go wrong, and in conjunction with KPIs gives them a tool for managing their operations.

The linkage between strategy, risk maps and KPIs is essential. 'None of this means anything unless it is translated from a table-top exercise into specific, measurable action,' says Mr Joy. The fact that senior management is behind the programme and that performance is actively tracked 'makes this a very tangible part of our business lives'. Moreover, says Mr Joy, 'it also helps that this just happens to be the most effective way I know of planning and managing a successful business.'

KPIs, not budgets

Diageo is minimizing its use of traditional budgeting. In its place, says Finance Director Nick Rose, a focus on key performance indicators 'provides a superior basis for managing a set of businesses.' While a relatively uniform set of KPI figures are tracked by the board and senior management for each division, additional, more focused subsets are developed to meet the needs of specific business managers.

Budget if you wish...

KPIs have replaced traditional budgeting at all Diageo affiliates. Budgeting 'is a thing of the past,' says Guinness's Ray Joy. Instead of a formal budgeting process, the company develops five-year plans 'with detailed first years' explains Mr Joy. 'The basic budget falls out of that.' The point is, 'We've scaled back the detail and rigour and the wasted resources of the classic budgeting process,' explains Mr Joy. 'We can focus – and senior management can focus – on our larger objectives and risks rather than on detailed breakouts.'

Meanwhile, operating divisions are free to pursue more detailed budgeting as needed. As Mr Joy explains, 'If the businesses say, "that's fine, but I still need to control my advertising and promotional investment with an annual grand plan", that becomes their choice as opposed to a mandate from finance.'

...But KPI you must

Instead of budgets, managers at Diageo rely on sets of KPIs known as 'KPI packs'. 'Those big dials let us know what is and isn't working in the business – it's much more effective than managing via big books of numbers,' says Mr Joy. Risk maps and KPIs are developed with the five-year strategic plan firmly in mind. Moreover, KPIs are more or less detailed depending on where they are used in the business. Finally, 'KPIs are being developed to manage specifically in the context of the risk footprints,' says Mr Joy. 'It's all about

Continued ...

getting the right quality product at the right customer service level at the lowest possible economic cost. We create KPIs, a balanced scorecard if you will, to make sure we get that balance right. The risk footprints enable us to focus on the key means of measuring and managing our effectiveness.'

CALL IT EWRM

Is Diageo practising EWRM? 'I can't think of a better term for it,' says Mr Rose. The company already uses a common risk language and deploys uniform processes. Similarly, the company seeks continual improvement in its programme. 'We are always looking for refinements,' he explains.

In the next phase, Diageo is looking for ways to aggregate its risks. 'That's a natural next step,' says Mr Rose. Right now the company has a 'significant project underway to look at how to aggregate all forms of risk: financial, interest rate, foreign exchange, traditional catastrophe/insurable risk, or broader-based business risks in the footprint,' says Mr Rose. No market action has yet been taken, 'but we believe that eventually all of these risks can be managed, at lower cost, under a sort of umbrella. The steps we are taking we hope will lead to a broader enterprise-wide risk strategy.'

The above practices have been evolving at Diageo and at Guinness for some time. But it has only been the past 18 months where the company has deployed resources to formalize the programme. So far, the results are exceptional, says Mr Rose. 'We feel all the business units, and Diageo itself, are much the better for it,' he explains. 'Risk is a big part of daily business life. Anybody that doesn't understand the broader business risks around their business and isn't doing something to manage risk proactively, holistically – even opportunistically – frankly, they're not using good commercial judgment and practice.'

The company is undertaking a 'significant project to look at how to aggregate all forms of risk'.

7

Continuously improve risk strategies, processes and measures

The man who makes no mistake does not usually make anything.

William Connor Magee, Irish orator

If you rest on your laurels, they become a funeral arrangement.

Chris Wasden, Managing Director, Azurix

So far we have introduced a common language and a uniform process. Together with a risk management infrastructure, which comprises the firm's risk management capabilities, these lay a foundation for improving risk strategies, processes and measures. But we need something more to focus on, identify and stage the appropriate improvements over time. That is why a focused approach to continuous improvement is of paramount importance.

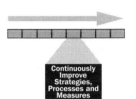

Continuously Improve Strategies, Processes and Measures

The business risk management process (BRMP), competently executed, is a systematic approach to building and improving risk management capabilities and is a catalyst for continuous improvement. But the desired risk management capabilities must be explicitly – and given finite resources, selectively – pursued.

Management faces two challenges in sustaining a dynamic mindset of continuous learning and renewal in its risk management:

1. *Define the target for initial efforts.* Just how capable do we want our risk management to be as we improve our strategies, processes and measures for each of our priority risks? Do we vary our risk management capabilities by risk? Do we rely on a few well-qualified individuals to regularly put out fires? Are our risks prioritized, our processes well-documented and our staffs cross-trained? Is our most relevant management information flowing smoothly into the hands of appropriate decision-makers and action-takers? There are conscious choices to be made here. To aid the process, we will introduce a tool – the Risk Management Capability Maturity Continuum.

2. *Stimulate continuous improvement after we have hit the target.* Once we have determined the desired capabilities for managing a particular risk and attained those capabilities, is the game over? No, it has only begun. For this to work, risk management must be embraced by the organization. As Nick Chown of the British Post Office explains, 'You can't have business unit managers thinking "thank God, the risk managers are here, so we can relax now and get back to our real jobs."' Risk management needs to become a recognized source of value that is owned by the businesses. Says Mr Chown, 'this is an iterative process – not a one-off exercise – with the organization learning at every stage.'

In this regard, we will discuss the three enablers introduced in Chapter 6 – (1) benchmarking performance and standards to identify best practices, (2) four-way interactive communications and knowledge sharing, and (3) employee learning – that facilitate the improvement process.

THE RISK MANAGEMENT CAPABILITY MATURITY CONTINUUM

It is not about adopting the most sophisticated tools, 'it is about choosing the most appropriate tools'.

Risk management capabilities are the qualities acquired or developed to systematically identify, source, measure, manage and monitor business risks. They address the priority risks that are inherent in the firm's business model. Continuous improvement of risk strategies, processes and measures is about enhancing risk management capabilities. In other words, given our risk management strategies, what capabilities are really needed in terms of processes, people, technology and knowledge? It is not about adopting the most sophisticated tools available, 'it is about choosing the most appropriate tools,' says Chris Valentine of Cable & Wireless.

Yes, most managers would agree that it is unnecessary to deploy the most advanced techniques for all risks. After all, no firm has the resources to do that, nor is there a viable business reason to do so.

The Risk Management Capability Maturity Continuum provides an effective framework for discerning present and desired capabilities.

For each type of individual risk or aggregate group of related risks, management must evaluate the current state of the firm's risk management capabilities. From there, management must make a conscious decision: how much added capability do we need to achieve our risk management objectives? Further, what are the expected costs and benefits of increasing our capabilities? The goal is to identify the firm's most pressing exposures and uncertainties and to focus improvement activities on the capabilities required to manage those exposures and uncertainties.

But to achieve that goal, we need a tool to help us think clearly about the problem of matching the firm's capabilities with its desired risk management solutions and vice versa. The Risk Management Capability Maturity Continuum illustrated in Figure 7.1 is adapted from Watts S. Humphrey's vision of software process maturity.[1] Applied successfully to software, we have found that this tool also provides an effective framework for discerning present risk management capabilities and targeting desired capabilities. The higher up this continuum a firm's capabilities, the greater its prospects for successfully managing business risk. Conversely, the lower its risk of failure.

To explain the application of this tool to risk management, the five 'states' along the continuum are listed in Table 6.1, starting at the bottom and working up.

---

1. Watts S. Humphrey (1994) *The Capability Maturity Model: Guidelines for Improving the Software Process*. Carnegie Mellon University Software Engineering Institute.

Fig. 7.1 Risk Management Capability Maturity Continuum

	Continuum	Capability attributes	Method of achievement
Process evolution ↑	**Optimizing**	(Continuous feedback) Risk management a source of competitive advantage	• EW strategy – emphasis on taking and exploiting risk • World-class processes • Knowledge accumulated and shared
	Managed	(Quantitative) Risks measured/managed quantitatively and aggregated enterprise-wide	• Rigorous measurement methodologies/analysis • Intensive debate on risk/ reward trade-off issues
	Defined	(Qualitative/quantitative) Policies, process and standards defined and institutionalized	• Process uniformly applied across the firm • Remaining components of infrastructure • Rigorous methodologies
	Repeatable	(Intuitive) Process established and repeating; reliance on people reduced	• Common language • Quality people assigned • Defined tasks • Initial infrastructure components
	Initial	(*Ad hoc*/chaotic) Dependent on heroics; institutional capability lacking	• Undefined tasks • Relies on initiative • 'Just do it' • Reliance on key people

Source: adapted from Carnegie Mellon University Capability Maturity Model

Table 6.1 Descriptions of states in the Risk Management Capability Maturity Continuum

Initial	• Capabilities are characteristic of individuals, not of the organization
	• Risk management process is characterized as *ad hoc*
	• Few processes are defined
	• Effectiveness depends on individual efforts and heroics
	• Success depends on exceptional and seasoned managers and cannot be repeated without the same competent individuals
	• When these individuals walk out the door and leave, so do the firm's capabilities
Repeatable	• Necessary process discipline exists to allow for repeat of past successes in similar situations
	• Basic risk management processes are established
	• Basic risk controls are installed
	• Resources are specifically allocated to risk management efforts
	• Guidelines on managing risks are established
Defined	• Risk management process is uniform across the company
	• Processes for both risk mitigation and risk oversight activities are documented and integrated

	• All groups use an approved, tailored version of the organization's defined risk management process
Managed	• Risks are managed quantitatively and aggregated at the corporate level
	• Risk exposures can be better anticipated through time-tested models
	• Aggregate risk limits are established and allocated to operating units
	• When pre-defined limits are exceeded, actions are taken to correct the situation
Optimizing	• Entire organization is focused on continuous improvement
	• Organized efforts are made to remove inefficiency; formal cost/benefit analysis is applied to all risk management practices
	• Best practices are identified and shared across the organization
	• Effect of diversification across multiple risk types is understood and exploited
	• Management employs effective change enablement processes
	• Risk strategy evaluated on an enterprise-wide basis to balance risk and rewards

Each firm must decide where on the continuum it wants to be with respect to *each* type of risk it intends to manage. What represents best practice in the context of a particular risk at one company may be insufficient or overdone in the context of the same risk at another company. For instance, value at risk (VaR) may represent best practice for a trading business where management desires a *managed state* of capability. For the same risk (such as currency risk) in another business, however, VaR may be more robust than necessary because the exposure is not significant enough to warrant its use.

The *desired state* of capability may also vary by risk. For purposes of managing certain mission-critical operating risks, such as nuclear power plant operations, management may desire the *optimizing state*. For certain hazard risks that warrant the purchase of insurance with very little internal process development, it may only require a *repeatable state*. For certain information technology risks, such as integrity and availability risks, a *defined state* may be considered adequate.

The point is that every risk does not require the same degree of capability to accomplish management's objectives. Managers can use the Capability Maturity Continuum by first plotting the 'current state' for each of the firm's key risks. Next, they plot the 'desired future state' and develop plans to close the gaps between the two states, as defined, over time. Where appropriate, the process of migrating toward the desired capabilities is incorporated into the business planning process. In essence, the firm makes conscious decisions 'risk by risk' as to how far along the EWRM journey it wants to go. For example, does management want to measure a particular risk quantitatively and aggregate risk measurements on an enterprise-wide basis? Does management want the entire enterprise focused on continuously improving its management of a particular risk? Will effective risk controls and monitoring get the job done?

The Capability Maturity Continuum illustrates how enhancing EWRM capabilities requires the adoption of new business practices over time through staged improvements (see Figure 7.2).

Fig. 7.2 Enhanced EWRM capabilities result from staged improvements over time

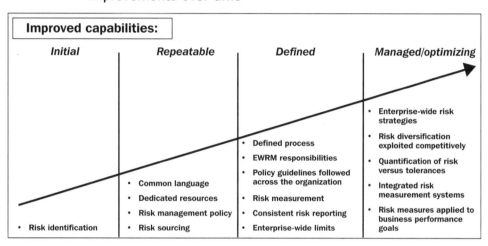

(Adapted from Watts S. Humphrey (1994) *The Capability Maturity Model: Guidelines for Improving the Software Process*. Carnegie Mellon University Software Engineering Institute.)

This idea of 'staged improvements' is very consistent with the journey metaphor on which this book is based. Implementing EWRM is not something that occurs overnight. The continuum illustrates the orderly progression necessary to improve risk management capabilities.

The benefits of EWRM also accumulate as risk management capabilities are enhanced, as illustrated in Figure 7.3.

Fig. 7.3 Benefits of EWRM accumulate as capabilities are enhanced

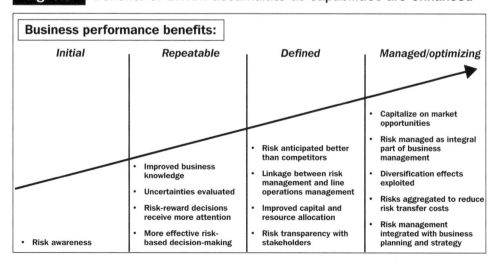

The Capability Maturity Continuum can also be applied to the six key components of risk management infrastructure introduced in Chapter 6. For example, a firm at the *initial state* of development may exhibit the attributes shown in Figure 7.4. Moving to the *repeatable state*, the company's risk management capabilities would be improved to reflect the enhanced attributes shown in Figure 7.5.

Fig. 7.4 Attributes of risk management capabilities at the *initial state*

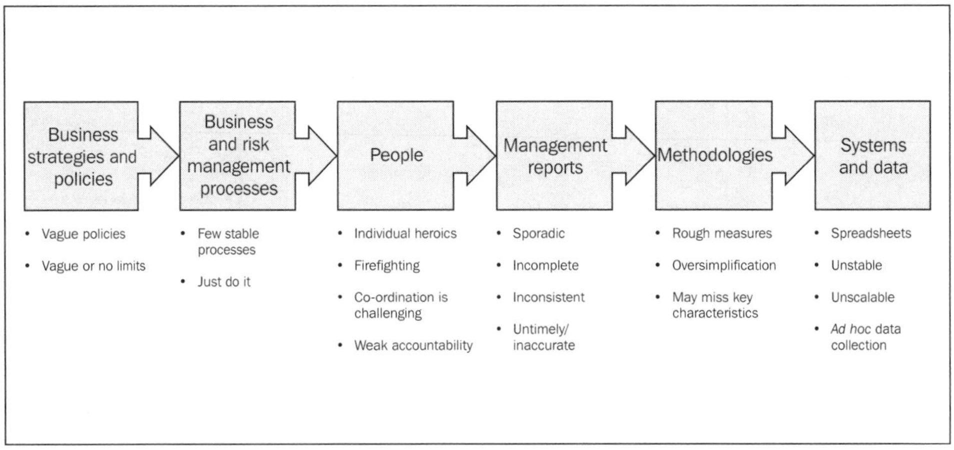

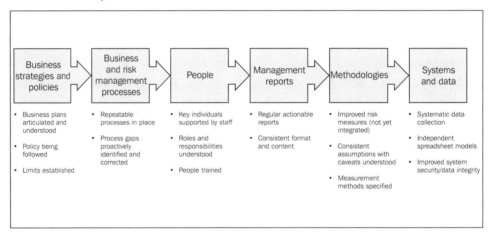

Fig. 7.5 Enhanced attributes of risk management capabilities at the *repeatable state*

The point is that each state on the continuum reflects further enhancements in attributes. Recognize: If your capabilities for managing a particular risk are at the *initial state* and you desire capabilities at the *defined state*, there are two ways you can close the gap. First, you can implement the improvements all at once. Alternatively, you can improve risk management in stages by first advancing your capabilities to the *repeatable state* and then onward to the *defined state*.

Our point of view is that the staged approach to the design and implementation of improved capabilities is preferable. Why? It is the more systematic of the two approaches from a change management standpoint and the one that is least disruptive to the organization. The deployment of capability maturity with managing software solutions has also proven that it increases the chances of a successful implementation.

Each successive stage for each type of risk describes a company's risk management capabilities in terms of its defining attributes. The consistent use of the Capability Maturity Continuum allows for a more focused definition of the current and desired states and promotes comparability and understanding across the organization. Moreover, it moves us away from the misguided notion that there is a single set of 'best practices' out there that apply to a given risk in any and all circumstances. While the collection of 'best practices' certainly augments the improvement process, it does not supplant the need for critical thinking when addressing the question, 'What are our desired capabilities?'

A staged approach is preferred.

When using this continuum, it is important to understand not only the *existence* but also the relative *stability* and *soundness* of risk management capabilities. Management should also be realistic when assessing desired capabilities. The objective is to configure the organization's risk management with its core competencies. Simply stated, the firm's capabilities must support its risk management goals and objectives. All told, the Capability Maturity Continuum coupled with the six components of infrastructure provide an overall framework for defining the appropriate level of risk management capabilities and the relative *sophistication* of these capabilities *for each priority risk*.

But what's the catalyst for making improvements? Continuous improvement is much more than a philosophy and mindset to seek a better way to accomplish a task. It is a process supported by clearly stated strategies and policies, well defined processes, experienced personnel, appropriate subject matter experts, effective reporting and monitoring, and relevant measurement methodologies. All of these infrastructure components provide a 'current state' baseline for managers to compare against the 'desired future state' to identify gaps.

When gaps arise in the risk management infrastructure and processes, action plans are developed to implement improvements and, for serious shortcomings and issues, bring the situation under control on a timely basis. Accountable risk and process owners then execute these risk plans in accordance with established timelines.

THE ENABLERS OF CONTINUOUS IMPROVEMENT

The Risk Management Capability Maturity Continuum can help establish targets and identify gaps that drive significant improvements in risk management. But what happens after the desired capabilities are achieved? Continuous improvement itself is an ongoing discipline driven by three enablers. We discuss them below.

Benchmarking

Benchmarking is a methodology that compares what a firm and its operating units do within a specific process such as risk management to what competitors or 'best of class' organizations do. This comparison is most effective when applied to superior performers, but EWRM also enables internal benchmarking between related business entities. As Calie Ehrke, Administrative Manager of Holderbank subsidiary Alpha Ltd, explains, 'one thing we really appreciate about this programme is that we are able to compare best practices and share knowledge [with affiliated companies]. That is already starting to pay off.'

Benchmarking contributes greater value if the firm's risk strategies and processes are well defined, risks are measured rigorously, risk management process performance is evaluated against management's risk tolerance or standard, and the most knowledgeable risk and process owners are involved in the exercise. Again, EWRM meets these requirements since it equips companies with precisely this sort of information and interaction. Still, depending on how it is defined and scoped, benchmarking can be a time-consuming and expensive process that should be focused primarily on critical areas.

In a well-implemented EWRM environment, risk owners will themselves be driven to improve the management of their assigned risks and will be capable of assessing the role and cost/benefit of benchmarking. But this does not abdicate senior management's role. 'The board and senior management still have to have a finger in setting the priorities and monitoring improvements,' says Mr Chown.

Once improvement opportunities have been identified, they are prioritized and progress is tracked against established timetables and periodic checkpoints. Audit activities (internal audits, risk compliance activities, external audits or regulatory audits) can provide assurances that improvements are being made timely. However, it is up to management to take the initiative to act on the results of continuous improvement activities, hold the appropriate personnel accountable for followup and monitor the actions taken. Benchmarking data should therefore be communicated to all appropriate process/activity owners and risk owners.

Four-way interactive communication and knowledge sharing

We have indicated throughout this book that a continuous transfer and exchange of information about risk up, down and across the enterprise is a vital enabler of EWRM. This information provides insights as to the existence, nature, significance, likelihood, acceptability and manageability of risk as well as the firm's risk strategies, measurement methodologies and processes for managing risk. It also fosters the sharing of best practices. The previous chapter focused on how *technology* enables this process. In this chapter, we discuss the interaction of *people*.

Top down communication is an integral part of four-way communication. All stakeholders in the BRMP, e.g. the board, senior management, risk management owners and business process owners, must be able to freely communicate about business risk issues. Executive management's top-down communications emphasize strategic direction ('Where are we going?'), overall organization performance ('How are we doing?'), employees' risk management responsibilities ('How do you fit in?') and the purpose of risk management.

Top-down communications include formal and informal processes. They work best in an environment supported by a framework that includes many of the following:

- a common risk language;
- a small, balanced family of measures (the 'balanced scorecard') that addresses cost, quality, time *and risk* across the organization, its processes and its people;
- performance goals supporting continuous improvement and stimulating innovation;
- frequent communication of goals, results of monitoring risks and performance measures, reports on the firm's progress and periodic employee feedback; and
- the use of appropriate media to communicate strategic direction, overall organization performance and employee duties and responsibilities, e.g. intranet websites, group-wide meetings, workshops, training, bulletins, quality circles, cross-functional teams and real-time supervision.

Upward communication is also important. Management should provide employees with a process for communicating information upward regarding what is happening in the external environment and internally within the business. For example, information received from managers and employees about competitors, markets, customers, suppliers and channels should be considered as input to the strategic management and business planning processes. In addition, employees should have clear reporting lines to communicate risk management recommendations, issues and concerns to someone other than a direct superior *without fear of retribution*. The process protects anonymity, if that is desired by the employee, and provides recognition for contributions resulting in process improvements.

This communications channel is vital because without it, senior managers lose touch with reality. There mustn't be any hesitancy on the part of managers and employees to report risk incidents or the threat of a risk incident. A 'shoot the messenger' culture defeats this process.

Finally, management facilitates *horizontal communication* across operating units and divisions, functions and departments. To illustrate, sales personnel communicate customer requirements to design engineering, manufacturing engineering, production and marketing. The process ensures that reported issues concerning products, services or other matters are addressed on a timely basis. For example, customer service personnel process customer complaints, and the appropriate managers and process/activity owners are made aware of the nature of the reported concerns so that actions can be taken to correct the problem. Cross-functional communications ensure that engineering, production, sales and other personnel understand the problems reported, and form cross-functional teams to determine their root causes and identify opportunities for improving products and processes.

Effective four-way communications and knowledge sharing, as illustrated in Figure 7.6, identifies conditions that must be acted upon. It is a powerful catalyst for stimulating continuous improvement. Senior management is responsible for establishing the environment that facilitates four-way communications. Once that environment is in place, it is the responsibility of all managers and employees to participate.

Fig. 7.6 Four-way interactive communications and knowledge sharing

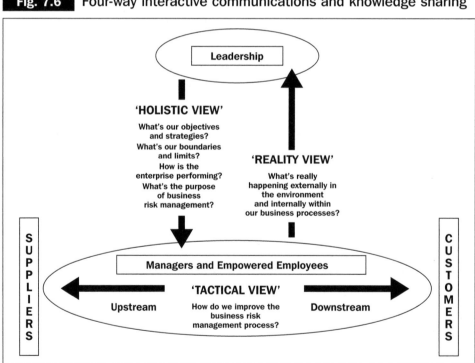

Employee learning

The journey to EWRM is a change process that is supported by organizational and individual learning. A continuous learning attitude and process helps all employees embrace and understand the firm's common language and uniform processes. In this regard, MarineMax includes risk management training in its

MarineMax University. Meanwhile, Enron conducts regular training sessions related to its rigorous risk assessment processes. Companies pursuing EWRM consider knowledge sharing, education and training vital to their efforts.

Effective employee learning assists operating unit managers as well as risk and process owners in many ways. For example, it helps them build awareness of the company's risk management vision, strategy, policies and processes, as well as gain an understanding of the information systems that support the execution of each of those components. It also contributes to (but alone cannot achieve) buy-in and ownership.

Employee learning should emphasize the following areas:

- company business risk management strategies and policies;
- the company's business risk language and risk assessment framework – and the supporting rationale (focusing on the need for application and buy-in);
- key self-assessment processes and how they can be integrated with day-to-day business activities;
- effective use of the risk measurement methodologies selected by the firm;
- the components of risk management infrastructure and their use in building and improving risk management capabilities;
- participation in established communication channels to enable the flow of risk information within the enterprise; and
- the firm's commitment to continuous improvement and what it means to the firm's risk management and to the individual employee.

SUMMARY

Implementing a common language and a business risk management process is not enough. Management must determine the capabilities needed to achieve the firm's vision of the desired future state of EWRM for each of the key risks and systematically build and improve those capabilities through staged improvements in risk strategies, processes and measures over time. The Risk Management Capability Maturity Continuum introduced in this chapter is a useful tool for this purpose.

The firm must also commit to improving continuously its risk strategies, processes and measures. There are three enablers of the continuous improvement process, and this chapter has briefly discussed each of them.

For those risks and groups of related risks for which management decides to develop capabilities along the lines of either the *managed state* or *optimizing state*, further steps can be taken along the journey to EWRM – aggregate risk measures, link to business performance and formulate an enterprise-wide risk management strategy. This is the focus of our next chapter.

Enron: the leading edge in EWRM

Nowhere in the research for this book did we encounter an industrial organization further along in the journey towards EWRM than Enron. For example:

- Enron requires its business units to adopt uniform processes for the identification and management of risks.

- Its energy trading operations, though vast, are conducted within an environment and culture featuring stringent and sophisticated controls.

- Enron aggregates and redistributes its business, financial and energy risks to those units most competent in a given risk area through a process it refers to as 'syndication'.

- The company uses an internal 'underwriting' team to work with business managers to fully evaluate and understand the risks of new projects.

- Capital allocations require full board approval and are evaluated based on probabilistic RAROC (risk adjusted return on capital) analyses.

- The company evaluates new investments both on a discrete and an enterprise-wide portfolio impact basis.

- Once capital is allocated, investments are continually re-evaluated against projected performance.

- All risk processes exist in an environment of continuous feedback and improvement.

- The Enron board is fully-briefed on the group's risks, and consequently, the company is able to move quickly on opportunities that would be cause for trepidation in less sophisticated organizations.

> Enron evaluates new investments both on a discrete and an enterprise-wide portfolio impact basis.

Two of the key players in Enron's EWRM odyssey are Richard Causey and Richard Buy. Richard Causey, EVP and Chief Accounting Officer, leads the group responsible for all accounting activities across the company – including analysis of capital allocation and investments. The role also includes all back office activity relating to the group's extensive trading operations, as well as oversight for internal control audits, which are largely outsourced.

Richard Buy is EVP and Chief Risk Officer and his group is responsible for continual review of all risks being taken on by the company. Credit and market risks are a big piece of this job – again owing to Enron's trading operations – but no less important is the focus on the analysis of risk relating to new investments and business ventures. It is a true co-ordinated effort by which Messrs Buy and Causey and their respective teams lead Enron's deployment of EWRM.

Enron begins its dissection of risks by breaking things down to three broad categories: market risk, credit risk and operating risk. Because this report focuses on EWRM for industrial companies, this case will give less emphasis to the management of trading risks (market and credit), and devote the most attention to the analysis of new investments. Of course, investment analysis and capital allocation are only a piece of the operating risk equation. But as Mr Causey explains:

> *Out of necessity, we're leaving out an awful lot of things relating to operations – in particular the controls we have in place. Recognize, if those controls weren't there, then the information coming out of the businesses isn't complete or accurate and you could throw this whole EWRM concept out the window. Good controls and an integrated audit function: those are the conditions precedent for EWRM.*

'We take risks to generate profit, but we never bet the farm.'

MARKET AND CREDIT RISKS

Owing to Enron's vast trading operations, the management of market and credit risks are high on the company's list of priorities. Trading operations are essential to the group. Not only are they a means of distributing the electricity and natural gas produced by the company, but sophisticated trading techniques also generate significant profit in and of themselves.

The group utilizes a full raft of controls similar to those associated with financial instrument trading, e.g. authorization to trade specific commodities, segregation of duties, trading limits and notification of limits violations. Energy markets are even more complex. Along with the issues associated with factors such as yield curves, duration and demand shifts, imagine a highly volatile commodity that cannot be stored (electricity), trades on a regional basis and where physical delivery takes place in the next 30 minutes. Consequently, in addition to stringent controls, Enron relies a great deal on the expertise and professionalism of its traders.

'The culture here,' says Rick Buy, 'is that if you take a trading risk and don't let us know about it beforehand, or if you willfully violate policies, even if you make money, you're fired.' Mr Causey and Mr Buy are confident that their controls and culture obviate the potential for a breakdown comparable to other headlines in financial and energy trading. 'We take risks to generate profit,' says Mr Buy, 'but we never bet the farm.'

The group also manages a sophisticated model for credit risk. 'There will be losses stemming from counterparties failing to perform from time to time as opposed to market risk,' says Mr Buy. Consequently, 'we have developed pricing methodologies to assess these risks, and at all times we hold capital in reserve to account for that.' All told, 'we feel we have a very good handle on what it takes to run a world-class trading operation,' says Mr Buy.

STRUCTURED TRANSACTIONS

An important part of Enron's EWRM programme is what the company refers to as the analysis and management of 'structured transactions'. These transactions take place on both the trading side of Enron and in its operations. In fact, because of the nature of the industry, just about any investment in plant and equipment, e.g. a generating facility, will be accompanied by a pricing contract or at least, will require additional capital for the management of that asset's pricing risks.

A structured transaction might involve the evaluation of a derivative or derivative-like transaction undertaken to reduce risk – or in some cases increase exposure to a given risk dimension – in some part of the business. For example, the company recently evaluated and executed a credit derivative designed to reduce exposure to a major European customer. Alternatively, a structured transaction might be a contract – complex or otherwise – between Enron and another buyer or seller of energy or gas. An example might be a long-term electricity supply contract in the Philippines featuring various pricing for various levels of demand. In Enron parlance, 'anything that requires our capital and that is not an ISDA [International Swap Dealer's Association] standard derivative deal is a "structured transaction",' explains Mr Buy.

> 'If it takes our capital to get it done, we are going to look at it closely to understand why it's being done.'

While trading is a significant activity for the company, 'at the end of the day, we're still an industrial company,' says Mr Causey. Consequently, a high volume of the structured transactions reviewed by Mr Buy and Mr Causey are investments in new enterprises, for example, plant and equipment. This could be a merchant power plant in the US or an investment in a Brazilian utility or the purchase of gas turbine generation equipment. In both cases, the capital needed to undertake the investment would have to include trading reserves for managing the energy or other financial risks associated with the investment. The bottom line: the review of structured transactions is a classic capital allocation situation. Says Mr Buy, 'if it takes our capital to get it done, we are going to look at it closely to understand why it's being done.'

There are two major components of the structured transaction review process. The first one the company refers to as 'underwriting'. Underwriting is a critical review of the actual assumptions, risks, terms and structure of the deal – and is a highly evolved practice at Enron. The second, closely related activity is the analytical review. This features the use of RAROC, VaR (value at risk) along with a rigorous probabilistic analysis of both the individual transaction and its effect on Enron overall. 'We review how good it can get, we review how bad it can get, and every place in between,' says Mr Causey. 'This is where my team and Rick [Causey]'s team work together very closely,' explains Mr Buy.

Underwriting

Enron runs its internal structured transaction approval process in a manner that would be envied by any investment bank or venture capital firm. Any significant allocation of Enron capital undergoes its 'underwriting' process. Internal underwriters work with the business unit managers to develop proposals for the use of company capital. The work follows a uniform set of processes designed to unveil both the risk and value potential of any proposed investment. The outcome of this rigorous process is a 'DASH' or Deal Approval Sheet. As Mr Buy explains, 'every deal that gets approved has a DASH that has been reviewed, approved and signed by the board.' Adds Mr Causey, 'without a DASH, signed and in our hands, they will not get any funding.'

'We review how good it can get, we review how bad it can get, and every place in between.'

The DASH is a two to three page document detailing the expected and required returns from an investment. Alongside these fixed information points, the DASH also provides a set of probabilistic analyses showing how the transaction might fare under various scenarios (see RAROC below). Noteworthy, beyond the hard and fast statistical and financial analyses, the DASH also includes a thorough, intense qualitative discussion of 'the assumptions behind the numbers', explains Mr Causey. 'What are the ten or so key variables that could make this deal work or not work?' In other words, for every new allocation of capital, the company executes a thorough mapping of the accompanying risks.

The value, says Mr Buy, is not so much in the output as it is 'in the level of critical analysis' that goes into the output. 'This is very different from having a business manager come in and say "here's my deal, now let me drive the discussion, and by the way, we're not going to touch on any of the five risky things I'm hoping the rest of you won't bring up",' he explains. Mr Buy adds:

We succeed – and the DASH becomes an effective tool – when people are in a room, sitting down, thinking and arguing not about their hurdle rate but about the things that could make this deal a grand slam or a flop. Here is the opportunity, here are the risks – they've been identified – here they've been modelled, here is how they impact the rest of the company, and here we are discussing the result, critically.

DASHs are required for all structured transactions. The approval process is tiered, requiring higher levels of review and authorization contingent on the amount of capital needed. The largest transactions require full board approval. The process not only helps business managers focus more clearly on the risks of their proposed actions, it also empowers the board to make informed decisions about risks and strategies. 'Senior management has got to know what risks are out there,' says Mr Buy. Adds Mr Causey, 'they need to be able to make an informed, conscious decision.'

The irony of the above risk assessment process is that the company is not at all risk averse. To the contrary, 'we're one of the bigger risk takers in our industry if not the world,' says Mr Buy. Mr Buy and Mr Causey believe this risk-taking culture goes back to the early days of Enron when Jeffrey Skilling, now President and COO, was given capital to start a new business for the company. 'I think Mr Skilling has a deep respect for risk-takers,' says Mr Causey. But even so, when Enron takes risks today, 'We do it with knowledge: knowledge of each business; knowledge of risk; knowledge of the enterprise,' explains Mr Buy. 'A rattlesnake may bite us every now and again, but we knew it was there and how much it might hurt.'

> The underwriters 'certify that these are the risks associated with this project'.

The risk underwriters

The DASH process is complex. But it is not an attempt to throw roadblocks in the way of risk-taking. Rather, it is a means of focusing the company's resources on the need to understand the risks being taken and to balance risk with value creation – and thereby make superior business decisions.

Internal consultants...

Facilitating the DASH process is a team of skilled internal consultants known as 'underwriters'. Their brief is twofold. First and foremost, it is their job to become intimately familiar with any proposed use of the firm's capital and to distill this information into a structured analysis that is reliable and meaningful to decision-makers on the board. The underwriters collect information relating to any investment as well as execute the detailed and probabilistic financial and economic analyses that ultimately populate the DASH.

Second, it is the underwriters' task to assist business managers with the process. 'You could call them hand holders,' explains Mr Buy. But it is much more than that. The underwriters work with the business managers to facilitate the identification and evaluation of all of the risks and business assumptions associated with an investment. Ultimately, when the DASH is presented to the board, these internal consultants have 'underwritten' the risk of the project. As Mr Buy explains, 'they're putting their name up there alongside the business manager. They're saying, "I certify that these are the risks associated with this project".'

Continued ...

Beyond identifying risks, the underwriters also help business managers develop risk mitigation and management strategies. For example, as risks are identified, the underwriters work with other business managers in the group to help 'syndicate' the risks associated with a project. To illustrate, the underwriting group would consult with a trading group on the pricing risk associated with an investment in power generation, and their agreement resulting from that consultation becomes part of the DASH.

...representing the board

The underwriters are there to represent the board's need to understand the risk and value-creation potential of any project. At the same time, they facilitate the process making it clearer for business managers. One way this is accomplished is through regular 'roadshows' designed to further clarify the need for and workings of the process. 'Managers who embrace this process are going to succeed,' explains Mr Buy. Like any growth organization, Enron is constrained by available capital and personnel. 'But we are always trying to send the message: if you have a good deal, we'll find the capital.'

Underwriters have become so valued that they are now continually recruited to join business units. But this is great for Enron. 'All of this becomes institutionalized,' says Mr Causey. 'It moves people from headquarters out to the wheels. It becomes a very effective way of improving risk assessment capability at the operating level.'

> 'We are always trying to send the message: if you have a good deal, we'll find the capital.'

Analytic review

Analysis is an essential component of underwriting the DASH process. All structured transactions are reviewed rigorously in order to determine how they will fare under a range of scenarios. Projects are also analyzed in terms of their impact on the company overall.

Here, Enron has developed its own quantitative methods for translating the risks of any investment into a specific capital equivalent. In other words, for any investment evaluation – for any DASH – the amount of capital allocated is not the actual cash 'out the door' but rather the full amount of capital considered 'at risk'. With capital as the driver, 'our formula translates positional risks into equivalent capital risks and we approve them as though they were a capital deal through the normal transaction approval policy,' explains Mr Causey.

For example, a typical fuel supply agreement could include the offer of fixed prices, a handful of accompanying derivatives to manage those risks, credit risk, market risk as well as additional capital perhaps in the form of fuel storage tanks.

Here, Enron uses a RAROC (risk adjusted return on capital) process to look at each piece of the transaction. This includes the VaR (value at risk) associated with the derivatives, the credit risk, the actual capital employed and all related risks. The analysis then assigns weightings and examines covariances in a probabilistic model (see box below).

Together, these analytical processes create Enron's view of the actual capital needed to execute the transaction on a risk-adjusted basis. 'We are not just adding all of the risks together,' explains Mr Buy. 'We are creating a probabilistic view of how much capital is actually necessary. That is our risk adjusted capital, and we treat it just as though it was cash going out the door.'

In addition to the probabilistic analysis, underwriters working for Mr Buy also generate an analysis of what 'the market' would want to see in terms of a return on the transaction. 'We do an independent assessment of what the return would be if we had to lay the position off in the market in an orderly manner – not a fire sale but not over a five-year horizon either,' explains Mr Buy. 'We then compare those two returns, the probabilistic and the market rate, to evaluate our final numbers.'

The outcome of the above analyses is then presented alongside the qualitative discussions of risk. Together, these qualitative and quantitative analyses make up the DASH, ultimately presented to Enron's board for approval.

In addition to DASHs relating to project proposals, the Enron board also conducts quarterly reviews of the overall business amounting to a true enterprise-wide examination of the risks, opportunities and performance of the company. All of the above processes serve two purposes. One, they provoke operating managers to think more emphatically in terms of both value creation and risk. Two, they provide the Enron board with clear statements of the risk and return inherent in the company's trading and business operations. In short, they provide the board and operating management with accurate and focused yet holistic information to make informed choices.

> 'We are not just adding all of the risks together, we are creating a probabilistic view of how much capital is actually necessary.'

Investment analysis: the Enron processes

Before a deal is brought to the board's attention, Enron's 'underwriters' have helped the proposing business unit address a battery of rigorous analyses. First, the company looks at risks – delineated in any project's Deal Approval Sheet (DASH) – via RAROC, VaR and probabilistic analysis. Second, the company takes an EWRM view, and looks at the impact of the investment on the enterprise as a whole.

Probabilistic modelling

One set of analyses is referred to as probabilistic. Companies often boil down their investment analyses to a single NPV (net present value) number. But this

Continued ...

---

does not take into account the interactions of the variables and underlying assumptions. In a probabilistic analysis, values for key assumptions are treated as a range and not as a fixed forecast. Then the analysis is executed as many as 1,000 times using random values within the variable parameters to generate a range of potential returns.

Enron uses RAROC and VaR measures to develop values for its risks then plugs everything into its own algorithms, partially enabled by a commercial programme called Crystal Ball. As for the range of probability assumptions, 'common sense is as good a tool as any,' says Mr Buy. For example, an operating company might say they can cut costs by 20 per cent or increase revenues 50 per cent as a result of a proposed investment. 'Could it happen? Sure, but is it realistic?' explains Mr Buy. So the analysis would instead use a range of outcomes giving the full 50 per cent revenue increase only a small probability.

With probabilities and values established, Crystal Ball helps the company generate hundreds of random iterations. One great thing about so many iterations, says Mr Causey, is that 'if something has a chance of blowing up, it probably will, and we'll get to see what blew it up.' While the process seems relatively straightforward, in practice, there are many challenges. For example, asks Mr Buy, 'What do you do when you're simulating a company's performance and you hit a scenario where it defaults? Do you shut it down? Do you intervene? Take any highly leveraged transaction – and even some not so highly leveraged – they blow up frequently and you have to have scenarios for that.'

Enterprise-wide modelling

Beyond the discrete impact of an investment, the company looks at the impact on Enron overall. 'Working with Mr Causey's group, we look at the impact of this transaction on the overall picture in terms of consolidated cash flow and earnings,' explains Mr Buy. 'How does it fit? How does it fit the budget for the year or for the next few years? We never look at anything in a vacuum.'

The impact on the company overall, or the impact on an individual business unit, are important considerations. The company will approve a 'marginal deal,' something that might not be approved on a stand-alone basis, in a variety of situations. For example, 'we've built power plants that on their own are questionable but overall they offset a short in the system somewhere,' explains Mr Buy.

Alternatively, a project may fit in with a broader business strategy. 'Business managers sometimes yank the "strategic" cord,' explains Mr Causey. 'They make the strategic assertion: it's a below market deal, on its own it's just a slab of stone on the ground, but overall it's a foundation for a larger business.'

Continued ...

Such deals do get approved, but the business unit managers have to recognize that they will be held accountable for the long-term success of the strategy. 'The board has a long memory,' explains Mr Causey. 'If all we ever see are these "foundation deals", the funding well can run dry.'

What gets done?

In the end, deals that have a higher than market return don't always get done, and deals that have a lower than market return certainly are not automatically rejected. 'We don't run the business entirely by the numbers,' explains Mr Buy. 'It's not paralysis by analysis, it's just informed decision-making and rational bet placement.'

'It's not paralysis by analysis, it's just informed decision-making and rational bet placement.'

In the end, Enron's portfolio represents risky business. 'We do take risks,' explains Mr Buy. He adds:

The power business is a very volatile business – some of these investments are very risky, and we could lose money. But our models are very robust, we know what our risks are, and we know the worst-case scenarios. We take risks, but we manage them actively and with our eyes open. That's why we've been so successful.

THE FUTURE

Although Enron is well ahead of the pack on EWRM, the company is not content. Mr Buy and Mr Causey believe that continuous improvement must be an objective for the risk management processes. For example, one area where work is needed is in VaR. Right now 'we have to look at various pockets of risk and pull things together manually,' explains Mr Buy. 'We can't easily generate a VaR for the business at large. We spend countless hours pulling it all together manually.' Another area is in the application of Internet technology. What is envisioned, says Mr Causey, 'is an application that will show the effects of a trade or an investment on the entire company.' In the same vein, adds Mr Buy, 'we'd like to have the underwriting process in template form with descriptive text explaining what is needed and why.'

Risk acumen is a principal driver in the firm's successful transition to a world leader.

Ultimately, Enron believes its risk acumen is a principal driver in the firm's successful transition from 'regulated pipeline', explains Mr Buy, to a world leader in energy markets, water and related fields. 'We maintain it is our risk orientation – our risk mentality – that is the engine behind this company. People can dismiss EWRM, our approach, but to our thinking, that's just putting your head in the sand.'

Taking it all the way

> *Life always gets harder toward the summit – the cold increases, responsibility increases.*
>
> Georg Wilhelm Nietzsche, German philosopher
>
> *Tomorrow's risk managers will be decision analysts. In a risk society, risk is an integral part of making decisions, not a separate entity to be managed.*
>
> Professor Larry Phillips (Professor of Operational Research – London School of Economics)
>
> *First weigh the considerations, then take the risks.*
>
> Count Helmuth Graf von Moltke, German General

The journey is not over, *but we are moving into uncharted territory*. Once risk management is being applied effectively to individual risks and groups of related risks – a major task in its own right – there is an opportunity to further align strategy, processes, people, technology and knowledge to improve risk management capabilities.

For its most vital risks, those where management has chosen to attain *managed* or even *optimizing* states on the Risk Management Capability Maturity Continuum, three additional steps may be taken: aggregating multiple risk measures, linking aggregate measures to business performance and formulating enterprise-wide risk management strategy. Representing the cutting-edge – there are no known prototypical companies – these steps are logical ones to conclude the progression towards EWRM.

AGGREGATE MULTIPLE RISK MEASURES

In Chapter 5 we discussed various measurement techniques and acknowledged, but did not fully explore, aggregation for results. This step of our journey improves methodologies for measuring individual risks which are pooled for aggregation purposes within an overall enterprise-wide 'portfolio'. In essence, choices for managing risk at the operating unit level or for specific functions and departments should be influenced by their potential impact on the organization as a whole – and vice versa.

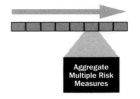

Evaluating and managing risks that arise as market conditions change and managers pursue new opportunities is what business risk management is about. To do so from an enterprise-wide approach means that some way must be found to understand the aggregate effect of risks existing throughout the organization, and then manage them as a portfolio. That is, companies at this stage will look to manage the total pool of risk, rather than the individual risks separately. This

Companies at this stage look to manage the total pool of risk, rather than the individual risks separately.

approach is already being applied in trading or investment environments for the management of market and credit risks. But as EWRM unfolds for many companies, similar techniques are increasingly being developed and applied to operational and other business risks.

Aggregation of multiple risks makes sense for activities directed at achieving a common enterprise-wide purpose. There are several reasons why:

■ *Risks add up whether evaluated piecemeal or in total.* If aggregated, managers are positioned to understand whether risks are increasing or decreasing as conditions change, both relative to each other or in the aggregate versus the firm's established risk tolerance. Conversely, very little perspective is gained from examining gross rather than net effects or smaller exposures in isolation.

Aggregation is powerful because it can alter management's focus and allocation of resources. For example, it enables the organization to quicken its response time in addressing favourable opportunities or adverse changes in the environment. Acting at the aggregate level gives a manager greater leverage, lower transaction or operating costs and the ability to streamline and optimize operations and to plan contingent risk management strategies. Aggregation also provides senior managers with the ability to act rapidly in a business environment which is quickly leaving the slow but steady behind.

■ *Increased efficiency and better decisions.* Aggregation methods provide the quantitative means to transfer, avoid and securitize risk. Transfers of risk, for instance, are more efficient when risks are netted or offset. For example, currency exposures can be pooled to determine the company's 'net' exposure – when that practice corresponds with the organization's operations. When exposures are pooled, they form a kind of portfolio that more accurately portrays the realities of the business. The goal, ultimately, is to evaluate total returns relative to total risks leading to more informed decisions.

This 'total risk focus' leads to increased confidence that management is making decisions based on a complete view of the business. To broaden the currency exposure example, credit risks can be aggregated with currency risks so that the common measure is focused on how credit risk increases or decreases as currency rates change. Huge shifts in currency rates may cause shifts in exposure to particular counterparties because the market revaluations may affect their ability to pay their debts.

■ *Improved reporting and capital allocation.* Analyses that are performed to identify the relationships between and among risks and their key drivers so that risks can be aggregated lead to more robust risk reporting. They help managers make better choices when allocating capital to those business activities providing the greatest prospects for attractive returns relative to *all* risks taken, and disallowing those activities that do not. The alternative is ineffective

This 'total risk focus' leads to increased confidence that management is making decisions based on a complete view of the business.

intuitive guesswork, which will not get very far given the complex interrelationships among risks and the variables affecting them.

- *Simplicity*. If executives can communicate the health of the organization in a single number – or a few numbers – they have a device which everyone can understand and apply. Aggregation is a way of summarizing a very complex set of relationships – the activities in the enterprise. The greater the ability to express in simple terms the organization's state of affairs, the greater will be the ability to effectively manage its course in an increasingly competitive marketplace.

Because there are so many different types of risks, aggregation is tough. Each risk must be assessed, quantified and related to every other risk the organization faces in order to aggregate them into one or more common measures, such as when a manager analyzes the risk of a stock portfolio by its alpha and beta rather than on the basis of the individual stocks themselves. Even taking risks for which there are established models, such as for price and credit, combining these into a common measure (like the stock portfolio's alpha and beta) is not easy. That said, how do we then fold in such things as operating risks and environment risks? Furthermore, correlating risks can be time consuming. Even the challenge of performance evaluation weighs in: how can the value of potential enterprise-wide 'offsets' be translated into incentives (or penalties) for specific operating units?

Difficulties aside, various attempts, such as value-at-risk type models, have been made in these areas, and our understanding of how to aggregate risks is steadily improving. Aggregation is not the end result but rather is the means to the end, the end being improved enterprise performance and viable enterprise-wide risk management strategies which make the information useful – and which may justify the effort in collecting and analyzing it. Managers, therefore, must evaluate just 'how high up' they want to aggregate. For every enterprise-wide measure of risk they have, such as over the entire enterprise or over each operating unit, a strategy is needed; otherwise, why aggregate?

> Choosing the right level of aggregation can depend on who will be using the measure.

Choosing the right level of aggregation can depend on who will be using the measure. Operational level employees, such as traders, inventory control managers or marketing managers, need very specific information to do their jobs. Senior management, on the other hand, need less detailed information, but they need it on a broader scale to be able to evaluate such questions as 'Did the total risk to our company increase or decrease? If so, by how much?' *Sacrificing some precision for the purposes of aggregation may be acceptable depending on the intended use.* Thus, in designing these measures, they must be targeted appropriately to the intended audience.

In essence, taking an enterprise-wide view translates into managing aggregate risks; this means that the organization's goals are defined in terms of the aggregate measure of these risks, affecting such things as performance incentives, cross-functional teamwork and knowledge sharing. The manager's focus, then, is on managing the aggregate measure, not irrelevant factors which have no influence on the measure. The bottom line is that selecting the right measure, or set of measures, is critical to the organization's success.

There is another key factor influencing a decision to aggregate. As mentioned in Chapter 2, it only makes sense to aggregate when the components included in the measure are directed towards the same common goal. If an organization's operating policy is to manage autonomous operating units, each acting as a stand-alone profit centre, then it is inappropriate to develop an aggregate measure over these units. In such circumstances, management has elected not to implement risk management solutions across operating units; therefore, having an aggregate measure is pointless. In essence, enterprise-wide goals and operating unit incentives must be aligned; if they aren't, the management capability provided by aggregation is not effectively deployed.

Let's now turn to some of the ways to aggregate multiple risk measures using a combination of a rigorous methodology and the application of judgement. The firm's navigation of the EWRM journey will lead to other approaches.

Risk pooling approaches

There is an alternative to aggregating risk into a single number, a 'holy grail' approach that presents daunting technical challenges. We think it is more feasible to aggregate risks whose interrelationships are well understood within logical families or pools.

A firm using this approach first determines the interrelationships among its key risks. Risks are either positively or negatively correlated when they have common risk drivers. Otherwise, they are uncorrelated. Management then 'pools' the different risks to assess the alternatives for managing the collective risks represented by the pool. The pooled risks could be managed as a portfolio, just as one would with an investment portfolio. Alternatively a hedge based on an aggregate index, such as a broad stock, bond or commodity index, could be used (as opposed, for instance, to hedging the individual component risks separately).

If risks are insurable, it is often cheaper to hedge the entire pool of risks than to insure each risk separately. In the case where the exposures in the risk pool are uncorrelated, the net cost of transferring them to an independent party, such as through hedging or insurance, may be less due to the benefits of diversification. For example, Honeywell created a structure that combined both casualty and foreign exchange risk into a single insurance transaction. This combined transaction resulted in considerably less transfer costs than the total cost of insuring each risk separately.

As David Fields, a Managing Director at AIG Risk Finance explains, 'When you combine two or more risks with low or even negative correlations, the incidence of loss decreases, and we can create a lower premium approach.' Although the jury is still out on the success of similar structures – specific market conditions play a critical role – the concept warrants evaluation as it is an inevitable consequence of EWRM. No question, says Mr Fields, 'we see corporations looking more closely at pooled risks, and we ourselves are responding and getting more creative.'

Similarly, a company could use its natural offsets enterprise-wide to obviate the need for hedging or insurance entirely. Rio Tinto plc is confident that management of a pool of investments in metals and geographies (a driver of foreign exchange risk) is an operational solution that represents its best possible hedge. The firm therefore accepts its price risks – no derivatives are needed – based in large part on assessments of its global risk pool.

In general, it will be cheaper to manage pooled risks rather than individual risks because of a few basic factors. In addition to the effects of diversification, transaction costs are lower (entering one trade rather than many), and monitoring and programme costs are reduced. Pools of aggregated risks may also be thought of as kinds of indices or benchmarks, in which case all the tools and techniques associated with benchmarking come into play.

When there are multiple pools of risks, it is a matter of expert judgement and leadership for senior managers to look at the different risk pools and make educated assessments about how an exposure in one pool may impact on other pools. Unfortunately, there isn't much guidance available for this crucial activity.

Enterprise-wide risk tolerances

Unbridled risks can result in excessive performance variability and unacceptable loss exposure. One method for achieving consistency of performance is setting risk tolerances. In effect, risk tolerances address the question, 'How much variability are we willing to accept as we pursue our business objectives and execute our strategies?' Guidance on this question is important as it helps managers assess their exposure in terms of the downside risk they are empowered to accept as they seek the upside inherent in executing their business strategy. The resulting analysis ultimately leads decision-makers to evaluating their options for managing downside exposure as they take the risks inherent in their business model.

Enterprise-wide risk tolerances are translated into specific risk limits to set the boundaries of acceptable risks that may be undertaken. As managers pursue opportunities for growth and new sources of profitability, risk tolerances and limits are an effective tool, in combination with a methodology for aggregating risk measures, for countering 'succeed at all costs' pressures on managers to produce results. Tolerances and limits should be sufficiently broad to permit operational flexibility, but at the same time ensure that the aggregate risk profile of the firm remains within the parameters mandated by the board.

Enterprise-wide tolerances can be communicated in many ways. For example, they can be included as an integral part of the risk management policy statement made available to all managers and key employees.

Hurdle rates

While certainly not a new idea, firms often set 'hurdle rates' to screen capital projects when using discounted cash flow (DCF) techniques. This screening is a starting point for assessing the relative merits of multiple capital projects more systematically. It provides increased assurance that any project selected can be expected to generate returns at least equal to, if not exceeding, the cost of capital. There are three issues to watch, however.

■ Sole reliance on financial models can cause firms to overlook difficult-to-quantify factors vital to sustaining competitive advantage, such as product innovation, quality, reputation and technological leadership.

■ Research has indicated that companies often tend to set hurdle rates arbitrarily far above the cost of capital, leading to underinvestment. Some would argue that a 'good' project is one that provides a return greater than the cost of capital. On the other hand, the projection of expected cash flows isn't an exact science, so a higher hurdle rate raises the bar. The question, then, is how much higher? Part of the answer to that issue lies in the company's risk tolerance; the lower the risk tolerance, the higher the hurdle rate must be over the expected cost of capital. After incorporating its risk tolerance and margin for estimation error, management should be careful about setting the hurdle rate any higher, otherwise underinvestment may result.

■ Hurdle rates must not be used as a hard and fast rule across all projects. If management has a single hurdle rate for the entire enterprise, the DCF model will not take into account appropriate project risks. While admittedly subjective and difficult to do, hurdle rates should be set on a project-by-project basis or at least on a business unit or divisional basis to reflect the different risk profiles. For example, in a business where the primary strategy is growth, projects with lower net present values are probably more acceptable than they would be in a business with a cash generation strategy. Companies should still take on their most attractive capital projects first and recognize that the cost of capital for subsequent projects, e.g. 'maintenance' projects needed to sustain the implementation of existing strategies, might not be the same as the cost for their primary projects.

Hurdle rates are not infallible. They cannot remain fixed over time as economic conditions change. In addition, potentially marginal investments can often be made to appear attractive as internal business units compete for capital. However, companies like Enron find that the human element, i.e. an effective, highly interactive risk assessment, often adds perspective and balance to an otherwise acceptable projection.

'At risk' frameworks

Value at risk (VaR), earnings at risk (EaR) and cash flow at risk (CFaR) methodologies are becoming more accepted by corporate enterprises and regulators as tools for:

■ facilitating the allocation of capital based on risk;

■ measuring performance taking into account the risks inherent in a portfolio; and

■ strengthening the links between performance, accountability and established risk thresholds.

These methodologies assist managers in considering critical factors when managing risk, e.g. the sensitivity of existing portfolio positions to market rate changes beyond specified limits, the liquidity of a portfolio, the contribution of each unit or product to both risk and return and the interrelationships between risks. All told, these techniques help managers consider the exposure of earnings or cash flow to loss and achieve the firm's target leverage and desired return on allocated capital.

Risk adjusted performance measurement

Once a firm has quantified its exposures, such as by using a technique like VaR, what do managers do with this information? One of the most meaningful uses of risk information is as a factor for adjusting the relative value of different business activities. Risk adjusted return on capital is a technique which specifically incorporates the riskiness of a business activity, such as an investment, into the measurement of the expected returns from that activity. Hence, a more risky investment (say, an investment in a power plant operating in a developing foreign country) would have to generate a higher return than a less risky investment (say, US treasuries) in order to be considered equivalent. Risk adjusted return on capital, or RAROC, tells you just how much greater that return would have to be for each level of risk. It also tells you whether your allocated capital is adequate to cover the risks.

However, there are issues with respect to RAROC. Since there is no one correct way to compute the expected riskiness of a project or to adjust for risk, the exact number you get will depend on the approach you take in the computations. Using RAROC, risk is quantified based on probability distributions of returns observed in historical data, consistent with VaR and other statistical models. The intended result is to aggregate and price risk and allocate capital based on the variability in expected returns. By its nature, RAROC is not an infallible tool and must be applied with judgement, care and knowledge of the business.

As firms take their journey to where they aspire to be in terms of EWRM, there is a growing awareness of the importance of quantifying risk, integrating risk measurement and linking risk management actions to enhanced enterprise performance and shareholder value. Although it has its limitations (and what tool does not?), RAROC provides a means of evaluating return, risk and capital trade-offs and comparing performance across different units or activities of the organization which are subject to different levels of risk. Hence, RAROC is also a tool which can be useful in creating benchmarks for the organization. Its power, therefore, lies in consistency of application.

Companies like Enron have developed proprietary applications of RAROC, as a measure of both performance and the capital needed to support a structured transaction based on its underlying market and credit risks. The Orange County debacle in the US in the early 1990s is a classic example of how investors can forget that superior performance of investments over a given period of time can be attributed to their assumption of greater risks through a strategy that may not yield consistent results as time goes on. Therefore, a RAROC approach adjusts returns for the capital at risk across asset classes. Managers can then use that information to establish limits on trading, investing or other business activities.

A world without equity

If there were no risks, there would be no equity. As Azurix's Managing Director Chris Wasden explains, 'Equity is the price of uncertainty. If there were no uncertainty, everyone would be able to fund themselves with AAA bonds.' Moreover, equity is specifically needed to cover unexpected risks. Anything that can be covered by traditional insurance or insurance-like structures becomes a certainty – no equity is required.

So how much equity is needed in a given project? That is dependent on the way a company manages its uncertainties. 'If you apply the rating agency point of view for individual decisions, you are going to completely misallocate your capital – you will not accurately account for uncertainty,' asserts Mr Wasden. 'You'll have too much for some projects, too little for others.' What companies need is a probabilistic approach to the management of equity

Continued ...

capital. 'If you're a AAA company, and you want to keep that rating, a project needs enough capital to give you something like a 99 per cent comfort level that it will not need additional equity.' For a BBB company, 'maybe you'd drop that to 90 per cent,' says Mr Wasden. But the bottom line is that it is a task of the board and CEO to allocate capital effectively. At Azurix, 'every project has to survive the RAROC process,' says Mr Wasden. Other boards and CEOs should demand a similar process from their organizations.

Summary

The purpose of these and other risk aggregation methodologies is to establish a common basis for organizing the array of information that managers need to make the critical choices. There are many factors that interfere with the ability of managers to make decisions. When risk management is effective at providing better information for decision-making through time-tested models, performance variability and loss exposure are reduced. When methodologies enable the allocation of established aggregate risk limits to operating units, corrective action can be taken when predefined limits are exceeded.

> Risk aggregation methodologies establish a common basis for organizing the information that managers need to make the critical choices.

These capabilities achieve four things:

1. *Robust risk reporting*. Risks are aggregated at multiple levels – by business unit (aggregating multiple risk types), by risk (aggregating the same risk on an enterprise-wide basis across all business units) and by specific investments and projects.

2. *Greater investment confidence*. With these capabilities, a firm can pursue opportunities with greater confidence knowing that it understands the risks inherent in its normal future operations and that those risks are being managed effectively.

3. *Greater integration and alignment*. As aggregate measures are effectively linked to enterprise performance, more integrated risk management solutions are possible.

4. *Higher valuation*. All of this gives management a more compelling story to communicate to investors, which in turn can lead to higher price/earnings multiples in share valuations.

LINK TO ENTERPRISE PERFORMANCE

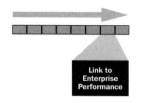

Link to Enterprise Performance

The next step – the linkage of aggregate measures to enterprise performance – is ultimately a move towards value creation. We have defined business risk as the exposure to uncertainty that a firm must manage as it creates value. The less that is known about the current and future state of a market, venture or project, the less the firm's ability to predict future outcomes; therefore, the more the net cash flows arising from those potential outcomes must be discounted when estimating their present values. Any process that helps management more effectively evaluate, understand and manage its exposures to uncertainty will lead to better decisions, greater value creation and higher valuations.

Information from aggregating multiple risks, as discussed above, is vital to this process as it reduces the 'disconnects' and facilitates alignment among board members, executive and business unit management, operating personnel and corporate staff functions. In this sense, 'improved enterprise performance' is a benefit of risk aggregation.

Through EWRM, managers up, down and across the organization use a common language, effective assessment tools and frameworks, and clearly stated strategies and risk tolerances as a foundation for making decisions about balancing risk, return and growth. They identify best practices internally and externally and share them across the enterprise. The bottom line is that the *organization* 'learns once' and shares experiences so that risk management is continuously improved. The resulting benefits are the reduction of unacceptable risks and strategic errors, more timely corrective actions and better management of the risk profile of the business through such tools as RAROC.

Whatever the organization's proxy for value, the most important contribution that business risk management can make is to help managers make better choices as their businesses face an increasingly uncertain future. Risk management strategies should, therefore, support the firm's value creation objectives by managing the performance variability inherent in its normal future operations, protecting accumulated wealth from unacceptable losses and leveraging the firm's core competencies to produce greater value.

There is a school of economics that argues that certain risk management actions are not in the best interests of investors. The argument asserts that investors more efficiently manage more efficiently their own exposure to the risks faced by an investee company by diversifying their own portfolios; therefore, investors are actually worse off if companies hedge or insure in those areas in which investors can do the same according to the specific criteria of their investment objectives. For instance, if an investor buys stock in a gold mining company which hedges its gold reserves, the stock would not be an effective vehicle for diversifying via gold appreciation. Hence, its value as a 'gold play' would be diminished. These costs to investors may possibly be offset by the stronger commitment managers have in the company's success if its viability is not compromised through market changes over which it has no control. This issue is made even more complicated when part of managers' compensation is tied to the company's stock price (which helps align the interests of managers and investors, although managers, in this case, would have an extremely diversified portfolio).

But where does this argument leave the manager of the firm in a world in which 'execution' and 'delivering on commitments' is vital to value creation? Performance variability can be a good or a bad thing, depending on the nature of the risks and rewards at stake and the reasons for the variability (for instance, no one desires variability due to poor operating performance). If investors generally desire performance variability for their portfolios, such as the 'gold play' in the example above, but variability for an individual company threatens its business health, what can management do? In practice, high earnings multiples follow superior strategy, a compelling storyline and superb execution that ultimately lead to hard profits and predictable returns. Losses and failure to deliver on promises drive investors to redirect capital to other opportunities, which lie in abundance. That is the stark reality. Thus, the practical answer is that risk management has to become more integral to the process of managing a business, not some appendage whose relevance is questioned.

> **The linkage of aggregate measures to enterprise performance is ultimately a move towards value creation.**

The linkage of risk management actions to improved enterprise performance is achieved by measuring the effects on business performance of changes to a firm's risk profile from implementing alternative risk management strategies. This approach focuses on:

- improving the expected return for the enterprise as a whole; or
- holding the expected return constant and altering the firm's risk characteristics by reducing:
  - the firm's net exposure;
  - the variability of the firm's expected returns caused by specific sources of uncertainty (such as currency rates);
  - the likelihood of financial distress in the event of realized changes in key variables (such as interest rates for a highly leveraged company); or
  - other uncertainty in the attainment of the expected return.

We believe that this is the direction that progressive companies will take. A strong focus on improving performance will inevitably lead to organized efforts to remove all significant inefficiencies. Thus, we expect companies to apply formal cost/benefit analyses to all risk management practices.

Measuring success

It isn't easy to measure the effects of alternative risk management strategies on a firm's risk profile. In the treasury area and in financial institutions, firms use VaR-based methodologies to accomplish this objective for different types of price risk. Much research, however, is required to extend this approach to other risks. The ultimate testimonial occurs when a firm outperforms its industry, in part, because its risk management capabilities are recognized as a differentiating skill.

Some assert that this measure is impossible to develop because of the myriad factors that enable a firm to perform better than its competitors. But how will we know when we are improving performance through the value contributed by business risk management, since we do not yet have a standard measurement framework? Based on input from 25 executives representing companies participating in the *New Dimensions on Business Risk* research introduced in Appendix 1, we suggest ten ways below.

Integration of risk assessment into strategic and operating processes

Clear evidence that risk assessment is integrated and internalized by managers into their normal activities would provide a strong indicator of effectiveness. For example, if managers make business risk an integral part of their opportunity-seeking agenda as they evaluate alternative deal structures, proposed process improvements, new systems, new products and new markets, the enterprise becomes more anticipatory and forward-looking. The Enron case provides an excellent example of a proactive focus on risk when evaluating structured investments. Another example is integration of risk management with the business planning and strategic management processes, as illustrated by the Holderbank case.

Improved risk identification

We have shown that risk mapping, coupled with a common language, provides a highly visible means of initiating and sustaining a dialogue about risks at all levels of the firm. Process and activity owners armed with the appropriate tools and processes are going to identify risks more effectively and contribute more to the enterprise's performance over time (as opposed to process and activity owners who approach the issue of risk as an afterthought). Over time, better risk identification will reduce the retention of risk out of ignorance, thereby reducing the company's exposure to unacceptable surprises that can impact on the financial market's assessment of its performance.

Continued ...

Implementation of more effective analytical and early warning techniques

Increased emphasis on more systematic, quantitative and predictive analytics leads to more informed decisions. Better decisions, in turn, lead to improved business performance over time. Greater use of methodologies for anticipating risk and assessing the impact of alternative scenarios on future expected results leads to increased effectiveness in escalating issues to the attention of appropriate executives.

Improvement in specific risk measures

The shift from 'guessing' to 'knowing' is a clear improvement, as is that from 'reacting' to 'being prepared'. Management reporting which tracks key risks provides evidence of improved performance over time. Information about risk – risk strategies, risk measures, risk processes, risk incidents, best practices, status of improvement plans and other relevant matters – made available at all levels of the organization through web-enabled database technology facilitates the knowledge-sharing aspects of an EWRM approach. Use of risk aggregation tools replaces intuitive guesswork with fact-based analysis.

Reduced number of risk incidents

If a firm can demonstrate fewer risk incidents than the industry average, it has clear evidence of superior performance. Workplace safety is a good example of a risk where such benchmarking is possible. In some cases, Y2K for example, the expectation is compliance – no more, no less. Some have questioned the level of Y2K expenditures. But consider the impact on reputation and image had a company's mission-critical systems not been Y2K-compliant. It is paradoxical thinking to invest in a risk reduction strategy and then be disappointed when 'nothing happens'.

Reduced performance variability

If a firm encounters fewer surprises in reported results due to (a) a more systematic and proactive risk evaluation process, (b) improved measures and (c) internal controls that prevent risk incidents at the source, this experience may be attributed to the firm's risk management programme. Reduced variability over time may, all other things being equal, contribute to higher price/earnings multiples versus peer companies that sustain greater volatility in reported results.

Continued ...

Reduction in cost of capital and improvement in shareholder value

As analysts, rating agencies, regulators and other institutions learn to differentiate between various firms' risk management capabilities, EWRM-equipped organizations will enjoy a relatively lower cost of capital. If a firm's risk management is viewed as a differentiating skill relative to its peers, then the company's borrowing costs should decline and its share valuations should increase accordingly.

Increased risk sensitivity and awareness

A cultural shift in the organization leading to an increased focus on and reinforcement of risk management goals and objectives is an indicator of effectiveness. For example, to achieve a demanding goal for a certain number of days of injury-free time in a manufacturing organization, a cultural shift is needed to modify behaviour. Another situation is when a utility plans the implementation of a process to prevent power outages in the future. In these instances, risk management is actually integral to managing the business as it addresses obstacles that may prohibit the achievement of a business priority declared by management.

Integration with KPI reporting

We see a number of firms integrating risk management with key performance indicators (KPIs) – for example, Diageo/Guinness. Another example is a North American energy firm that prepares risks maps for each of the KPIs on its balanced scorecard. This innovative approach offers executives a comprehensive prioritization of risks by KPI. Steps are then taken to address the significant risks that could cause the firm to fall short of its performance goals. This linkage can only help improve performance over time.

The continued success of the firm

Finally, some believe that building and sustaining competitive advantage and producing incremental increases in EPS is, in itself, an indirect measure of risk management effectiveness. Other traditional measures used in this regard include cash flow, ROI, ROE and shareholder value added. Useful non-financial measures include customer satisfaction and retention, employee satisfaction, channel throughput, market share and brand image. Whatever measures are used, the firm should track its performance relative to its competitors over time. The notion is that if the firm is managing its risks effectively and continues to be successful in a competitive marketplace, then the two must be related.

FORMULATE ENTERPRISE-WIDE RISK STRATEGY

Business strategy provides the context for formulating risk management strategy. In this final step, it is important that risk strategies do not conflict with business objectives, key strategies and performance goals, and vice versa.

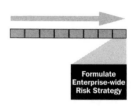

Formulate Enterprise-wide Risk Strategy

Risk strategy formulation, as presented in Chapter 5, is typically applied to individual risks and groups of related risks. Throughout this book, we have pointed to examples of companies that are integrating risk management with business planning and strategic management. Diageo/Guinness, Holderbank and Hydro-Quebec see risk management as a discipline for defining specific actions in their business plans that are focused on managing risk. As a company implements an effective risk assessment process consistently across the enterprise, comparison and aggregation become possible and capital allocation becomes more meaningful. As Ron Dembo of Algorithmics points out, 'If everyone in the organization uses the same frameworks, then the investment choices become clearer.'

Formulation of an enterprise-wide risk management strategy is something any firm can do at anytime regardless of how far it travels along the EWRM journey. The point we want to make is this: the enterprise-wide strategy formulation process is more meaningful when it is supported by aggregated risk measures and a clear understanding of how risk management improves business performance. That is why we have positioned this step as the last one to take on the pathway to EWRM.

This last step in the journey is not the end, but a new beginning.

This last step in the journey is not the end, but a new beginning. New insights are gained from the process of formulating an enterprise-wide risk strategy. These insights, in turn, spawn new risk management capabilities. New or enhanced processes, competencies, reports, methodologies and systems may be needed to execute the strategy – and the linkage of risk and opportunity is further enhanced.

To capitalize on the enhanced understanding made possible by more rigorous risk management, there are several 'frontiers' in which a broader application of enterprise-wide strategy can be developed to further align strategy, processes, people, technology and knowledge. We point out three below.

Evaluating risk capacity and appetite

Effectively managing the relationship between capital, risk and reward within the boundaries of a firm's risk strategy is a significant opportunity for business risk management. One approach for developing this capability is to evaluate the capacity to bear risk and appetite to take risk, and allocate capital based on this analysis. This approach is described below.

1. *Define the firm's 'capacity to bear risk'*. Capacity represents the risk the organization is capable of undertaking. Capacity is a complex issue that some

213

may even consider contrived. It is a function of many things – the people, processes and technology used to measure, monitor and manage risk, the environment in which the firm is operating as well as its economic capital, long-term business strategies, debt capacity, earnings/cash flow sensitivity to financial commitments and other factors.

2. *Measure the firm's 'appetite to take risk'.* The firm's risk appetite or willingness to take risk reflects both its capacity to bear risk as well as a broader understanding of the level of risk which it can safely and successfully manage for an extended period of time. It is the extent to which a firm exposes its capital to the exploitation of strategic opportunities and retention of performance variability and loss exposure. Prudence and common sense are vital when evaluating risk appetite. For example, does it make sense to take all of the risk an organization is capable of undertaking without reserving capital for new investment opportunities? Is it appropriate to retain a significant risk when options for transferring it are available at reasonable cost? From a strategy standpoint, it is valuable to have a notion of at what point the firm's limit for risk bearing would be encroached upon.

> Risk appetite must always be less than the firm's ability to bear risk.

3. *Allocate capital according to the firm's tastes for risk bearing.* Some companies, principally commercial banks and other financial institutions, allocate capital (either equity or regulatory capital) to major sources of risks. In fact, banking regulations in most developed countries require commercial banks to allocate regulatory capital to lines of business. The objective is twofold: (a) optimize the balance between preserving capital and generating growth and profits, and (b) improve returns via a superior capital allocation process. Management then decides whether risk-taking should be aggressive or in moderation relative to available capital and alternative risk–return opportunities.

Most executives would agree that risk appetite must always be less than the firm's ability to bear risk, otherwise the firm puts itself in significant danger of financial distress, even bankruptcy. However, when the firm's appetite for risk bearing is low, e.g. a 'cash cow' maintenance strategy, it is equivalent to leaving money on the table if competitors successfully navigate more risky and profitable growth strategies to develop new markets and products. Conversely, a company with a high appetite for risk may even dilute value and face financial distress when risk outruns investor preferences or its risk management capabilities. The firm's challenge, therefore, is in choosing the appropriate middle ground in its quest to efficiently deploy capital, and in monitoring and updating that choice over time.

This thinking can lead to a useful capital allocation framework that managers can use when evaluating strategy.

Effects of pooling on risk strategy

To take the development of risk strategy to a higher level, the firm should aggregate its risks into logical pools and develop strategies – *retain* (self-insure, internally finance), *transfer* (insure or hedge), *reduce* (disperse or control), etc. – that are relevant to those pools. The objective is to measure and evaluate the pooled risks as a portfolio to determine the appropriate risk strategy. Pooling of risk contributes to more effective strategic thinking because the focus is on managing the most important key drivers influencing the risks included in the pool.

Identifying sources of competitive advantage

In this book, we have pointed out that EWRM contributes to establishing sustainable competitive advantage. Enron is an excellent example of a firm that views effective risk management as a source of competitive advantage. As illustrated in Case 5, Enron exploits risks in new markets and, through new innovative products and services, risks that may even intimidate other firms.

Firms that seek to implement business risk management as a source of competitive advantage strive for vastly different results than firms that view risk management as a mere cost centre for purchasing insurance and derivatives. These companies see risk management as a means of pursuing opportunity (which may *increase* the firm's exposure to performance variability) as they simultaneously *reduce* loss exposure to an acceptable level. For example:

> **Firms that seek to implement business risk management as a source of competitive advantage strive for vastly different results.**

■ Integrating an enterprise-wide business risk management process with business planning enables the firm to more effectively exploit its risks. Several case illustrations in this book focus on the merits of such integration, which better positions the company to exploit market opportunities.

■ Implementing a methodical risk assessment will position the firm to stay on top of, and better understand, its risks. That is half of the battle, for once a firm identifies and understands its risks, it can take proactive steps to manage them. Several of the companies described in the case discussions point out how vital it is to identify risks in a timely manner and incorporate appropriate responses to those risks in the business plan. If management is highly confident that risks contributing to performance variability and loss exposure are being managed effectively, the firm is better positioned to allocate capital to exploit strategic opportunities more vigorously than competitors lacking that confidence.

■ Finally, configuring risk-taking with the firm's expertise and core competencies makes good business sense. Enron is an excellent example of a firm that is noted for taking risks, but is also keenly aware of what its capabilities are. These capabilities are reinforced through a superior and intensive risk assessment process.

Firms will need to experiment with these concepts to devise practical frameworks. Taking the formulation of risk strategy to an enterprise-wide level elevates the contribution of business risk management.

Again, formulation of an enterprise-wide risk management strategy is more meaningful when it is supported by aggregated risk measures and a clear understanding of how risk management improves business performance. Thus, it is the last step of our EWRM journey to link risk and opportunity.

A call for research, experimentation and advancement

There are many open questions, but that does not mean a company can afford to sit on the sidelines. The discipline of measuring risk makes a valuable contribution to risk management. EWRM itself promotes research, analysis, communication and dialogue and it is only through these processes that quantum improvements will be achieved. Below are some of the areas that warrant further experimentation and research.

- What are the most useful ways to aggregate risks? Do we aim at the enterprise as a whole or at specific business units? Is aggregation really feasible given the complexities of different risks? Do we target aggregation to meaningful families or pools of risks that are distinguishable by the nature of the measurement methodologies and management solutions unique to them?

- What are the best available metrics or indicators of successful or superior risk management? What metrics make the most sense for measuring risk management effectiveness? How can these metrics be translated into benchmarks useful across an industry or, more generally, across non-financial corporations?

- How do we practically link effective risk management and the various shareholder value measures and systems so that companies can effectively apply an integrated methodology to their business? Can this methodology be operationalized into an actionable framework for decision-making?

- What is the relationship between internal risk capital and market value? Internal capital must be available as a cushion to absorb unexpected losses from risk events. However, a firm's market value will decline or stagnate due to the realization of risks that (a) do not affect its peers or (b) make other industry sectors more attractive.

- How do we measure a firm's capacity to bear risk? What guidelines should be considered in determining a firm's appetite for risk? What is the

Continued ...

relationship between a firm's capacity to bear risk and its appetite for risk, and, in particular, how does the external environment, e.g. the industry, competitors, customers, regulators, suppliers, financial markets, etc., affect this assessment?

- What is the relationship between the firm's appetite for risk and its equity capital? What are the practical measures that should be used for allocating capital, subject to the firm's appetite for risk and investors' preferences for risky investments? What are the superior methods for evaluating total capital against total quantified risks? What are the practical alternatives for allocating capital to operational risks?

- How does a firm choose risk tolerance? What alternative frameworks are available? How are risk tolerances related to allocated capital?

- What are the alternative methods for disaggregating allocated capital by risk? For example, once a business unit is assigned its risk-based capital, it must assign risk limits for each of its risks and delineate those limits by time period – overnight, monthly, quarterly and annually. The total of all risk limits will ordinarily exceed total capital and established risk tolerances due to the probability that all risk events will not occur simultaneously.

Our posing the above questions is not intended to suggest that we have presented an exhaustive list. There are many opportunities for research and experimentation in risk management. Nor do we intend to suggest that there hasn't been any thinking, research, experimentation and progress by companies, academics and consulting firms on these issues. But our intention is to raise the bar to one of practical application by most companies in a rigorous and systematic manner.

> There are many opportunities for research and experimentation in risk management.

SUMMARY

While there are no perfect EWRM prototypes, there are companies that have begun the journey. As they move forward, there is an increasing awareness of the importance of (a) aggregating the effects of multiple risks on the business, (b) understanding the effects of comprehensive risk management strategies on enterprise performance, and (c) evaluating strategic alternatives for the enterprise as a whole. These last three steps are the culmination of the journey to EWRM, enabling managers to evaluate exposures and sources of uncertainty on an aggregate basis with better information. These steps enhance the understanding of senior managers of the contribution of risk management to the success of the business, while developing enhanced risk strategies that benefit the enterprise as a whole. Although these are cutting-edge tasks, the real challenge remains – getting started, the subject of the next and final chapter.

Hydro-Quebec: getting started – the transition to a risk-conscious culture

- Managing risk and opportunity as one: a cultural shift
- Understanding the risks of entering a new business: focusing on growth and international investment
- Starting the journey with a mandate from the top and a change model

With revenues of $5.7 billion, Hydro-Quebec (HQ) is not only Canada's but also one of the world's largest power producers. As a public utility, the firm's mission has been to satisfy the electricity needs of Quebec's population centres in the south by tapping the vast hydroelectric generation potential represented by the province's rivers in the far north. In so doing, the company has overcome numerous technical challenges, for example pioneering long-distance power transmission. But today, most of the economically viable rivers 'are already dammed,' says HQ CFO Daniel LeClair. Perhaps more importantly, the world of regulated, monopolistic electricity markets is careening towards a world of competitive merchant power. 'Clearly,' says Mr LeClair, 'commercially – and culturally – we have to change.'

'Commercially – and culturally – we have to change.'

Commercial change is being fuelled by broader business initiatives and investments. One chosen avenue for the company is the pursuit of clean and renewable power resources – a competitive response to ageing and less environmentally palatable coal and nuclear plants. For example, in the autumn of 1998, the firm began work with multiple partners to build a 100 megawatt wind farm on Canadian soil. The accompanying project financing is the first of its kind to obtain an investment grade rating from the Canadian Bond Rating Agency. Commercial change is also being propelled by a shift towards international investment. This, says Mr LeClair, 'is the real growth engine' for the company.

But to succeed commercially, the company realizes it must simultaneously change its culture – dramatically. As a regulated utility, though highly capable of managing operating risks, the company's managers are accustomed to a relatively risk-free commercial environment. The shift to a competitive culture 'introduces new opportunities but also new risks – and we have to be certain our organization is able to manage these risks capably,' says Mr LeClair. Consequently, the group has been searching for the means to change its culture to more capably manage its risks.

After much consideration of options by the board and senior management, the group decided to embark on the journey towards EWRM. Concludes Mr LeClair, 'we believe that by making our people more aware of our commercial position, by making them more understanding of what risk means and why we take risks – that will help us succeed in driving the desired behaviours, given the strategic direction we have chosen.' This case study looks at Hydro-Quebec's fast-evolving EWRM programme and offers an in-depth look at the commensurate activities of Hydro-Quebec International (HQI), the group's high-growth international subsidiary.

THE MANDATE

Senior management at Hydro-Quebec became interested in the powerful ideas behind EWRM in early 1998. Existing HQ risk management practices, the company realized, could be described as defensive or passive in nature, not to mention segmented. Its commercial practices were largely monopolistic. Both were the practices of an earlier era.

The objective today is to develop an approach that is more appropriate for a competitive global marketplace: one that is proactive, holistic and integrated. To support the transition, a new position, General Manager – Control and Integrated Risk Management, was created and taken by André-Richard Marcil. Reporting directly to CFO LeClair, his charter 'is to create a culture or risk-consciousness, and to give our business people the tools and support they need to achieve the greatest possible success,' says Mr Marcil.

In practical terms, the new 'business risk champion' sees a threefold task:

1. *Develop a vision.* Job one is to develop more fully the concept of integrated risk management – creating a vision that appeals to board members, senior executives and middle managers alike. This means advancing the concept of integrated risk management beyond the theoretical, essentially translating the journey into a series of practical objectives and milestones. This also means actively 'selling' the benefits of the programme to achieve broader understanding and commitment. 'We are not out to take over risk management responsibility,' says Mr Marcil, 'but rather to give the business units and the board an effective framework as well as access to the right tools.'

2. *Develop an enterprise-wide view.* The second task is to pull together a true portfolio view of the group's risks. This will initially focus on risk identification and valuation, but will ultimately require the development of practical tools for managing and optimizing risks. The most important word is 'optimization' says Marcil. 'We do not want to eliminate risk, rather we want business managers to understand risk conceptually and to be able to explain why they are taking a particular set of risks.' Then, enterprise-wide, 'we want to ensure our business units understand the tools available to them so that we can create an optimal risk position.'

Specific risk optimization strategies will need to be developed both for individual business units as well as for 'residual risks' at the group level. Risk modelling is also critical to the vision, and HQ is endeavouring to supplement 'simplistic' or 'deterministic' gauges with more 'probabilistic' approaches. The ultimate objective, says Mr Marcil, is an organization that continually, proactively, rigorously and optimally co-ordinates its processes for business planning, risk assessment and risk management.

3. *Assess trading and insurance.* The third task is to assess the state of the company's use of derivative instruments and insurance products. Unquestionably, the adoption of an enterprise-wide view will have an impact on the objectives and decision-making processes of the company's trading operations. However, the focus here is on operational optimization to reduce performance variability to acceptable levels as well as ensure adherence to established policies and controls.

Use of derivative products is accelerating at HQ. The company increasingly and necessarily trades energy products. But these markets are known for their complexity and new instruments such as futures on transmission rights (the rights to 'pipelines' between grids) arrive continually. Interest rate risk and currency risk are also being actively managed – the latter growing rapidly and more significantly in step with HQ's emerging international presence. As in any industrial company, insurance products are also an important element of risk strategy.

Mr Marcil's mandate is to take a broad view of the company's risks with the goals of supporting the management of those risks and focusing derivative trading and insurance operations on optimizing processes and controls. Executed capably, says Mr Marcil, a uniform set of procedures should satisfy both the trading units' need for speed and flexibility and top management's need for assurance that such matters are under control. Ultimately, the company wants to ensure that (a) business units understand their risks and know where to go to find the expertise to assist with the management of those risks, and (b) the groups that use capital markets to manage risks are capably managed and controlled.

> Facilitated discussions focused on the current state of risk management, the progress to date and the desired future state.

A 'GO/NO GO' DECISION

Over the first year and a half in his new position, Mr Marcil's charge was to prove the efficacy of EWRM. Top approval had been obtained for the first phases of the mission only and full backing would come only if early success became evident. Based on the first 18 months' progress, full backing was achieved in October 1999 at a meeting of the company's top executives. That facilitated discussions focused on the current state of risk management at Hydro-Quebec, the progress to date, and the potential achievement of a desired future state (see Figure C6.1 used during the meeting). After much interaction and deliberation, the board chose, says Mr Marcil, 'to move with all possible speed towards the future state.'

Fig. C6.1 Change model used to facilitate discussion at Hydro-Quebec (Adapted from Arthur Andersen's *New Dimensions on Business Risk* research)

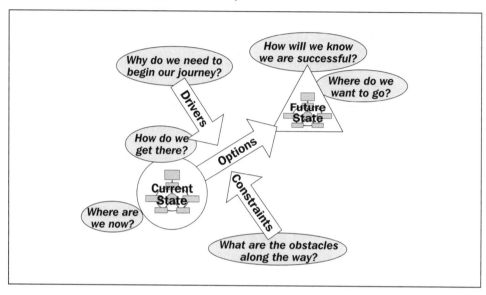

At the meeting, the board empowered Mr Marcil and his team to press on with the steps needed to achieve both immediate and long-term benefits. 'I believe it will take at least five years before we have a true EWRM-focused culture and processes,' says Mr Marcil. 'But within two years, we intend to move most of the way – so we are going to be very busy.'

This is not to say progress has not already been achieved. For the first four months beginning in April 1998, Mr Marcil and his team drafted their vision. The company had always managed its financial risks in an integrated manner, for example exploiting opportunities for netting currency and related financial risks. The goal, says Mr Marcil, is to emulate that structure for all risks. 'We need all managers to feel responsible for the risks relating to their businesses,' says Mr Marcil. 'We want them to view risk critically: what are the opportunities for improving performance, what are the risks, why are we taking these risks?' From there, the vision is that, once identified, conscious decisions are made relative to risks: retain and mitigate, reject and eliminate (avoid), transfer, or accept and exploit. The final piece of the vision is that the effect of these risks would be viewed in terms of a portfolio, 'just like we do already with financial risks,' says Mr Marcil.

The question becomes in practice, how can an EWRM approach give HQ's management teams the tools and insights to capably identify and manage the risk/return profiles of its opportunities for improving performance? Mr Marcil sees a five-step approach:

1. *Help business units outline their opportunities and risks.* The business environment must be clearly understood. If there is a better process than risk mapping (see Chapter 5) for this purpose, Mr Marcil is not aware of it. But even here, Mr Marcil and his team have experienced initial challenges. 'The biggest problem is getting people to admit they have any risks because no one has ever asked them before.' But persistence pays off. 'We say, "maybe you've never put it on paper before, but you know it's there, so let's get it out in the open and talk about it."'

   Another effective approach to initiating dialogue is to focus first on risks that are common to all business units. In this way, individual managers feel less threatened, since they recognize they are not alone and, thus, the ice is broken. Eventually, the process bears fruit enabling operating managers to see their risks in the context of their opportunities, 'often for the first time,' says Mr Marcil.

2. *Establish risk tolerances for priority risks.* Once the risk map is drafted, debated and finalized, the next responsibility for business units is to begin prioritizing risks. Vital to this process is the establishment of 'conditions for success': what are the levels where the risks become tolerable? Says Mr Marcil, 'It is very easy getting operating managers to specify the conditions of success in terms of opportunities, but much more difficult for them to think the same way about risks.' Establishing, expressing and managing risk tolerances for both operating units and the group at large 'is going to be one of our principal challenges for the next year,' says Mr Marcil.

3. *Evaluate options.* Regarding each critical risk, the business units are asked to define the full range of possible actions. Risk management options are discussed more fully in Chapter 5. It is important to understand the implications of each potential strategy. In this endeavour, Mr Marcil and his team adopt the role of consultant/advisor. The risk function is there to assist business unit managers in their decision-making, not to tell them what they must do. 'Our role', says Mr Marcil, 'is to facilitate an informed, conscious decision relating to how we manage the risks accepted.'

4. *Devise an action plan.* Once alternatives have been outlined, the business units have to make specific choices. Moreover, their decisions need to be explained and specified in business plans. 'We are not looking for a parallel process outside business planning,' says Mr Marcil. 'What we want now is for these two ideas, risk management and business planning, to go hand in hand – to be integrated.' Moreover, the business units recognize that, once identified, they are now accountable to see to it that the risks are managed. This is no mere one-off exercise: the success or failure of the risk strategies becomes a part of the business unit's overall evaluation and continuous improvement objectives.

> 'The biggest problem is getting people to admit they have any risks.'

223

5. *Manage risks on a portfolio basis.* As of today, in the early days of the work, the analysis is business unit by business unit only. Ultimately, efforts will be made to combine the risks of individual business units in search of natural offsets. Only at the 'corporate' level can such opportunities be identified and exploited.

Eventually, it is believed, certain actions at certain business units will prove redundant on an enterprise-wide level. Or, high levels of risk in one business unit's strategic investments might be sufficiently offset by low risk in other units. As all of these outcomes are identified and analyzed, the individual units will be made aware of the situation and be given the opportunity to reassess their proposed actions. Alternatively, certain forms of 'relief' or 'insurance' from the parent (in lieu of contemplated business unit actions) might become a part of a unit's business plan and evaluation criteria in order to achieve optimum results for the enterprise as a whole.

Uniformity in language and reporting is critical, as is clear risk 'ownership.' Overall, the goal is to so stimulate a continuous cycle of communication and creative thinking that the group's business risks become a truly optimized portfolio. 'The CEO has ultimate responsibility and he reports to the board,' explains Mr Marcil. But management intends the EWRM initiative to vest risk responsibility with those managers who are in the best position to manage the risks – as well as provide the processes, reporting and methodologies for optimizing those risks across the entire organization. 'We want each business unit to feel responsible for managing their own effectiveness.' Then, aided by Mr Marcil and the risk integration function, 'we will develop the common language and uniform processes that enable close co-operation, communication and knowledge sharing between business units. We will optimize our risk on a portfolio basis and be able to evaluate the effects of alternative risk management strategies on the overall organization.'

THE VISION APPLIED: HYDRO-QUEBEC INTERNATIONAL

So far the above steps have been implemented in two areas. The first is in the sale of electricity to adjoining power grids in the US and Canada. Although the company has substantial experience – it has been selling electricity in this way for over 20 years – this has nearly always taken place in a regulated manner featuring guaranteed sales and pricing conditions. As deregulation fuels a competitive pricing environment, it becomes important to apply a more disciplined approach to risk and opportunity assessment.

Though important to the company, the future growth potential of regional electricity marketing remains relatively limited. But this is not the case for the group's international subsidiary, HQI, which is seen as one of the group's high-potential breeding grounds for future growth. Providing consulting for the past 20 years, the group already has a strong international reputation. But now the company is embarking on an investment programme: acquiring, developing and operating physical assets world-wide. HQI has already invested or committed over $150 million abroad, but this is only a fraction of the $1.35 billion designated for investment over the next four years.

The development and management of international power projects is a complex, capital-intensive, competitive and therefore risky business. But for those with the right capabilities, it is also a lucrative opportunity. The developing world is power-starved. Meanwhile, even existing capacity is often inefficient or obsolete. By bringing its world-class development and operating capabilities to bear, HQI brings efficiency – benefiting both host nations and shareholders.

But direct international investment is a new activity for the group. This means taking on new and significant business risks that are clearly different from and in addition to the risks managed domestically. These risks require new competencies; therefore, HQI became a natural candidate for Mr Marcil's programme of comprehensive risk assessment and management. As Ghislain Giroux-Dufort, Director of Risk Management at the subsidiary, explains, 'It was obvious to everyone that with this new mandate at HQI, risk would be a major factor. So it was agreed, we should become a kind of proving ground and showcase for the larger initiative in risk management.'

Taking on new risks requires new competencies.

What are our risks and how do we manage them?

The first step, undertaken in the summer of 1998, says Mr Giroux-Dufort, 'was to review the basic strategy of the company and our major activities.' Utilizing a risk mapping process, the group developed a comprehensive ranking of the risks most likely to upset the achievement of business objectives. The 'big seven' key risks are as follows:

Human resources

As with the parent at large, the prime risk for HQI turns out to be human resources. HQI's staff had been accustomed to managing projects or budgets without a profit motive. But investing abroad, says Mr Giroux-Dufort, and pricing and managing for profitability requires an entirely new set of additional skills. 'It doesn't matter how capable you are at the technical aspects,' he explains. 'If you are unable to manage for profit, if you choose the wrong projects, you will fail.' To address this risk, HQI formed a human resource function focused on ensuring that the right competencies are in place for critical positions. Where gaps are identified, 'we are taking steps to complement those competencies, perhaps through training or hiring from the outside,' says Mr Giroux-Dufort.

Project selection (investment evaluation)

Noting work to be done on the second risk highlighted by the risk mapping process, the group hired a major consulting firm to assist with benchmarking the full range of related processes. As Mr Giroux-Dufort explains, 'we redesigned our investment process from A to Z – project identification, the modelling requirements, investment valuation, methodologies and all of the underlying assumptions and techniques. We felt this was important because our profitability depends not only on the management of assets but also on acquiring them at the right price.'

This is not to say existing processes were wholly inadequate. The group had always been equipped with numerous models and techniques acquired in the consulting business and from working with financial advisers and investment banks. However, HQI realized significant improvement was not only possible, but necessary. For now, the company is developing a more sophisticated risk adjusted NPV model – one that reflects the key risks of the international infrastructure investment and project management arena. Beyond this, the company hopes to supplement this model with a set of probabilistic models capable of projecting a range of returns for an individual project.

Ultimately, says Mr Giroux-Dufort, the group will develop a model that demonstrates how a potential investment fits in with the existing portfolio. 'We want the ability to view the investment on a risk adjusted basis incrementally, but also to look at the portfolio effects of one investment versus another.' How an investment melds with the existing portfolio is a critical component of project selection and capital allocation.

> **How an investment melds with the existing portfolio is a critical component of project selection and capital allocation.**

HQI's expanding portfolio

HQI has invested or committed almost 12 per cent of its $1.35 billion earmarked for international development over the next four years. Its portfolio so far includes assets in the following.

■ *Costa Rica.* Here the company has an up-and-running 10-megawatt hydroelectric plant, acquired in 1998. The group is engaged in the full range of generation and transmission.

■ *Senegal.* HQI has acquired the national electric company. The investment requires equipment and managerial upgrades, as well as significant further investment.

Continued ...

- *Peru*. The company is building long-distance transmission facilities to connect the north of the nation to the south (due for completion in 2000). This is a regulated project with guaranteed pricing and returns (although there is residual political risk).

- *Australia*. To arbitrage two markets, HQI is building underground transmission from Queensland to New South Wales. This is an unregulated, merchant endeavour.

- *China*. To gain a foothold in the world's most massive emerging economy, HQI has partnered with PSE&G to acquire and operate eight regulated hydroelectric plants.

Contractual risk

HQI is accustomed to writing contracts for professional services. However, these are relatively small contracts spread over a number of countries with relatively limited capital investment. Today, with the company pursuing a capital intensive presence in host countries, an assessment of contractual practices and risks is essential. This is a major change for the group. In a monopolistic, regulated environment, 'terms are set in stone for you – you dictate the conditions,' explains Mr Giroux-Dufort. But in unfamiliar local environments 'with their own rules' or in increasingly 'merchant' situations, obtaining the right contract language is critical. Accordingly, there are ongoing efforts to review and improve this area, and contractual risk is now addressed throughout the investment evaluation process.

Political risk

Infrastructure investments entailing 10, 20 or even 30 year lives (concession periods) are highly susceptible to risk: violence, war, expropriation, creeping expropriation (detrimental regulatory or economic changes initiated by the host government), various forms of confiscation and so on. The risk mapping process highlighted yet another element to this mix: 'The not so well defined risk that we might not have the right level of influence in the country to reduce the risk of potentially adverse changes by the government,' says Mr Giroux-Dufort. Here, HQI is working with a consulting firm to develop a model for managing political risk. For example, the company is looking at ways to analyze the obligations of various host governments in order to gauge and isolate the potential for political risk. Work is not yet complete, but the company is looking for ways to gather and analyze data from internal and external sources.

A closely related problem for the company is to evaluate more rigorously the cost-effectiveness of various insurance options from, for example, quasi-governmental organizations like MIGA or local export credit agencies (ECAs). For now the company purchases political risk insurance for all its investments – recognizing that the current portfolio of investments is not yet large nor diversified enough to fully cushion a significant political risk event. At a later stage, perhaps in three to five years, HQI will explore the reduction of coverage in this area, relying instead on a broad portfolio to absorb the costs of a significant political risk event.

Competitor risk

Looming large enough on its managers' radar screens to merit separate mention, the company is keenly aware it must improve its ability to make deals and manage projects in an increasingly competitive international environment. 'In the past, we did not have to analyze our competition or detail our strategic position,' says Mr Giroux-Dufort. Going forward, 'we now have to pay attention to these issues.'

Partnering risk

The company also recognizes that it must improve its ability to identify the best joint venture (JV) partners. 'What are the risks of a JV, who should we partner with and why, how can we be sure our interests are aligned with our partner's and are sufficiently protected – and who should we never partner with and why?' explains Mr Giroux-Dufort. Just as importantly, once a partner is identified, 'How can we work effectively with our partner to ensure the success of the relationship?' This risk is especially important in those countries where a significant amount of international investment and development activity often tends to be subject to corruption. Local joint venture partners and suppliers must, at a minimum, be creditworthy and have impeccable integrity and reputations, subject to appropriate background reference checks and a rigorous selection process.

Financial risk

Finally, although not initially highlighted, as the portfolio grows, the impact of foreign exchange and interest rate risks also increases. The company now has two professionals whose mission is to measure and quantify these and other financial exposures, evaluate hedging strategies, acquire appropriate tracking and modelling software and eventually manage these risks on a group-wide basis.

Communication and continuous learning: essential to the vision

Communications are particularly important in an organization with diverse cultures. At HQI, a third of the 100 member staff has been dealing with international consulting for many years. But two-thirds of the staff have been added only recently, with one-third arriving from the parent corporation and one-third from the outside. The challenge, says Mr Giroux-Dufort, is to bring these groups together to enable the company to build an international presence without taking on undue risk. Communication – spurred by top management's unqualified support – is driving the process. Here, HQI's President Michel Clair has met with the group at large on a number of occasions to stress the importance of the EWRM initiative. Regular briefings to discuss objectives, highlight progress and detail 'next steps' are a cornerstone of the group's efforts. There is even a regular newsletter serving as a channel to identify and discuss issues of vital concern.

Hand in hand with communication, HQI is also organizing training sessions to foster awareness and buy-in. For the group at large, these are not so much focused on specific risks but rather on the benefits and the checkpoints along the way to an enterprise-wide approach. These sessions will highlight, for example, changing policies, roles and responsibilities along with procedures. At HQI, there are one-hour modules for support personnel and three-hour sessions for professionals.

Beyond general awareness training, there are also more intensive sessions. Professionals at the company attend a five-hour workshop focused on specific risks. The goal, says Mr Giroux-Dufort, is to make certain that understanding is achieved 'both in terms of process and in terms of the tools available'. Ultimately, says Mr Marcil, the goal is to facilitate discussions of risk across processes and organizational boundaries. 'Many risks are common across business units,' explains Mr Marcil. 'The integrated risk management function is the co-ordinator in this case. We ask the units to share information, to help to identify offsets and to propose practical strategies.'

Ultimately, EWRM is all about people and continuous learning – and this is what makes training and communication so important. 'What we are building is the means to share individual experience,' says Mr Marcil. 'We are equipping managers with the knowledge and the tools they need. We are helping them to communicate through a common risk language. What we are building is something bigger and richer than individual experience – we are facilitating the sharing of knowledge.' Just as crucially, in the end, decision-making is a human experience. As Mr Giroux-Dufort explains, 'I'm very quantitative, but you cannot run a business just on the numbers. In the end you have to synthesize the issues and make a decision.'

THE END GAME

EWRM is still in its infancy at HQ and even at HQI. All of the above represents a sea change in mindset and operation. As outlined in the HQ vision developed by Mr Marcil and his team, HQI has taken the preliminary steps towards EWRM. It has conducted risk-mapping workshops and obtained organizational buy-in to the EWRM concept. It is now looking for ways to empower and incentivize its managers to survey the range of possible actions for risk mitigation and management – both on a business unit and group-wide level. Business managers recognize this: for fiscal year 1999/2000, they must include discussions of risks and risk actions in their business plans. Right now, says Mr Marcil, 'we are organizing training for middle managers so that they will better understand these tasks.' From there, the goal is to further develop the models and tools necessary to achieve the EWRM vision. 'That's the hard part,' says Mr Giroux-Dufort, 'and we are tackling it now.'

In the end, change enablement is probably the most important aspect of the approach being used by Mr Marcil, Mr Giroux-Dufort and their teams. Both Mr Giroux-Dufort and Mr Marcil believe risk consciousness is an ideal organizing principle and see an enterprise-wide approach as essential. 'Risk is inseparable from opportunity,' says Mr Marcil. 'The challenge is to make people aware of this, and make certain they realize that they are the closest and best qualified to identify, measure and manage risk – recognizing we are here to help when the challenge is more significant.' Only by attacking risks at both the business unit and group levels – a two-pronged approach – can a company truly optimize risk and return.

Although Mr Marcil and Mr Giroux-Dufort are pleased with progress to date, they are fully aware that the real work is yet to come. The appropriate people must be put in place to address skills gaps, communication channels have to be established, performance evaluation and planning relative to risk must be integrated, reporting must be standardized, modelling methodologies must be developed and perfected and supporting technologies must be implemented. Finally, processes must be developed to ensure a continual cycle of re-evaluation and refinement. 'Our vision and our function is all about helping the business units understand their risks, understand the strategic choices they are making and understand the potential synergy with the overall organization,' says Mr Marcil. 'Our vision is about learning. You must crawl before you can walk, and walk before you can run. We're just about ready to walk – and we believe one day we will run.'

> Change enablement is probably the most important aspect of the approach.

9

Getting started

> *The journey of a thousand miles must begin with a single step.*
>
> The Tao Chi
>
> *My advice to others? These are powerful ideas and they have enormous value. Don't take forever getting started.*
>
> Ghislain Giroux-Dufort, Director of Risk Management,
> Hydro-Quebec International
>
> *Without everybody embracing what we want to do, we haven't got a prayer.*
>
> Jack Welch, CEO, General Electric

Our intent is to encourage your firm to begin its journey to a more proactive, holistic and integrated approach to managing business risk. The objective of the EWRM journey is to evaluate and improve the firm's capabilities to identify and manage its uncertainties as it executes its strategies to achieve its objectives and create value. In short, the task is to make business risk management an integral part of the enterprise-wide agenda. Our advice is as follows:

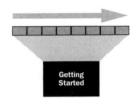

Getting Started

- Reorganize the *ad hoc*, reactive and fragmented activities of functions and departments operating as independent silos.

- Capitalize on emerging capabilities to redefine the value proposition of risk management, with emphasis on linking risk and opportunity.

- Manage individual risks or groups of related risks from a top-down enterprise-wide point of view.

- Seek to understand the interrelationships between risks and, based on that understanding, organize risks into appropriate families and pools.

- Develop more integrated risk management solutions, skilfully applying appropriate analytical frameworks and measurement methodologies to each risk family or pool.

- Practise a continuous improvement mindset.

EWRM will become the root differentiator between mere survivors and industry pace-setters.

The end result is an organization of incomparable capability in setting strategies, exploiting opportunities and creating wealth. In the new millennium, EWRM will become the root differentiator between mere survivors and industry pace-setters.

THE EWRM JOURNEY: HOW FAR DO YOU WANT TO GO?

Progress in virtually any endeavour is not possible without focusing on goals that stretch a firm's capabilities and its people. As in the axiom 'no pain, no gain', EWRM challenges an organization to strive for improvements in business performance and ultimately enhance shareholder value.

In this book, we have systematically explored eight stepping stones or phases:

- Adopt a common language.

- Establish goals, objectives and oversight.

- Assess risks and develop risk strategies.

- Design and implement risk management capabilities.

- Continuously improve the strategies, processes and measures for managing individual risks and groups of related risks.

- Aggregate multiple risk measures.

- Link risk management actions to improved enterprise performance.

- Formulate enterprise-wide risk management strategy.

Each step of the journey adds to the enterprise's capabilities and to the value proposition of business risk management.

EWRM is a cultural transition requiring a change process which must be managed as with any other similar initiative. As indicated in Chapter 2, the more steps the firm takes along the pathway to EWRM, the greater the requisite alignment of strategy, processes, people, technology and knowledge; hence, the more integrated the enterprise's risk management becomes and the greater its risk management capabilities.

How far a company chooses to go – and how fast – should be driven by the specific outcomes and benefits afforded by each phase of the journey. Figure 9.1 illustrates the stepping stones along the EWRM journey that we have explored in this book. Each step of the journey adds to the enterprise's capabilities and to the value proposition (benefits) of business risk management. But accompanying every advance in risk management capabilities is a corresponding increase in the degree of sophistication and the extent of commitment required. Therefore, each firm must decide – consciously – just how far along the EWRM journey it wishes to go. Then it must systematically align its strategies, processes, people, technology and knowledge (through staged improvements) to attain that plateau.

We have used the journey metaphor throughout this book to articulate a continuous learning process which cannot succeed unless it is initiated and sustained with vigour and persistence. The steps we have summarized above and illustrated throughout this book represent a journey that each organization customizes to its specific circumstances. It is our view that this notion of a journey as a 'future pulling' vision is a powerful one. It provides management with the confidence that each step leads the organization in the right direction, even though the approach to subsequent steps may not be crystal clear.

Fig. 9.1 The stepping stones along the EWRM journey: a synopsis

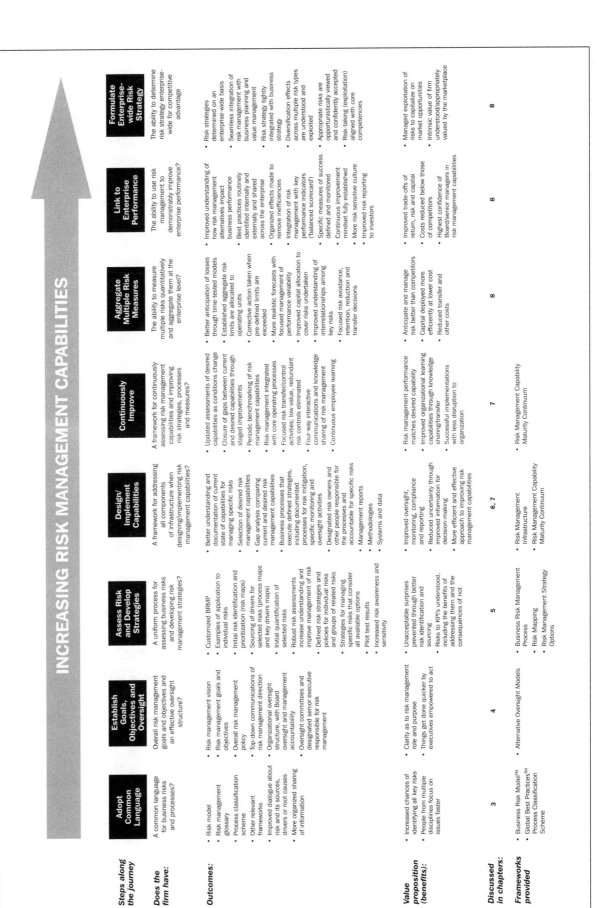

INCREASING RISK MANAGEMENT CAPABILITIES

Steps along the journey	Adopt Common Language	Establish Goals, Objectives and Oversight	Assess Risk and Develop Strategies	Design/Implement Capabilities	Continuously Improve	Aggregate Multiple Risk Measures	Link to Enterprise Performance	Formulate Enterprise-wide Risk Strategy
Does the firm have:	A common language for business risks and processes?	Overall risk management goals and objectives and an effective oversight structure?	A uniform process for assessing business risks and developing risk management strategies?	A framework for addressing all components of infrastructure when designing/implementing risk management capabilities?	A framework for continuously assessing risk management capabilities and improving risk strategies, processes and measures?	The ability to measure multiple risks quantitatively and aggregate them at the enterprise level?	The ability to use risk management to demonstrably improve enterprise performance?	The ability to determine risk strategy enterprise-wide for competitive advantage
Outcomes:	• Risk model • Risk management glossary • Process classification scheme • Other relevant frameworks • Improved dialogue about risk and its sources, drivers or root causes • More organized sharing of information	• Risk management vision • Risk management goals and objectives • Overall risk management policy • Top-down communications of risk management direction • Organizational oversight structure, with Board oversight and management accountability • Oversight committees and designated senior executive responsible for risk management	• Customized BRMP • Examples of application to individual risks • Initial risk identification and prioritization (risk maps) • Sourcing of drivers for selected risks (process maps and key drivers maps) • Initial quantification of selected risks • Robust risk assessments increase understanding and improve management of risk • Defined risk strategies and policies for individual risks and groups of related risks • Strategies for managing specific risks that consider all available options • Pilot test results • Increased risk awareness and sensitivity	• Better understanding and documentation of current state of capabilities for managing specific risks • Selection of desired risk management capabilities • Gap analysis comparing current and desired risk management capabilities • Business processes that execute defined strategies, including documented processes for risk mitigation, specific monitoring and oversight activities • Designated risk owners and other people responsible for the processes and accountable for specific risks • Management reports • Methodologies • Systems and data	• Updated assessments of desired capabilities as conditions change • Closure of gaps between current and desired capabilities through staged improvements • Periodic benchmarking of risk management capabilities • Risk management integrated with core operating processes • Focused risk transfer/control activities; low value, redundant risk controls eliminated • Four-way interactive communications and knowledge sharing of risk management • Continuous employee learning	• Better anticipation of losses through time-tested models • Established aggregate risk limits are allocated to operating units • Corrective action taken when pre-defined limits are exceeded • More realistic forecasts with focused management of performance variability • Improved capital allocation to cover risks undertaken • Improved understanding of interrelationships among key risks • Focused risk avoidance, retention, reduction and transfer decisions	• Improved understanding of how risk management alternatives impact business performance • Best practices routinely identified internally and externally and shared across the enterprise • Organized effects made to remove inefficiencies • Integration of risk management with key performance indicators (balanced scorecard) • Specific measures of success defined and monitored • Continuous improvement mindset fully established • More risk sensitive culture • Improved risk reporting to investors	• Risk strategies determined on an enterprise-wide basis • Seamless integration of risk management with business planning and value management • Risk strategy tightly integrated with business strategy • Diversification effects across multiple risk types are understood and exploited • Appropriate risks are opportunistically viewed and confidently accepted • Risk-taking (exploitation) aligned with core competencies
Value proposition (benefits):	• Increased chances of identifying all key risks • People from multiple disciplines focus on issues faster	• Clarity as to risk management role and purpose • Things get done quicker by executives empowered to act	• Unacceptable surprises prevented through better risk identification and sourcing • Risks to KPI's understood, including the benefits of addressing them and the consequences of not	• Improved oversight, monitoring, compliance and reporting • Reduced uncertainty through improved information for decision-making • More efficient and effective approach to improving risk management capabilities	• Risk management performance matches desired capability • Improved organizational learning capabilities through knowledge sharing/transfer • Successful implementations with less disruption to organization	• Anticipate and manage risk better than competitors • Capital deployed more efficiently at lower cost • Reduced transfer and other costs	• Improved trade-offs of return, risk and capital • Costs reduced below those of competitors • Highest confidence of Board/senior managers in risk management capabilities	• Managed exploitation of risks to capitalize on market opportunities • Intrinsic value of firm understood/appropriately valued by the marketplace
Discussed in chapters:	3	4	5	6, 7	7	8	8	8
Frameworks provided	• Business Risk Model™ • Global Best Practices™ Process Classification Scheme	• Alternative Oversight Models	• Business Risk Management Process • Risk Mapping • Risk Management Strategy Options	• Risk Management Infrastructure • Risk Management Capability Maturity Continuum	• Risk Management Capability Maturity Continuum			

KEYS TO NAVIGATING THE JOURNEY

Aligning strategy, processes, people, technology and knowledge to increase EWRM capabilities requires a disciplined approach that is consistent with the enterprise-wide view defined by the organization's structure and culture and management's operating philosophy. Although a variety of approaches can be used to implement EWRM, our experience has consistently shown that successful initiatives incorporate time-tested practices to plan, orchestrate and manage the change process. We have organized them as 'key success factors' in four categories as shown in Figure 9.2.

> **Successful EWRM initiatives incorporate time-tested practices to plan, orchestrate and manage the change process.**

Fig. 9.2 Key success factors when implementing EWRM

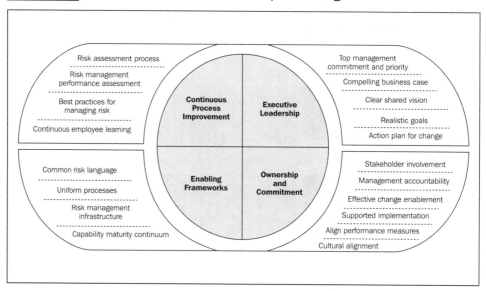

While we have discussed the importance of all of these practices throughout this book, we believe that those listed under 'Executive Leadership' and 'Ownership and Commitment' are the keys to getting the EWRM journey started. Effective change enablement assures that these key success factors are considered in the EWRM initiative. One point is especially critical: without top management support these initiatives will fail. As Roland Köhler, Chief Risk Officer at Holderbank, advises: 'If the Executive Committee is not 100 per cent behind the programme, do not accept the task.'

Sound change enablement techniques build awareness, buy-in and support for business risk management across the enterprise and enhance the success of the change effort by fostering a proactive, anticipatory risk management culture. A change focus is vital because, ultimately, successful implementation is about people internalizing and owning the new attitudes, knowledge and behaviours that an EWRM approach requires. While there are volumes of books and articles on change and scores of consultants in the marketplace that provide insight into the process, the reality that companies face is that change is often a painful, even chaotic, process. As change experts often point out, 'How do you change the tyres when the car is travelling 60 miles per hour?'

The following best practices are listed under 'Executive Leadership' and 'Ownership and Commitment'.

Executive leadership

- *Commit senior executives.* Support from the top is vital to instigate and sustain successful change. Senior management must commit to EWRM as a priority and demonstrate this commitment through consistent actions to create and sustain momentum for the initiative. The executives interviewed for this book have almost unanimously confirmed that this level of commitment is where everything starts. One example is illustrated by Hydro-Quebec, which used a facilitated workshop session to generate awareness of the benefits of EWRM among its senior executive team and build commitment for specific action steps for the initiative. As André Marcil, General Manager responsible for integrated risk management at Hydro-Quebec, points out, 'Without this unified support from the top, a true enterprise-wide initiative would not be possible.'

'If the Executive Committee is not 100 per cent behind the programme, do not accept the task.'

- *Develop a strong business case that clarifies why change is the only option.* Change under any circumstance is difficult to initiate, but unless the need to change is clearly understood, it will not happen. Organizational readiness and an undeniable case for change, as well as clear communications from top management that change is essential, are vital to getting started. In developing a business case, it is important to address the internal and external pressure points that create the need for change as well as the state of readiness and existing structures which can drive or constrain change. These factors reflect the organization's resiliency or ability to understand and embrace change. The business case provides the economic justification for action by articulating the organizational and personal benefits which can be achieved as well as the cost of inaction, i.e. why we need to begin our journey and what happens if we don't. It also considers the impact of change on performance goals and incentives.

- *Focus on the big picture with a compelling shared vision.* Once the need has been established, top management must provide a compelling, shared vision of the future state that provides direction for positive change. This vision should clearly describe the scope, goals and objectives for the EWRM initiative and articulate the 'what's in it for me' for everyone expected to contribute to the implementation process.

- *Set realistic goals.* Risk management objectives should not exceed the firm's risk management capabilities. Any gaps must be identified and addressed or else the change process will founder. The Risk Management Capability Maturity

Continuum introduced in Chapter 7 is a powerful tool for identifying gaps requiring attention. Managers should consider these gaps to ensure that change goals are realistic and needed improvements are appropriately staged over time.

- *Develop a clear plan of action.* A well-defined plan for change provides a clear roadmap to create value for the organization and milestones to monitor progress. As one executive commenting on the change process points out, 'If you don't know where you're going, any road will do; if you don't know where you are, a map is no good.' The change plan identifies what is to be accomplished, who is in charge and who is responsible for executing specific tasks. Aligning the components of infrastructure as we discussed in Chapter 6 – strategy, processes, people, reporting, methods and systems – provides a powerful framework for focusing the change effort.

Ownership and commitment

- *Obtain stakeholder involvement and commitment.* Identifying leaders throughout the organization and gaining their support is critical to successful implementation. An effective change process positions key stakeholders along a continuum from *awareness* to *buy-in* and ultimately to *ownership*. Senior management have a dual role of demonstrating leadership and finding the 'captains and lieutenants' throughout the firm who will lead the charge as role models. A workshop approach is one way to create management buy-in. Holderbank found the use of one and a half day meetings – supported by technology – highly effective in gaining the interest, confidence and support of local managers. 'There is no faster, more effective means to jump start your risk management implementation,' says Roland Köhler, CRO of Holderbank.

> **Understanding the people and accountability issues is one of the most vital steps of the change process.**

- *Establish accountability for results.* Understanding the people and accountability issues is one of the most vital steps of the change process. A goal of EWRM is to incorporate risk management into the daily agenda and decision-making processes of the organization. This means that, ultimately, every manager is responsible. This can only happen if goals are clearly articulated, and the appropriate individuals accept responsibility for achieving those goals and are held accountable for results.

- *Enable change by focusing on the 'human side'.* Too often, the change focus is limited to the 'technical side' such as the policies and limits, strategies, processes, measures, systems, data and reports. While important, these are not the only objects of change. As illustrated in the Holderbank case, there is also the important 'human' side of risk management that maximizes the use of a common language, effective communication, increasing risk awareness and sensitivity, and effective knowledge sharing as critical components of managing change. Communication about the ongoing progress of implementing EWRM should be simple and frequent to maintain momentum.

- *Support the implementation process.* The journey towards EWRM is a process which requires a systematic approach using sound project management techniques. The implementation process must be supported with dedicated resources, e.g. by the business risk management function discussed in Chapter 4, appropriate standards, best practices, relevant measures and effective feedback mechanisms. Quality assurance is also important as well as clear communication regarding the authority of the implementation teams, in effect, empowering them to do their jobs.

- *Align organizational, process and individual performance measures.* As discussed earlier, aligning the firm's reward systems and incentive plans with the change process through performance metrics is an important step. Virtually all executives interviewed concur. For example, as Paul Brink, Director of Risk Management at Dow Chemical, explains, 'You need an effective scorecard for the organization as a whole, you need agreement on that scorecard, and you need all subsequent scorecards to be built upon that foundation. If all the individual scorecards do not pull in the same direction, you get nowhere.' Unless individual performance measures are consistent with EWRM objectives, and unless the EWRM objectives are closely linked with overall business strategy, the desired results will not be achieved.

'If all the individual scorecards do not pull in the same direction, you get nowhere.'

- *Align the change process with the firm's culture.* EWRM cannot be seen as an independent initiative but must become a part of the culture – 'the way we do things here.' Management must build on current practices that support the risk management vision and develop new or improved processes, tools and techniques that will be accepted within the organization. Education and communication can be utilized to foster a more proactive, anticipatory culture supporting business risk management. Reinforcing messages and rewards must engage key risk owners and sustain their ongoing support. The use of pilots, i.e. the 'quiet splash', can provide a means of transitioning to new processes by demonstrating early successes and learning from mistakes. Experimentation and innovation, particularly with respect to measurement methodologies, can help integrate EWRM into the culture and establish ownership of results.

The above list of change enablement practices, if executed competently, leads to sustainable change. Together, they are summarized in Figure 9.3, including observations on the consequences should any one of them be neglected.

Fig. 9.3 Change enablement practices and consequences if ignored

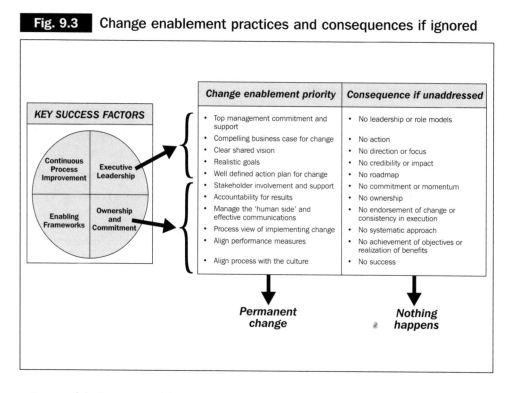

Successful change enablement is hard work. It combines both technical and human systems that align the goals and aspirations of people with the goals and objectives of the enterprise. The focus is on results, not just activity. Without careful management of change, there is a risk of suboptimal solutions, high resistance to desirable change, dysfunctional behaviour and failure to realize expected benefits.

KEYS TO GETTING STARTED: EWRM TRAIL MARKERS

EWRM is a journey, not a destination. It requires a disciplined and methodical approach to navigate successfully.

As André Marcil of Hydro-Quebec explains, his company, like nearly all EWRM early-adopters, is integrating risk management into the business planning process. 'Each unit must have a plan of action regarding their own risks,' he explains. 'We will be monitoring the results of those plans on a regular basis, and we'll be able to see how the process is moving. And this means we start with a good summary of a few major risks, document and measure those risks, and then decide what actions to take.' Hydro-Quebec's plan is to put in place a phased programme over three years, initially focusing on the most significant risks. According to Mr Marcil, 'For the second year, we will add another group of risks. And the third year, a third layer of risks. At the end of the three years, if we're successful, we should have a strong hold on about 80 per cent of our risks. If we achieve that, we'll be where we want to be.' This '80 per cent philosophy' is a good one for managers to consider as no firm has the resources to manage every single risk, so trade-offs are inevitable.

To get started, it is useful to translate the vision of a journey into a logical set of tasks that managers and risk owners can execute. These tasks target the business risks and processes that require the most attention, define the overall business risk management strategy and framework, and hold every line manager accountable for managing risk. The idea is to start with a comprehensive top-down view to target the most significant areas that can lead to early 'success stories'. A top-down approach also ensures that the implementation is consistent with the firm's objectives, strategies, organizational structure, operating philosophy (centralized versus decentralized, command and control versus empowering, etc.) and culture.

Start with a comprehensive top-down view to target the most significant areas.

- *Establish oversight structure.* Once senior management is committed, a working group of senior executives (a RMEC, for example), supported by a CRO, is empowered to build the organization's risk management capabilities. These executives are supported by a central staff function, such as a business risk management function. When chartering the RMEC and CRO, the CEO, executive committee and board of directors define the scope of EWRM, e.g. what does 'enterprise-wide' mean and what are its implications? The RMEC and CRO then perform the tasks below.

- *Define common language and framework.* The organization's risk language and process classification scheme provide a useful starting point for identifying risks and assessing the source of risks within business processes.

- *Target risks and processes.* Through an effective targeting process, the firm identifies the businesses and product groupings, business risks and business processes that require the most attention based on its business objectives and strategies. As a high level assessment, targeting helps the RMEC focus on those areas which expose the company to performance variability and losses affecting earnings, cash flow and capital within a given time horizon. Targeting leads to identification of industry and company 'trouble spots', historical problems and areas where there are likely to be significant changes. The result is a menu of prioritized operating units, business risks and processes on which to focus subsequent efforts.

- *Develop overall goals, objectives and processes.* Here the RMEC defines the business risk management vision, goals and objectives for the enterprise as a whole and its business units, as illustrated in Chapter 4, based on its understanding of the targeted units, processes and risks. The business risk goals and objectives provide a 'big picture view' of how to organize the firm's business risk management. From this broader view, an overall risk management policy is developed. To achieve 'buy-in' enterprise-wide, its development should be highly participatory. It is then approved by the board and implemented under the direction of the RMEC and CRO. The policy defines the risk management roles, responsibilities and accountabilities ('Every Manager Accountable'). A uniform process (such as the BRMP introduced in Chapter 5) is also developed for customization across the firm.

- *Assess risk management capabilities.* Successful firms already have talented personnel at work managing risk who may already have improvement initiatives underway. The current state of risk management is documented for use as a baseline to identify needed improvements. The six components of infrastructure and the Risk Management Capability Maturity Continuum introduced in Chapters 6 and 7 are useful tools for this purpose. This step also provides the opportunity to harvest best practices within the organization which can be shared and institutionalized throughout the enterprise. Once the current state is understood, the desired risk management capabilities are later developed by risk owners for review and approval by the RMEC so comparisons with the current state to identify gaps can be made. The RMEC is now positioned to develop an EWRM communications plan (see box). If there are priority risks that do not have a designated owner, a responsible manager should be appointed as soon as possible.

An EWRM communications plan

EWRM requires a change in mindset about risk and the role of risk management in the organization. It also requires a change in behaviour as managers learn to incorporate risk and an enterprise-wide view into their decision-making. To begin this transition, it is critical for the RMEC to develop a plan with the assistance of the CRO that outlines the key communications required as the firm operationalizes its new approach.

A well executed communications plan addresses the key questions on people's minds:

- What are we doing?
- Why is it necessary?
- How does the change relate to the firm's objectives and strategy?
- Why will the organization be more competitive?
- Is management really committed?
- Will the right people be involved?
- What is the change plan?
- Can it be done?

Continued ...

- How will it be supported?

- Is it being done fairly?

- What's in it for me?

- Will anyone notice if I don't participate?

- How will progress be measured?

- Will my compensation be affected?

- How will we know whether we are successful?

For example, communications will be needed to announce:

- the formation and purpose of the RMEC;

- the role and responsibilities of the CRO;

- the objectives of risk management across the enterprise and for specific units;

- key risks requiring attention;

- the planned phases over the near to intermediate term as the firm implements its EWRM approach and the enabling frameworks, tools and techniques available for use throughout the firm.

We see organizations making enabling frameworks available via an intranet website. Ongoing communication highlighting risk management opportunities, success stories and learning reinforce the impact of risk management on the business and help to achieve buy-in across the enterprise.

A communications plan also addresses the value proposition of risk management. For example, is it contributing to the establishment of sustainable competitive advantage? Is it improving business performance? Is it optimizing costs? If the answer to any of these and other questions is 'yes', the firm's communications should explain that contribution. The plan should also describe how the new EWRM approach is linked to enterprise performance and how the process and reward systems are aligned to support implementation. It should address who owns the priority risks and critical processes, as well as who has the responsibility for the vital oversight role. Finally, the plan should clearly convey that there is executive/senior management buy-in and support. A good communications plan helps establish EWRM as part of the firm's culture – 'the way we do things here,' as one CFO of a power generation company beginning its EWRM journey pointed out.

THE LAUNCH PAD

The five tasks described above do not deliver EWRM, but rather they create the stable launch pad required to take the journey forward. As Figure 9.4 illustrates, these tasks lead the firm to (a) identifying a well-defined set of risks and (b) assigning clear accountability for managing those risks. In addition, they complete the first two steps of the journey that we have outlined in this book – adopt a common language and establish goals, objectives and oversight. Finally they pave the way for the remaining steps. The five tasks and the resulting outcomes are summarized in the first row of Figure 9.4.

The second row of Figure 9.4 applies the process view of the BRMP introduced in Chapters 5 and 6 to define additional tasks for moving implementation forward *after* the tasks in the first row are completed. Combined together, the tasks summarized in Figure 9.4 provide a high-level work plan.

EWRM is a value-generating process that provides the discipline and tools for mastering risk as the organization creates value.

The second row tasks continue the implementation of an EWRM approach – sourcing and measuring risk, formulating risk management strategies, designing and implementing risk management capabilities, monitoring risk and performance, and continuous improvement. These tasks are 'drill down' activities applied by individual risk owners working in tandem with the CRO and the RMEC and under the appropriate oversight. If attempted *before* achieving the focus and accountability arising from the tasks in the first row of Figure 9.4, resources may be misallocated to the wrong risk areas. In essence, the top-down approach we recommend is to start with the five tasks in the first row to get organized and achieve 'quick hits' and successful results that build up momentum for a successful journey.

SUMMARY

Risk is a reality of life and life is constantly changing in the new economy. EWRM is a new strategic process that identifies and addresses the full range of business opportunities and risks. It is needed because the forces of the new economy are rewriting the rules of wealth creation and preservation. EWRM is a value-generating business risk management process that provides the discipline and tools for mastering risk as the organization creates value.

EWRM represents a sea change in organizational attitude and behaviour. As with any significant change, the adoption of EWRM is fundamentally a process of building awareness, developing buy-in and ultimately driving the acceptance of ownership throughout the organization. Change enablement is, therefore, a significant aspect of any initiative of this magnitude. The EWRM journey – enabled by the frameworks provided in this book, including an effectively functioning BRMP – leads the firm to improving its risk management capabilities.

Fig. 9.4 The launch pad to EWRM: A high level roadmap

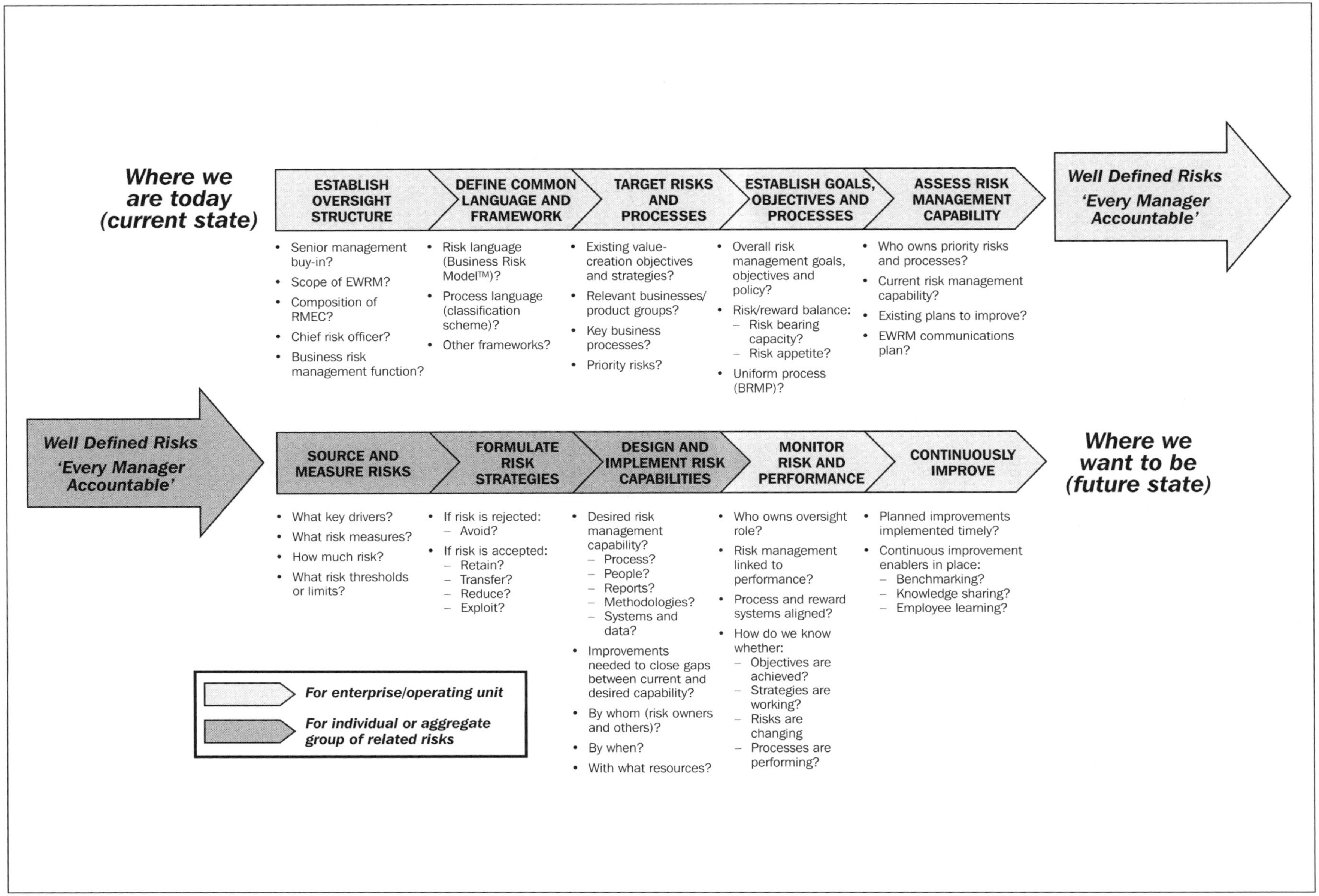

Where we are today (current state)

Well Defined Risks 'Every Manager Accountable'

ESTABLISH OVERSIGHT STRUCTURE	DEFINE COMMON LANGUAGE AND FRAMEWORK	TARGET RISKS AND PROCESSES	ESTABLISH GOALS, OBJECTIVES AND PROCESSES	ASSESS RISK MANAGEMENT CAPABILITY

• Senior management buy-in?
 • Scope of EWRM?
 • Composition of RMEC?
 • Chief risk officer?
 • Business risk management function?
	• Risk language (Business Risk Model™)?
	 • Process language (classification scheme)?
	 • Other frameworks?
		• Existing value-creation objectives and strategies?
		 • Relevant businesses/product groups?
		 • Key business processes?
		 • Priority risks?
			• Overall risk management goals, objectives and policy?
			 • Risk/reward balance:
			   – Risk bearing capacity?
			   – Risk appetite?
			 • Uniform process (BRMP)?
				• Who owns priority risks and processes?
				 • Current risk management capability?
				 • Existing plans to improve?
				 • EWRM communications plan?

SOURCE AND MEASURE RISKS	FORMULATE RISK STRATEGIES	DESIGN AND IMPLEMENT RISK CAPABILITIES	MONITOR RISK AND PERFORMANCE	CONTINUOUSLY IMPROVE

• What key drivers?
 • What risk measures?
 • How much risk?
 • What risk thresholds or limits?
	• If risk is rejected:
	   – Avoid?
	 • If risk is accepted:
	   – Retain?
	   – Transfer?
	   – Reduce?
	   – Exploit?
		• Desired risk management capability?
		   – Process?
		   – People?
		   – Reports?
		   – Methodologies?
		   – Systems and data?
		 • Improvements needed to close gaps between current and desired capability?
		 • By whom (risk owners and others)?
		 • By when?
		 • With what resources?
			• Who owns oversight role?
			 • Risk management linked to performance?
			 • Process and reward systems aligned?
			 • How do we know whether:
			   – Objectives are achieved?
			   – Strategies are working?
			   – Risks are changing
			   – Processes are performing?
				• Planned improvements implemented timely?
				 • Continuous improvement enablers in place:
				   – Benchmarking?
				   – Knowledge sharing?
				   – Employee learning?

Where we want to be (future state)

Well Defined Risks 'Every Manager Accountable'

For enterprise/operating unit

For individual or aggregate group of related risks

As it navigates its journey, the organization becomes more sensitive to changes in the external environment and within its internal business processes. This sensitivity in the culture is important because if there is one thing we can expect in the new economy, it is this: *opportunities and risks will continue to surface and change rapidly as the dynamic global marketplace evolves*. Therefore, developing an effective, enterprise-wide view of business risk management will always be a journey of continuous learning and improvement, not an event that comes and goes. Transforming business risk management to a truly enterprise-wide strategic process provides a source of competitive advantage, leads to improved business performance and optimizes cost.

So... let's begin

Our expectation is that readers of this book will lead their companies in taking a fresh look at their risk management to increase the risk sensitivity of their culture; link risk with opportunity and build differentiating capabilities that provide a source of competitive advantage. This cultural shift is vital as risk is inherent in *all* business activity – indeed, risk is the partner of opportunity. All opportunities have a cost – and risk is an integral part of that cost. That is why directors, CEOs and line managers must use practical and uniform processes and tools to evaluate risks and opportunities simultaneously. Their collaborative efforts to build EWRM capabilities will help them optimize their desire for growth and return with their tolerance for risk as they create value in the new economy.

For those companies that choose to begin their EWRM journey, we wish them well. We are confident that their efforts will be rewarded. For those companies that have already begun their journey, we hope to learn valuable lessons and insights from their successes. Finally, for those companies who are well down the road toward EWRM, we look forward to the positive results and advances from their pioneering efforts.

Appendices

The current state of risk management

In a 1995 research study co-authored by Arthur Andersen and the Economist Intelligence Unit, *Managing business risk: An integrated approach*, a world-wide survey determined that:

- fewer than 50 per cent of senior executives had 'high confidence' that their risk management systems are identifying and managing all potentially significant business risks;

- more than 50 per cent had made recent significant changes in those systems; and

- nearly 60 per cent planned significant changes within three years.

In June 1998, a subsequent study conducted by Arthur Andersen with the EIU, *Managing business risks in the information age*, reconfirmed the results of the earlier work.

These results also parallel the results of a still more recent study, *New Dimensions on Business Risks*, conducted by Arthur Andersen and a leading insurance underwriter in the autumn of 1998. Workshops and related survey activities with participating executives from 25 Global 1000 and middle market companies highlighted just a few of the opportunities and challenges:

- *Goals, objectives and oversight.* Risk management goals and objectives are not adequately articulated. Written policies do not clearly articulate an enterprise-wide strategy linking risk management to business strategy. Policies in general are more often developed in reaction to regulatory requirements and events than as a proactive and anticipatory approach to managing the business. Expanded board involvement to provide oversight over the process is considered highly desirable – making risk management an integral component of the corporate governance process. A lack of a common language – a means to improve communication – is a significant hindrance.

- *Risk assessment.* Risk assessment methods are generally *ad hoc* and inconsistent throughout the enterprise or are not well developed. Improvement is needed in risk measurement and in the linkage of risk management activities to enterprise performance.

- *Risk management strategies.* A more rigorous approach to formulating strategy for individual risks is needed. When a new risk is identified, the appointment of a risk 'owner' – someone accountable for managing and monitoring that risk – is often slow to occur, if at all.

- *Capabilities to execute selected strategies.* Risks are managed in 'silos' and in an unco-ordinated fashion across the firm and its business units. Some risks are better managed than others. Opportunities to aggregate risks into pools or families – to exploit diversification and other opportunities – are impeded by functional barriers. Performance and reward systems do not reinforce desirable risk management capabilities, behaviours and priorities throughout the enterprise and its units.

- *Monitoring.* Reporting about risk and risk management – information that could assist management in understanding the impact of risk on the firm's operating performance – is sporadic and inconsistent. Generally, the formal reporting that does exist is limited to hedging performance and compliance with established risk controls.

- *Continuous improvement.* These efforts are often narrowly focused on internal control. There is very little benchmarking activity and sharing of best practices.

- *Information for decision-making.* Virtually every executive stated the need for more and better information. 'Too much data, not enough information' is a common frustration.

The above shortcomings exist to some degree in many companies. With the business environment changing rapidly and the tools and processes available to manage risks evolving, directors, CEOs, senior executives and line managers should re-evaluate the value proposition of risk management.

The Arthur Andersen Business Risk Model™: abbreviated definitions of business risks

SECTION I: ENVIRONMENT RISK

Environment risk arises when there are external forces that could affect the viability of the enterprise's business model, including the fundamentals that drive the overall objectives and strategies that define that model.

1. *Competitor risk.* Actions of competitors or new entrants to the market impair the firm's competitive advantage or even threaten its ability to survive.

2. *Customer wants risk.* Pervasive customer needs and wants change and the firm isn't aware, e.g. increased demand for faster delivery or turnaround on products and services.

3. *Technological innovation risk.* The firm is not leveraging advancements in technology in its business model to achieve or sustain competitive advantage or is exposed to the actions of competitors or substitutes that do leverage technology to attain superior quality, cost and/or time performance in their products, services and processes.

4. *Sensitivity risk.* Overcommitment of resources and expected future cash flows threatens the firm's capacity to withstand changes in environmental forces (e.g. interest rates, market demand, changes in regulations, etc.) beyond its control.

5. *Shareholder relations risk.* A decline in investor confidence in the firm's business model or ability to execute its model threatens its capacity to efficiently raise capital or sustain share valuations.

6. *Capital availability risk.* Insufficient access to capital threatens the firm's capacity to grow, execute its business model and generate future financial returns.

7. *Sovereign/political risk.* Adverse political actions threaten the firm's resources and future cash flows in a country in which the firm has invested significantly, is dependent on a significant volume of business or has entered into a significant agreement with a counterparty subject to the laws of that country.

8. *Legal risk.* Changing laws threaten the firm's capacity to consummate important transactions, enforce contractual agreements or implement specific strategies and activities.

9. *Regulatory risk*. Changing regulations threaten the firm's competitive position and its capacity to efficiently conduct business.

10. *Industry risk*. Changes in opportunities and threats, capabilities of competitors, and other conditions affecting the firm's industry threaten the attractiveness or long-term viability of that industry.

11. *Financial markets risk*. Movements in prices, rates, indices, etc., affect the value of the firm's financial assets and stock price, which may also affect its cost of capital and/or its ability to raise capital.

12. *Catastrophic loss risk*. A major disaster threatens the firm's ability to sustain operations, provide essential products and services or recover operating costs.

SECTION II: PROCESS RISK

Process risk is the risk that the firm's business processes are not effectively acquiring, managing, renewing and disposing the assets of the business; are not clearly defined; are poorly aligned with the strategies driving the firm's business model; are not performing effectively and efficiently in satisfying customer needs; are not creating value; or are diluting value by exposing significant financial, physical, information and intellectual assets to unacceptable losses, risk-taking, misappropriation or misuse. These risks affect the success with which the firm executes its business model.

A. Operations risk

Operations risk is the risk that operations are inefficient and ineffective in executing the firm's business model, satisfying customers and achieving the firm's quality, cost and time performance objectives.

1. *Customer satisfaction risk*. A lack of focus on customers threatens the firm's capacity to meet or exceed customer expectations.

2. *Human resources risk*. A lack of requisite knowledge, skills and experiences among the firm's key personnel threatens the execution of its business model and achievement of critical business objectives.

3. *Knowledge capital risk*. Processes for capturing and institutionalizing learning across the firm are either non-existent or ineffective, resulting in slow response time, high costs, repeated mistakes, slow competence development, constraints on growth and unmotivated employees.

4. *Product development risk*. Ineffective product development threatens the firm's ability to meet or exceed customers' needs and wants consistently over the long term.

5. *Efficiency risk*. Inefficient operations threaten the firm's capacity to produce goods or services at or below cost levels incurred by competitors or world-class performing companies.

6. *Capacity risk*. Insufficient capacity threatens the firm's ability to meet customer demands, or excess capacity threatens the firm's ability to generate competitive profit margins.

7. *Performance gap risk*. Inability to perform at world-class levels in terms of quality, cost and/or cycle time performance due to inferior internal operating practices and/or external relationships threatens the demand for the firm's products or services.

8. *Cycle time risk*. Unnecessary activities threaten the firm's capacity to develop, produce and deliver goods or services on a timely basis.

9. *Sourcing risk*. Limited sources of energy, metals and other key commodities, raw materials and component parts threaten the firm's ability to produce quality products at competitive prices on a timely basis.

10. *Channel effectiveness risk*. Poorly performing or positioned distribution channels threaten the firm's capacity to effectively and efficiently access current and potential customers and end users.

11. *Partnering risk*. Inefficient or ineffective alliance, joint venture, affiliate and other external relationships affect the firm's capability to compete; these uncertainties arise due to choosing the wrong partner, poor execution, taking more than is given (resulting in loss of a partner) and failing to capitalize on partnering opportunities.

12. *Compliance (regulatory and other) risk*. Non-compliance with customer requirements, prescribed organizational policies and procedures or laws and regulations may result in lower quality, higher production costs, lost revenues, unnecessary delays, penalties, fines, etc.

13. *Business interruption risk*. Business interruptions stemming from the unavailability of raw materials, information technologies, skilled labour, facilities or other resources threaten the firm's capacity to continue operations.

14. *Product/service failure risk*. Faulty or non-performing products or services expose the firm to customer complaints, warranty claims, field repairs, returns, product liability claims, litigation and loss of revenues, market share and business reputation.

15. *Environmental risk*. Activities harmful to the environment expose the firm to liabilities for bodily injury, property damage, cost of removal, punitive damages, etc.

16. *Health and safety risk.* Failure to provide a safe working environment for its workers exposes the firm to compensation liabilities, loss of business reputation and other costs.

17. *Trademark/brand erosion risk.* Erosion of a trademark or brand over time threatens the demand for the firm's products or services and impairs its ability to grow future revenue streams.

B. Financial risk

Financial risk is the risk that cash flows and financial risks are not managed cost-effectively to (a) maximize cash availability, (b) reduce uncertainty of currency, interest rate, credit and other financial risks, or (c) move cash funds quickly and without loss of value to wherever they are needed most.

Price risk

Price risk is the exposure of earnings or net worth to changes in market factors (e.g. interest rates, currency rates, etc.) which affect income, expense or balance sheet values.

1. *Interest rate risk.* Significant movements in interest rates expose the firm to higher borrowing costs, lower investment yields or decreased asset values.

2. *Currency/foreign exchange risk.* Volatility in foreign exchange rates exposes the firm to economic and accounting losses.

3. *Equity risk.* Exposure to fluctuations in the value of equity securities or income streams from equity ownership in an incorporated entity.

4. *Commodity pricing risk.* Fluctuations in commodity prices expose the firm to lower product margins or trading losses.

5. *Financial instrument risk.* Exposure to excessive management costs or losses due to complexity or unintended consequences of financial instrument structures.

Liquidity risk

Liquidity risk is the exposure to loss as a result of the inability to meet cash flow obligations in a timely and cost-effective manner. It also includes the exposure of asset valuations or traded positions to an imbalance or lack of buyers and sellers in a particular market, i.e. an illiquid market.

1. *Cash flow risk.* Exposure to lower returns or the necessity to borrow due to shortfalls in cash or expected cash flows (or variances in their timing).

2. *Opportunity loss risk*. The use of funds in a manner that leads to the loss of economic value, including time value losses and transaction costs.

3. *Concentration risk*. Exposure to loss due to participation in a narrow market consisting of a limited group of counterparties resulting in inability to consummate transactions at reasonable prices within a reasonable timeframe.

Credit risk

The exposure to actual loss or opportunity cost as a result of the default (or other failure to perform) by an economic or legal entity (the debtor) with which the company does business.

1. *Default risk*. A counterparty to a financial transaction is unable to fulfil its obligations.

2. *Concentration risk*. Exposure of a significant portion of business to a company or group of companies that are similarly impacted by events.

3. *Settlement risk*. Different settlement times between the capital markets of the firm and its counterparties expose the firm to a short-term risk of counterparty default on obligations.

4. *Collateral risk*. The loss of value or inability to secure control of an asset provided to a firm as security.

C. Empowerment risk

Empowerment risk is the risk that managers and employees (a) are not properly led, (b) don't know what to do when they need to do it, (c) exceed the boundaries of their assigned authorities, or (d) are given incentives to do the wrong thing.

1. *Leadership risk*. The firm's people are not being effectively led, which may result in a lack of direction, customer focus, motivation to perform, management credibility and trust throughout the firm.

2. *Authority/limit risk*. Ineffective lines of authority may cause managers or employees to do things they should not do or fail to do things they should. Failure to establish or enforce limits on personnel actions may cause employees to commit unauthorized or unethical acts, or to assume unauthorized or unacceptable risks.

3. *Outsourcing risk*. Outsourcing activities to third parties may result in the third parties not acting within the intended limits of their authority or not performing in a manner consistent with the firm's strategies and objectives.

4. *Performance incentives risk*. Unrealistic, misunderstood, subjective or non-actionable performance measures may cause managers and employees to

act in a manner inconsistent with the firm's objectives, strategies and ethical standards, or with prudent business practice.

5. *Change readiness risk.* The people within the firm are unable to implement process and product/service improvements quickly enough to keep pace with changes in the marketplace.

6. *Communications risk.* Ineffective communication channels may result in messages that are inconsistent with authorized responsibilities or established performance measures.

D. Information processing/technology risk

Information processing technology risk is the risk that the information technologies used in the firm (a) are not operating as intended, (b) are compromising the integrity and reliability of data and information, (c) are exposing significant assets to potential loss or misuse, or (d) are exposing the firm's ability to sustain the operation of critical processes.

1. *Relevance risk.* Irrelevant information created or summarized by an application system may adversely affect users' decisions.

2. *Integrity risk.* All of the risks associated with the authorization, completeness and accuracy of transactions as they are entered into, processed by, summarized by and reported by the various application systems deployed by the firm.

3. *Access risk.* Failure to adequately restrict access to information (data or programmes) may result in unauthorized knowledge and use of confidential information, *or* overly restrictive access to information may preclude personnel from performing their assigned responsibilities effectively and efficiently.

4. *Availability risk.* Unavailability of important information when needed threatens the continuity of the firm's critical operations and processes.

5. *Infrastructure risk.* The risk that the firm does not have the information technology infrastructure (e.g. hardware, networks, software, people and processes) it needs to effectively support the current and future information requirements of the business in an efficient, cost-effective and well-controlled fashion.

E. Integrity risk

Integrity risk is the risk of management fraud, employee fraud, illegal acts and unauthorized acts, any or all of which could lead to reputation loss in the marketplace.

1. *Management fraud risk*. Intentional misstatement of financial statements or misrepresentation of the firm's capabilities or intentions may adversely affect external stakeholders' decisions.

2. *Employee/third-party fraud risk*. Fraudulent activities perpetrated by employees, customers, suppliers, agents, brokers or third-party administrators against the firm for personal gain (e.g. misappropriation of physical, financial or information assets) expose the firm to financial loss.

3. *Illegal acts risk*. Illegal acts committed by managers or employees expose the firm to fines, sanctions and loss of customers, profits and reputation, etc.

4. *Unauthorized use risk*. Unauthorized use of the firm's physical, financial or information assets by employees or others exposes the firm to unnecessary waste of resources and financial loss.

5. *Reputation risk*. Damage to the firm's reputation exposes it to loss of customers, profits and the ability to compete.

SECTION III: INFORMATION FOR DECISION-MAKING RISK

Information for decision-making risk is the risk that information used to support the execution of the business model, the internal and external reporting on performance and the continuous evaluation of the effectiveness of the firm's business model is not relevant or reliable. These risks relate to every aspect of the firm's value creation activities.

A. Process/operational information for decision-making risk

1. *Product/service pricing risk*. Lack of relevant and/or reliable information supporting pricing decisions may result in prices or rates that customers are unwilling to pay, or that do not cover development and other costs, or do not cover the cost of risks undertaken by the firm.

2. *Contract commitment risk*. Lack of relevant and/or reliable information concerning contractual commitments outstanding as of a point in time may result in subsequent incremental contractual commitment decisions that are not in the best interests of the firm.

3. *Measurement (operations) risk*. Non-existent, irrelevant and/or unreliable non-financial measures may cause erroneous assessments of and conclusions about operational performance.

4. *Alignment risk.* Failure to align business process objectives and performance measures with enterprise-wide and/or operating unit objectives and strategies may result in conflicting, unco-ordinated activities throughout the firm.

B. Business reporting information for decision-making risk

1. *Budget and planning risk.* Non-existent, unrealistic, irrelevant or unreliable budget and planning information may cause inappropriate financial conclusions and decisions.

2. *Accounting information risk.* Overemphasis on financial accounting information to manage the business may result in the manipulation of outcomes to achieve financial targets at the expense of not meeting customer satisfaction, quality and efficiency objectives.

3. *Financial reporting evaluation risk.* Failure to accumulate relevant and reliable external and internal information to assess whether adjustments to or disclosures in financial statements are required may result in the issuance of misleading financial reports to external stakeholders.

4. *Taxation risk.* Failure to accumulate and consider relevant tax information may result in non-compliance with tax regulations or adverse tax consequences that could have been avoided had transactions been structured differently.

5. *Pension fund risk.* Incomplete and/or inaccurate information pertaining to compensation and benefits (i.e. pension plans, deferred compensation plans, retiree medical plans, etc.) may preclude the firm from meeting its defined obligations to employees on a timely basis and result in a loss of morale and reputation, work stoppages, litigation and additional funding requirements.

6. *Investment evaluation risk.* Lack of relevant and/or reliable information supporting investment decisions and linking the risks undertaken to the capital at risk may result in poor investments decisions.

7. *Regulatory reporting risk.* Incomplete, inaccurate and/or untimely reporting of required financial and operating information to regulatory agencies may expose the firm to fines, penalties and sanctions.

C. Environment/strategic information for decision-making risk

1. *Environmental scan risk.* Failure to monitor the external environment or formulation of unrealistic or erroneous assumptions about environment risks

may cause the firm to retain business strategies long after they have become obsolete.

2. *Business model risk*. The firm has an obsolete business model and doesn't recognize it and/or lacks the information needed to make an up-to-date assessment of its current model and build a compelling business case for modifying that model on a timely basis.

3. *Business portfolio risk*. Lack of relevant and reliable information that enables management to effectively prioritize its products or balance its businesses in a strategic context may preclude a diversified firm from optimizing its overall performance.

4. *Valuation risk*. Lack of relevant and reliable valuation information may preclude owners or prospective owners from making informed assessments of the value of the firm or any of its significant segments in a strategic context.

5. *Organizational structure risk*. Management lacks the information needed to assess the effectiveness of the firm's organizational structure, which threatens its capacity to change or achieve its long-term strategies.

6. *Measurement (strategy) risk*. Non-existent, irrelevant or unreliable performance measures that are inconsistent with established business strategies threaten the firm's ability to execute its strategies.

7. *Resource allocation risk*. An inadequate resource allocation process and the information supporting it may preclude the firm from establishing and sustaining competitive advantage or maximizing shareholder returns (e.g. channelling scarce resources toward those opportunities that provide the best prospects for balancing risk and reward).

8. *Planning risk*. An unimaginative and cumbersome strategic planning process may result in irrelevant information that threatens the firm's capacity to formulate viable business strategies.

9. *Life cycle risk*. Lack of relevant and reliable information that enables management to manage the movement of its product lines and monitor the evolution of its industry along the life cycle threatens the firm's capacity to remain competitive.

Risk controls process framework

In Chapter 5, we have introduced five overall risk management strategies; one of those strategies is 'Reduce'. While 'Control' is a risk reduction strategy. Risk control processes are primarily directed at reducing the likelihood that an undesirable risk incident will occur to an acceptable level, as defined by management's risk threshold.

The risk controls process framework illustrated in Figure A3.1 provides guidance for risk owners to consider when designing risk controls. This appendix summarizes the high points of that guidance.

Fig. A3.1 The Arthur Andersen Risk Controls Process Framework

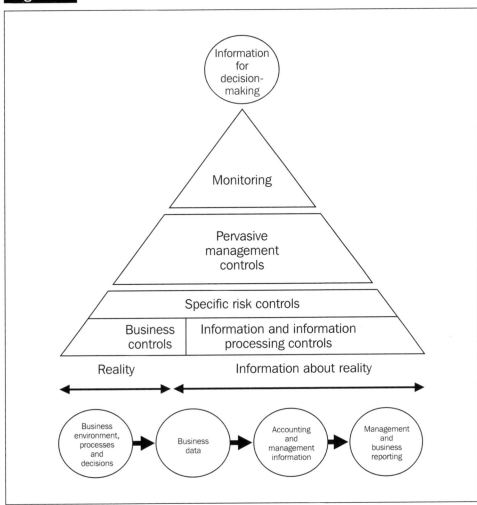

The components of the risk controls process framework comprise the strategic, management and business process controls of a business.

The information for decision-making sphere above the framework recognizes the importance of communicating relevant and reliable information between risk owners and senior management. The flow of information below the framework differentiates *reality* (what's actually happening in the external environment and internally within the processes of the business) and *information about reality* that is used to manage the business.[1] Given these points, the framework works as follows:

- *Specific risk controls.* At the base of the framework, these risk controls are comprised of the business controls and information and information processing controls for preventing, detecting and correcting errors and risk incidents. Business controls manage the 'business reality' risks which the firm faces in the environment and within its processes for executing its business model, as defined by the Business Risk Model™. There are three components of business controls: (a) strategic, (b) operational, and (c) legal and regulatory compliance. Information and information processing controls address the risks relating to the flow of information from the capture of relevant business events, transactions, facts and other data all the way through to their ultimate inclusion in financial and internal management reports.

- *Pervasive management controls.* The next layer of the framework relates to the control processes that are pervasive throughout an organization. These risk controls provide a vital 'front line of defence' protecting the integrity of business processes and the information supporting those processes.

- *Monitoring.* At the top of the framework, we have those tasks executed by process and activity owners to monitor and test the performance of risk controls. Monitoring also provides information for decision-making to senior managers from process and activity owners.

The components of the risk controls process framework comprise the strategic, management and business process controls of a business, as illustrated in Figure A3.2.

Although risk control processes can be used in any organizational structure that management chooses, do not confuse them with 'command and control' environments. While pervasive management controls provide focus and boundaries for empowering employees, the risk controls process framework itself can be used as a tool for integrating risk control into the firm's business processes so that employees are empowered in responsible and focused ways. For example, starting at the base of the framework and working up:

- *Business controls: strategic control.* Empowerment is not about eliminating leadership. Managers are needed to keep the firm in touch with the realities of the external environment and align the activities of empowered employees with those realities. This activity is the purpose of strategic control processes that are integral to the strategic management function. These processes:

---

1. Robert N. Anthony (1988) *The Management Control Function.* Harvard Business School Press, p. 7.

- monitor the external environment;

- assess strategic implications of changes in the environment;

- formulate strategies in response to changes in the environment;

- acquire/allocate resources to execute strategies;

- monitor organization/business unit performance; and

- continuously improve the strategic control process.[2]

Strategic control processes are an adaptation of the BRMP to the management of changes in environment risk factors on business strategies and the alignment of the firm's processes and activities with those strategies. In a dynamic environment, these processes are needed to stimulate innovation in an empowering culture because the strategies driving today's business models will quickly become yesterday's lessons in the new economy.

Fig. A3.2 Components of the Risk Controls Process Framework

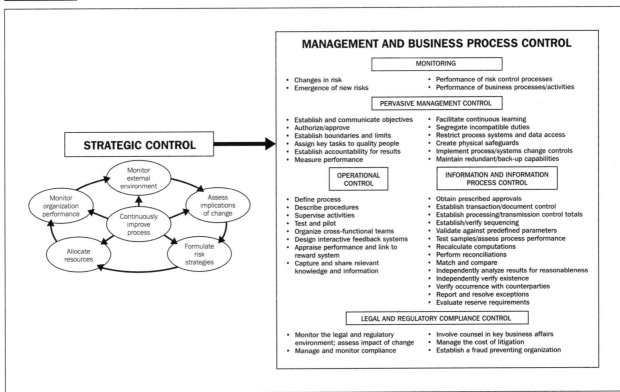

- *Business controls: operational control.* Operational controls are the processes, tools and techniques that focus risk assessment activities, facilitate cross-functional communications and co-operation, build effective

---

2. Economist Intelligence Unit (1995) *Managing business risk: An integrated approach*, written in co-operation with Arthur Andersen, pp. 15–20.

problem-solving and quality improvement teams, stimulate innovation and process improvement, and recognize and reward employees who consistently produce superior results. As defined by a major UK company, these control processes include management systems, procedures and work instructions, supervision, testing and piloting. Empowered employees use them to satisfy customers, improve quality (including safety), reduce costs and compress cycle time.

■ *Business controls: legal and regulatory compliance control.* These risk controls reduce the risk that empowered employees will commit ethical violations or fail to comply with laws and regulations leading to loss of reputation and market opportunities to the firm.

■ *Information and information process control.* These processes provide assurance that the information used by empowered employees is reliable for use in decision-making.

Risk controls, pervasive and specific, are either preventive or detective, and can be positioned at either the source of the risk (preventive) or downstream from the risk source within a business process (detective). Risk controls are also systems-based or people-based. The hierarchy shown in Figure A3.3 should be considered during the risk controls design assessment, particularly in dynamic environments involving large volumes of transactions (such as in eCommerce and eBusiness environments).

Fig. A3.3 Hierarchy of risk controls

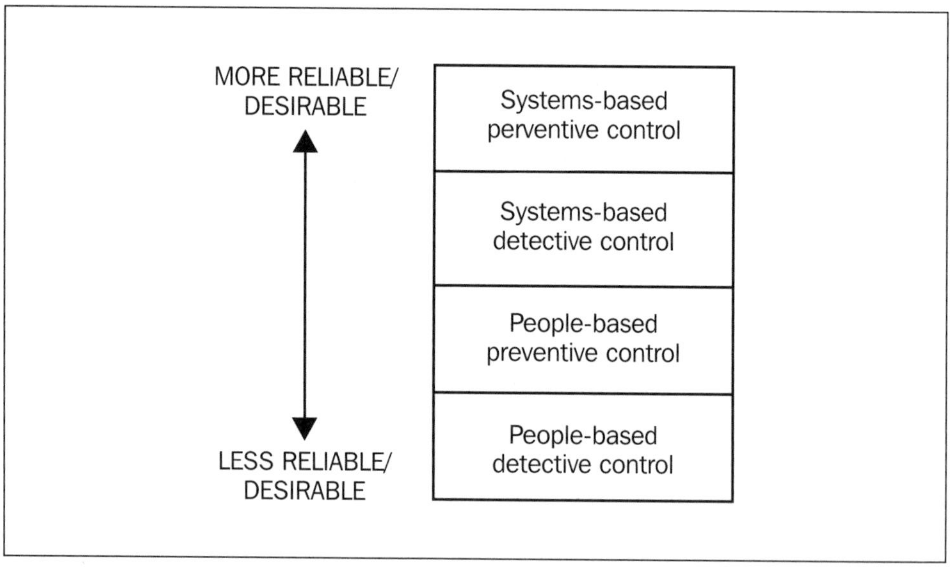

As transaction volumes and the velocity and complexity of risk increase, systems-based risk controls are often more reliable than risk controls that are people-based. Systems are less prone to mistakes than human beings, *if*

designed and secured effectively. Furthermore, a shift toward an anticipatory, proactive approach to controlling risk requires greater use of preventive controls than the reactive 'find and fix' approach embodied in a detective control. Effectively designed control processes that prevent risk at the source free up people resources to focus on the critical tasks of the business.

■ *Pervasive management control*. Pervasive controls define the 'sandbox' within which empowered employees function. As Figure A3.4 illustrates, the 12 pervasive controls are used in practice to select the best people for a given set of tasks, define the terms of empowerment, set boundaries, limits and restrictions, and establish accountability for results.

Fig. A3.4 **Pervasive management controls: supporting an empowering envrionment**

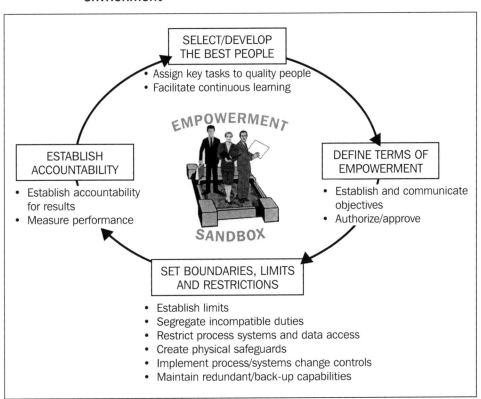

As 'anything goes' within the confines of a sandbox, the purpose of management control is to define and enforce the framing boundaries. Those who argue that such confinement is not consistent with an empowerment culture have the burden of articulating why a responsible CEO should be willing to give licence to anyone to do anything they choose without focus, boundaries or limits. Of course, it makes absolutely no sense to do so. Robert Simons articulated very well the tension imposed by defining objectives, boundaries and limits:

> *Boundary systems ... delineate the acceptable domain of activity for organizational participants. Unlike belief systems, boundary systems do not specify positive ideals. Instead, they establish limits, based on defined business risks, to opportunity seeking ... Although boundary systems are essentially proscriptive or negative systems, they allow managers to delegate decision making and thereby allow the organization to achieve maximum flexibility and creativity. In many ways, boundary systems are a prerequisite for organizational freedom and entrepreneurial behavior.[3]*

- *Monitoring*. Finally, to ensure that a control process is working, effective monitoring is needed. As one manager at Motorola told us, 'Empowerment means accountability', therefore accountability for results and monitoring play a vital role in an empowerment culture.

All told, effective risk controls are vital in an empowerment environment. It remains management's responsibility to focus employees on strategic, operational and financial goals and to protect the firm's physical, financial, customer, employee/supplier and organizational asset holdings. Elsewhere, we introduced the term 'self-control' as a substitute for the term 'empowerment' and broke down the definition of that term to illustrate its application within a business. Although we will not repeat that analysis here, it is worth noting that empowerment is not the end in itself, but is only a means to an end, the end being 'self-control'. The term 'self-control' is more descriptive of what many firms strive to achieve, which is to drive risk assessment and control throughout the organization in a rapidly changing environment and with clear objectives, accountabilities, boundaries and limits.[4]

3. Robert Simons (1995) *Levers of Control: How Managers Use Innovative Control Systems to Drive Strategic Renewal*. Harvard Business School Press, pp. 33–41.

4. Economist Intelligence Unit (1995) *Managing business risk: An integrated approach*, written in co-operation with Arthur Andersen, pp. 35–40.

Glossary

Accept. See 'risk acceptance'.

Acceptable tolerance levels. The range of possible future outcomes that achieve stated performance goals and objectives.

Appetite. The risk-taking perspectives of different managers as they make choices. For example, a firm that is willing to take on new risks in response to market opportunities by exploiting new markets, channels, external relationships and products has a higher risk appetite than, say, a firm that chooses 'business as usual' by resisting change and maintaining its existing risk profile. The notion of 'risk appetite' is made much more explicit in an organization that uses techniques such as risk adjusted return on capital (RAROC) that force debate on how much risk is being taken and why and then evaluates those risks against the expected rewards and capital allocation requirements. In the context of specific risks, 'tolerance' and 'threshold' are terms that are often used.

Assess. See 'risk assessment'.

Avoid. See 'risk avoidance'.

BRMP. Acronym for 'business risk management process'.

Business control. The control processes put in place to manage environment risks and reduce process risks to an acceptable level. These processes include strategic control, operational control and legal and regulatory compliance control.

Business model. How companies create value and take on risk through their unique combinations of assets and technologies. Assets fall into five categories for purposes of understanding business models: physical, financial, customer, employee/supplier and organizational. As individual assets have unique risk and reward profiles, so too does the asset portfolio that makes up each business model. The synergy of assets has the capacity to produce results greater than the sum of the parts, depending on how a company invests and how it manages risk. And the reverse is always the case, as a portfolio that is concentrated in the wrong assets can actually dilute value.[1]

Business process. A process (a) consists of inputs, activities, outputs and interfaces with other processes, (b) is supported by people, methodologies and technology, and (c) is designed to achieve one or more specified objectives. Every business can be decomposed into operating, management and support processes.

---

1. Richard E. S. Boulton, Barry D. Libert and Steve M. Samek (2000) *Cracking the Value Code: How Successful Businesses are Creating Wealth in the New Economy*. HarperCollins.

Business risk. The level of exposure to uncertainties that the enterprise must understand and effectively manage as it executes its strategies to achieve its business objectives and create value.

Business risk management process. A systematic process for building and improving risk management capabilities. It is used by executive management to manage the risks of the enterprise and by process/activity owners to manage the risks within their respective business processes and activities. It includes key tasks essential to an EWRM environment: establish goals, objectives and oversight; assess business risk (identify, source and measure); develop business risk management strategies; design and implement risk management capabilities; monitor process performance; and continuously improve risk management capabilities. All of these tasks are supported by information for decision-making.

Capability. See 'risk management capabilities'.

Capacity. In conjunction with risk management, the aggregate financial ability of a firm to absorb or withstand losses from risk incidents. Capacity to bear risk is a function of many things, such as economic capital, long-term business strategies and debt capacity. For example, firms hold equity in order to respond to unanticipated investment opportunities and provide a cushion to absorb unexpected losses arising from performance variability or loss exposure.

Common language. A framework of mental models that simplify and focus communication. Multiple disciplines within a business use it to initiate and sustain a continuing dialogue about business risks and processes and risk management capabilities. It is particularly useful in supporting the risk identification process.

Comprehensive. A term used in risk management to convey that the firm's risk management coverage of its business risks is broad and complete. A 'comprehensive' risk management approach covers many or all of the significant business risks across the entity, which may be a business unit or division or even the enterprise as a whole. An EWRM approach is comprehensive.

Consequence. A negative or positive outcome or result of a single causal event, or two or more related causal events.

Control. See 'risk control'.

Deterministic. These scenario analyses modify portfolios and forecasts to reflect the effects of situations or events that may or may not occur in the future. For example, a deterministic approach might show the change in earnings for a defined scenario relative to a base case in terms of both absolute and percentage amounts without an assessment of the probability that the particular scenario will happen. The methodology is particularly useful when evaluating extraordinary, highly unlikely events or stressful situations.

Dispersion. An option for mitigating risk that distributes financial, physical (facilities and stocks) or information assets deployed by the firm's business model over a widely dispersed geographic area, making it less likely or impossible to incur an unacceptable loss from fire, windstorm, earthquake, war, theft or terrorist acts. Geographic dispersion of assets needs to be balanced against operating objectives driving the concentration of assets to achieve needed efficiencies.

Diversification. A versatile management tool for shaping a firm's aggregate risk profile. For example, a firm may diversify its portfolio of businesses, its geographic sources of revenue, its product mix, its customer mix, its R&D portfolio, its sources of supply and its asset allocation by type of financial asset.

Drivers. Underlying causal factors that 'drive' risk, creating sources of uncertainty. Determining the type and nature of the significant drivers is often a critical step towards the development of a risk measurement methodology. See also 'root cause' and 'source'.

Enterprise-wide risk management. A structured and disciplined approach that aligns strategy, processes, people, technology and knowledge with the purpose of evaluating and managing the uncertainties the enterprise faces as it creates value. 'Enterprise-wide' suggests an elimination of functional, departmental or cultural barriers so that a truly holistic, integrated approach is taken to manage risk with the intent of creating value.

Environment risk. Arises when there are external forces that could either significantly change the fundamental assumptions that drive a firm's overall objectives and strategies or, at the extreme, render its business model obsolete.

Event. Something that happens through the interplay of a combination of factors (external environment, strategy and organization, people, processes, materials, facilities and equipment, technology and information). Events can have positive or negative consequences. Negative consequences include process failures, errors, waste, losses, injury, death and other undesirable effects.

Exposure. Arises when any asset or source of value of the enterprise is affected by changes in key variables and/or the occurrence of well-defined risk events or scenarios. The enterprise is exposed to risk when a realized change in a variable or occurrence of an event will result in a change in one or more of its key performance indicators. The greater the realized change in performance, either positive or negative, the greater the exposure. A firm may be exposed to performance variability on account of its strategies, processes, market positions and other sources of earnings and cash flows.

EWRM. Acronym for 'enterprise-wide risk management'.

Four-way interactive communications and knowledge sharing. Transfers or exchanges of information, knowledge and best practices about risk up, down and across the enterprise.

Frequency. A term used in the context of the future, present and past. If used in the context of future occurrences of an event: see 'likelihood'. If used in the context of the present or past, it is the number of times that an event occurs or has occurred.

Hazard. See 'loss exposure'.

Holistic. A term used in risk management that emphasizes the strengthening of the linkages, co-ordination and interrelationships among individual risks (or groups of related risks) and the components of an organization that contribute to managing risk. A holistic risk management process is therefore, by definition, one that is not fragmented into functions and departments, but is organized with the intention of optimizing the performance of the process, unit or enterprise in managing a single risk or aggregate group of related risks. An EWRM approach is holistic in its perspective of business risk management. Depending on the capabilities desired by management, an EWRM approach may also be holistic in its perspective of risk.

Incident. See 'event'.

Information and information process control. These control processes address the risks relating to the flow of information from the capture of relevant business facts through their ultimate inclusion in financial and management reports.

Information for decision-making risk. This component of business risk on the Business Risk Model™ arises when information used to support business decisions is incomplete, out of date, inaccurate, late or simply irrelevant to the decision-making process.

Infrastructure. See 'risk management infrastructure'.

Inherent risk. The risks associated with any business activity.

Integrated. A term used in risk management to describe an approach or methodology that aggregates and organizes risk data, information, measurements and analyses into a larger framework for decision-making that adds rigour and robustness to the process. All applications of EWRM are integrated approaches applied to a single risk, to a group of related risks or comprehensively to all significant risks of the enterprise.

Likelihood. The probability that, or frequency with which, an event is expected to occur over a given time horizon.

Loss exposure. Uncertainties arising from physical phenomena (weather, earthquake, fire, flood, etc.), dependencies on processes and systems, handling of hazardous materials or exposure to conditions, accidents or malicious acts (sabotage, terrorism, etc.) that could cause loss of or damage to physical assets, injury or death to employees or other people, business interruption or loss of reputation. These risks are often labelled as 'downside risks' because the distribution of potential future outcomes is heavily skewed toward adverse consequences. Every foreseeable outcome results in a negative net cash flow.

Monitoring. The activities of managers as they oversee and review process performance, changes in the environment, changes in internal processes and compliance with established policies and limits.

NPV. Acronym for net present value.

Performance variability. Uncertainties affecting the quality and sustainability of future earnings that are inherent in the firm's normal ongoing operations. These uncertainties can result in a range of events that could give rise to positive or negative outcomes. Firms manage these risks to ensure that their potential impact on business performance falls within an acceptable range (or tolerance).

Pervasive management control. These risk controls are implemented across the firm's units and processes to ensure that managers and employees are focused on the right objectives and activities, have the requisite knowledge and skills, do not perform incompatible duties (authorization, custody and record-keeping) in the same function, and protect physical and financial assets and information integrity. They provide a vital 'front line of defence' protecting the integrity of business processes.

Pools. See 'risk families'.

Probabilistic. This analysis approach attempts to assess portfolio performance over a period of time, taking into account the interactions of the key underlying variables and assumptions. It offers a means of assessing the likelihood of a particular change in financial performance as well as the magnitude of that change. This approach is most effective in evaluating financial risk when the underlying risk factors can be statistically modelled, but it is less effective than the deterministic scenario approach in evaluating extraordinary, unlikely events or stressful situations where uncertainty cannot be easily evaluated statistically.

Process risk. Arises when business processes do not achieve the objectives they were designed to achieve in supporting the firm's business model.

Propensity. Refers to the extent to which a firm exposes its capital, earnings and cash flow to performance variability or loss exposure. In other words, propensity is the willingness of a firm to assume risk. Firms that have a low propensity to take risk are 'risk averse', while firms that have a high propensity to take risk are 'risk-takers'.

Reprice. Including a risk premium in the pricing of products and services, when market conditions allow, to compensate the firm for risks undertaken.

Residual risk. The exposure to uncertainty remaining after the effective implementation of all risk management strategies. Sometimes used to refer to the level of risk before considering risk transfer strategies.

Retain. See 'risk retention'.

Risk. The distribution of possible outcomes in a firm's performance over a given time horizon due to changes in key underlying variables. The greater the dispersion of possible outcomes, the higher the firm's level of exposure to uncertain returns. These uncertain returns can have either positive or negative consequences. The organization's sensitivity to risk is a function of (1) the significance of its exposures to changes and events, (2) the likelihood of those different changes and events occurring and (3) its ability to manage the business implications of those different possible future changes and events, if they occur.

Risk acceptance. A conscious, rational and often supported decision to accept a risk. Risk is accepted for many reasons. For example, the firm's processes are effective in managing the risk, the risk is inherent in the firm's strategies and day-to-day business, the firm has sufficient equity capital or operating margin to absorb the financial impact if an undesirable risk incident should occur or the firm possesses sufficient information to understand the risk well enough to justify accepting it. Once accepted, the risk may be retained, reduced, transferred or exploited.

Risk assessment. The set of tasks in which risk is identified, sourced and measured. Sometimes used in a more limited context to refer solely to risk identification and prioritization.

Risk avoidance. Avoiding risk is a decision to divest a business or product or terminate a process or activity to eliminate unacceptable risks, prohibit high-risk business activities or implement preventive process improvements that make it impossible for a well defined undesirable event to occur.

Risk control. Risk control processes are the monitoring activities, pervasive management controls, business controls and information and information process controls that reduce the likelihood of an undesirable risk event occurring to an acceptable level. These processes require supervision, enforcement and periodic re-evaluation.

Risk event. See 'risk incident'.

Risk exploitation. Management decides to take the risks inherent in its choice to enter new markets, introduce new products, merge with or acquire another firm or exploit other market opportunities, all of which result in shaping the firm's risk profile differently, even to the point of increasing the firm's exposure to risks it desires to take in accordance with its business model.

Risk families. A natural grouping of risks sharing fundamental characteristics, e.g. common drivers, positive or negative correlations or other characteristics that make the risks susceptible to the application of common measurement methodologies and risk management solutions.

Risk financing. The process by which a firm pays for the outcome of an undesirable risk incident. There are two forms of financing, one external and the other internal. External financing results from a legally enforceable transfer of risk to an independent third party through financial instruments (i.e. insurance or hedging). Internal financing funds risk through current and/or future operating cash flows.

Risk identification. The process of defining what can happen that fundamentally affects the success of the firm's business model, which includes the risks inherent in the pursuit of targeted opportunities for increased growth and return. The focus of executive management when identifying risk is on the environment. The focus of process/activity owners is on the processes and activities that they manage.

Risk incident. An event that results in or has positive or negative consequences for the business.

Risk management. The management activities which are authorized, designed and executed to provide reasonable assurance that the possible outcomes arising from business risks fall within acceptable tolerance levels. Risk management activities identify, source, measure and monitor risk, formulate risk management strategies and implement capabilities to avoid, retain, reduce, transfer and exploit individual risks and groups of related risks.

Risk management capabilities. The processes, people, reports, methodologies and systems needed to implement a particular risk management strategy. The term 'capability' is used interchangeably with 'infrastructure'.

Risk management infrastructure. Six key components – strategy, business and risk management processes, people, management reports, methodologies and systems, and data – that define risk management capabilities. To maximize risk management capabilities, these components must be effectively aligned. The term 'infrastructure' is used interchangeably with 'capability'.

Risk management system. The components of the firm's systems that are concerned with measuring and managing risk, including business planning, risk control processes, monitoring and feedback mechanisms, dedicated risk management personnel, technology (including support systems architecture and databases), methodologies and risk-focused knowledge sharing and communications processes.

Risk measurement. Methodologies and techniques used to quantitatively or qualitatively determine the likelihood and consequence (including financial impact) of possible outcomes or events over a given time horizon under alternative scenarios and provide information for informed decision-making to managers.

Risk mitigation. Steps taken by management to reduce the pain or limit the adverse effects of a risk incident. See also 'risk control' or 'risk reduction', both of which are terms with which 'risk mitigation' is often used interchangeably. Mitigation is sometimes used in a broader sense to include 'risk transfer'.

Risk reduction. Taking action to reduce risk to an acceptable level, as defined by management's risk tolerance. Approaches to reduce risk vary, but are generally focused on decreasing either (a) the likelihood of an undesirable event occurring, or (b) its impact on the business should it occur. For (a), risk reduction is accomplished by controlling the risk through internal processes. For (b), it is accomplished by spreading the risk, i.e. disperse assets geographically.

Risk retention. Planned retention of risk is a purposeful, conscious and intentional decision to accept the consequences in the event an undesirable risk incident occurs. Unplanned retention of risk occurs when the firm doesn't know of its existence.

Risk securitization. A process for transferring risk, such as weather related derivatives (options contracts, for instance) or preferred stock with payouts indexed to the incidence of some operational risk. It is usually targeted to operational risks, as the maturity of the capital markets facilitate the transfer of interest rate, currency and other price risks.

Risk taking. The act of selecting and executing strategies whose outcomes are subject to uncertainty and result in significant exposures. This act may result in increasing the firm's exposures to uncertainty.

Risk transfer. Transfer of risk occurs when the firm passes a risk through to an independent financially capable third party at a reasonable economic cost under a legally enforceable arrangement. Transfer can be accomplished in many ways, e.g. through the insurance markets, by hedging risk in the capital markets, by sharing risk through joint venture investments or strategic alliances, through an outsourcing arrangement accompanied by a contractual risk transfer and by indemnifying risk through contractual agreements.

Risk treatment. A term normally used to refer to the specific strategy selected for managing a risk. While often used to refer exclusively to risk reduction strategies, it is sometimes broadly applied to encompass risk transfer and other strategies.

Root cause. The fundamental reason(s) why, how and where an event or scenario occurred or could possibly occur. See also 'source'.

Scenario. A well defined event which could occur in the future and affect the value of the firm's asset portfolio comprising its business model, the viability of its business strategy and the operating effectiveness and efficiency of its business processes. Scenarios are useful in evaluating 'what if' questions. Depending on the complexity of the underlying variables, they may require modelling tools to fully understand their potential impact on the firm should they occur.

Severity. The significance of a risk to a business based on criteria selected by management.

Source (or sourcing). The process of determining why, how and where risks are created, either outside the organization or within its business processes. Risk sourcing is the process of understanding a risk and its interrelationships with other risks as well its drivers or root causes.

Threshold. See 'tolerance'.

Time horizon. The period of time which management considers when assessing the severity or likelihood of a particular risk or group of related risks and evaluating risk management options.

Tolerance. Tolerable risk is an acceptable level of risk to the firm, as defined by management in terms of a loss amount, an error rate or some form of rating. The term 'tolerance' refers to the ability of a firm to accept or withstand performance variability or loss exposure from a given source and can be expressed in terms of the following question: 'What is the firm's tolerance for deviations of actual results from plan?' Risk tolerances can also be expressed in terms of the acceptable level of loss, as addressed by the question: 'What risks are we willing to accept as we pursue our business objectives and execute our strategies?'

Transfer. See 'risk transfer'.

Transparent. Risks are efficiently priced using methodologies that (a) are applied consistently across the organization (or multiple organizations), (b) are clearly understood and accepted by decision-makers and other relevant parties, (c) facilitate sensitivity analysis and (d) enable comparisons, aggregation and monitoring for results.

Uncertainty. Managers do not know in advance the magnitude and direction of change in the value of a key underlying variable, i.e. interest rates, commodity prices, technological innovation, currency rates, human performance, etc. or the likelihood that a well-defined significant event or scenario will occur within a given time horizon. Uncertainty refers to any situation in which all possible outcomes are identified and the related probabilities are assessed, but we simply do not know which event will occur.

Value at risk. A form of probabilistic analysis that measures risk in terms of the likelihood that the hypothetical value of a portfolio will differ from its expected market value at some future time. To compute VaR, it is necessary to obtain a measure of the portfolio value's sensitivity to underlying variables (e.g. spot prices, load volumes, currency rates, interest rates, etc.) over a given time period, and to measure the statistical variability (the volatility or standard deviation) of the portfolio value with respect to those variables.

Bibliography

Anthony, Robert N. (1988) *The Management Control Function*. Harvard Business School Press.

Banham, Russ (1999) 'Kit and Caboodle: Understanding the skepticism about enterprise risk management', *CFO Magazine*, April, pp. 63–70.

Boulton, Richard E. S., Libert, Barry D. and Samek, Steve M. (2000) *Cracking the Value Code: How Successful Businesses are Creating Wealth in the New Economy*. HarperCollins.

Drucker, Peter F. (1999) *Management Challenges for the 21st Century*. HarperCollins.

Economist Intelligence Unit (1995) *Managing Business Risk: An Integrated Approach*, written in co-operation with Arthur Andersen.

Grose, Vernon L. (1987) *Managing Risk: Systematic Loss Prevention for Executives*. Omega Systems Group.

Grove, Andrew S. (1996) *Only the Paranoid Survive: How to Exploit the Crisis Points that Challenge Every Company and Career*. Doubleday.

Haubenstock, Michael (1999) 'Organizing a financial institution to deliver enterprise-wide risk management', *The Journal of Lending and Credit Risk Management*, February, pp. 46–52.

Humphrey, Watts S. (1994) *The Capability Maturity Model: Guidelines for Improving the Software Process*. Carnegie Mellon University Software Engineering Institute.

Institute of Chartered Accountants in England and Wales (1999) *No Surprises: The Case for Better Risk Reporting*. ICAEW.

Shapira, Zur (1995) *Risk Taking: A Managerial Perspective*. Russell Sage Foundation.

Simons, Robert (1995) *Levers of Control: How Managers Use Innovative Control Systems to Drive Strategic Renewal*. Harvard Business School Press.

Stewart, Thomas A. (2000) 'Managing risk in the 21st century', *Fortune*, 7 February, pp. 202–6.

Index